KU-062-978

RACE CONSCIOUSNESS

AFRICAN-AMERICAN STUDIES FOR THE NEW CENTURY

Edited by
JUDITH JACKSON FOSSETT
and JEFFREY A. TUCKER

With a Foreword by
NELL IRVIN PAINTER
and ARNOLD RAMPERSAD

and an Introduction by
ROBIN D. G. KELLEY

NEW YORK UNIVERSITY PRESS

NEW YORK AND LONDON

NEW YORK UNIVERSITY PRESS
New York and London

Copyright © 1997 by New York University

All rights reserved

Library of Congress Cataloging-in-Publication Data
Race consciousness : African American studies for the new century /
edited by Judith Jackson Fossett and Jeffrey A. Tucker ; with a
foreword by Nell Irvin Painter and Arnold Rampersad ; and an
introduction by Robin D.G. Kelley.
p.   cm.
Includes index.
ISBN 0-8147-4227-0 (cloth : alk. paper). — ISBN 0-8147-4228-9
(pbk. : alk. paper)
1. Afro-Americans.   2. Afro-Americans—History.   3. Afro-
Americans—Study and teaching.   I. Fossett, Judith Jackson, 1965–   .
II. Tucker, Jeffrey A., 1966–   .
E185.R23   1996
305.896'073—dc20   96-42999
                              CIP

New York University Press books are printed on acid-free paper,
and their binding materials are chosen for strength and durability.

Manufactured in the United States of America

10 9 8 7 6 5 4 3 2 1

RACE CONSCIOUSNESS

WITHDRAWN

2 0 MAY 2002

LIVERPOOL JMU LIBRARY

3 1111 00773 1548

WITHDRAWN

for Ruth J. Simmons,
mentor and friend

CONTENTS

NELL IRVIN PAINTER
and ARNOLD RAMPERSAD

FOREWORD

**AFRICAN-AMERICAN STUDIES
ENTERS THE NEW CENTURY**

Who knows what will happen to African-American Studies in the new century? The twentieth century witnessed the extraordinary flourishing of a field of study that began small. In the nineteenth century it arose mainly to deny racist dogma that was contemptuous of people of African descent and envisioned us as fit primarily for forced, uncompensated labor. Sad to say, after all these years, books, and scholars, such ideas persist among a large section of the population. African-American Studies, still bearing the burden of vindicating the race—to use a nineteenth-century formulation—is still very much engaged scholarship, at least for most of us who are black.

When we entered the field in the early 1970s—what now seems to have been almost an eon ago—it bore little resemblance to what we call African-American

Studies today. Indeed, it barely had a name. The study of the history and culture of African Americans was the province of a small number of black scholars and an even smaller number of whites. Certain differences existed between the two major subfields within African-American Studies, history and literature. The dean of African-American history was John Hope Franklin, whose best-selling text, *From Slavery to Freedom,* had first appeared in 1947 and maintained its eminence through multiple editions. However, white scholars also played an important role in history. Slavery, among the most fertile and prestigious topics in American history, had attracted major white talents, such as Herbert Aptheker, Dorothy Sterling, Gerda Lerner, and Herbert Gutman. Although none in any sense followed a traditional career, they were able to influence a number of younger academics, black and white, and generally helped stimulate the field of African-American Studies without always intending to do so. In addition, many of these whites were of the Left politically and brought an unusual zeal for social justice to their profession.

The situation was somewhat different in literature. In the late 1960s, J. Saunders Redding of Hampton Institute and then Cornell University was perhaps the most respected literary authority, and the white scholar Robert Bone, with his provocative history of black American fiction, probably the most frequently cited. Fewer white literary academics maintained a serious professional commitment to the study of black writing than white historians to the study of black history. In both cases, we younger students of history and literature in the late 1960s and early 1970s found ourselves largely on our own. We struggled with many factors, not least of all with the resistance to "political" questions that had become ingrained in literary study with the triumph of the values of the New Criticism starting in the 1940s and the resistance to Marxist scholarship among Cold War historians. In a period of difficult transition, black scholars such as Charles Davis at Yale, Donald Gibson at Rutgers, and Hollis Lynch at Columbia helped smooth the way for the younger generation, who eventually would make at least a passing knowledge of black literature and history almost fashionable in the American academy.

With the rise of the Black Power movement in the late 1960s, along with the Black Aesthetic and Black Arts movements, the task facing younger scholars in African-American Studies seemed straightforward. Using sources that mainstream scholars had overlooked or distorted, we would reveal the truth about our people. Who exactly were "our people" and what constituted "truth" became questions only much later. In the early 1970s, race meant blackness, and we all knew what we meant by that term. We could talk about "the black community" and "the black church" without being challenged, though the time had passed for easy usage of "the Negro," a common formulation in the work of black as well as white writers in the 1960s. In the new Afro-American (as we called it then) scholarship of the early 1970s, black opposed white, without inordinate delving into the process of acquiring racial identities or into intraracial divisions.

With the recession of the mid-1970s and with increasing controversy about the standards and values of the field, the enrollment of graduate students doing African-American Studies declined. We began to 'worry that we might have no successors, as year after year passed with very few students following in our footsteps. For various reasons, some bright young men and women never completed their dissertations; others failed to receive tenure and even turned away from the academy. Even more frightening were the early deaths and serious illnesses of colleagues we had thought too young to face mortality. By the time we ourselves of that "first" generation had reached the ranks of senior scholars, we sometimes felt like dinosaurs.

Reports of the demise of African-American Studies turned out to be premature. By the mid-1980s younger people interested in the field started turning up in graduate schools, sometimes encouraged by ourselves and our colleagues, but mostly arriving on their own initiative and with a far more mature sense of the demands of university life. Energetic, bright, serious, they built on our work and the new fields that had grown up in tandem with African-American Studies: Women's Studies, Cultural Studies, Postcolonial Studies, Gay and Lesbian Studies. By the mid-1990s, they had remade African-American Studies.

Scholarship of the late 1980s and early-to-mid-1990s has revolutionized the epistemology of the field. Whereas we in the early 1970s took race for granted, much of the new work investigates the making of races, including the race called white. "Gender" is no longer a euphemism for women, and the process of gendering black men engages many young thinkers. No one can say "the black man" to mean all black Americans, as was possible only a generation ago. Black Women's Studies has emerged as a vibrant field in its own right, reshaping African-American Studies and Women's Studies as well. No longer do we write as though all people of African descent were heterosexual, for some of the most exciting work has come from black gays and lesbians happy in their gayness. Gay and Lesbian Studies encourages a concentration on the study of the body that suits Black Studies perfectly in many respects, since so much of American culture is preoccupied with the black body, literally and figuratively.

A decade ago post-structuralism, or what detractors termed "theory," appeared antithetical to African-American Studies. However, the detractors have lost this round, if not the entire battle. Following the lead of literary critics, historians and, to a lesser degree, sociologists and political scientists have sat at the feet of anthropologists, French post-structuralists, and, increasingly, the legal scholars of what is now called critical race theory. Theory is no longer controversial, because asking how we know what we know and investigating differences within the "Negro race" enrich our field immeasurably. In addition, a growing body of splendid biographical writing is one of the most visible signs of the sophistication of today's African-American Studies.

Now, as opposed to a generation ago, the lenses of African-American Studies turn on individuals and phenomena of any race or group. African-American Studies still connotes a study centered on race; however, "race" no longer means simply blackness, nor do we take what race means for granted. In the early 1970s few could have foreseen such an expansion of our then-new field. In the mid-1990s we are absolutely delighted by the excellence of the new scholarship. Bravo!

JUDITH JACKSON FOSSETT
and JEFFREY A. TUCKER

PREFACE: IN MEDIAS RACE

THE COLOR/CULTURE OF SPECTACLE

Marion Barry. Mike Tyson. Arthur Ashe. Magic Johnson. Clarence Thomas. Anita Hill. Rodney King. Lani Guinier. Michael Jordan. Michael Jackson. Joycelyn Elders. Henry Foster. Colin Ferguson. O. J. Simpson. Louis Farrakhan. Colin Powell.

Consider the widespread media attention, internal and external dialogues, personal psychic time, and private conversation devoted to these African-American individuals in the last decade of the twentieth century. These well-known black figures have served as grist for the mill of cultural spectacle, fodder for the programmers of television and talk radio, and subjects for seemingly limitless column inches in print media and on magazine covers. Why does there seem to be a growth industry in African-American celebrity? In the same time frame, we observe the explosion in another kind of cultural production—a strand of conservative political rhetoric that implores society to move beyond race as a salient category in American culture. This argument asserts that since race matters less and less as we move into the twenty-first century, we can instead permanently consign chattel slavery, race-based segregation, and discrimination, as well as the struggles against them, to America's distant past. However, when we see events such as the widespread coverage of the 1991 Rodney King beating at the hands of white police officers in Los Angeles, the subsequent acquittal of those officers and the resulting civil unrest in the summer of 1992 in which issues of race, gender, and sexuality, especially black masculinity, flourished, how do we reconcile these events with the political view that the difficult work of healing racial divisions was already accomplished through the gains of the civil rights movement and has therefore rendered further ministrations to society's racial wounds unnecessary? Most simply, we cannot. Despite extravagant posturing to the contrary, both the sweep of American history and the small window afforded by a focus on the decade of the 1990s illustrate that American society finds itself always in the midst of race—*in medias race*—battling a kind of cultural schizophrenia, fascinated and obsessed with racial difference on the one hand and in denial of its existence on the other.

Although not the only group of people who function as objects of intense media scrutiny, African Americans who find themselves displayed so spectacularly in public serve as prisms through which the nation views issues of race and gender. In other words, America, as a culture in the grip of racial schizophrenia, seizes the spectacle as an opportunity to work through the troubling, destabilizing reality of racial difference. But the process of effectively working through racial difference requires a vocabulary and cognitive apparatus with which to effect a kind of racial "talking cure." Interestingly enough, the problematic of talking about race does not necessarily stem from a lack of a precise racial vocabulary. Indeed, American society has developed a kind of racial glossary, but that glossary makes cultural sense only when race is characterized as the "problem" or "problems" that black people and culture present to larger American society. The ability to speak of race in terms of constructions of "blackness," "whiteness," or other kinds of racialized subjectivity has not proliferated through the wider culture. Instead, we hear and read something like the following: "What are we going to do about welfare mothers?" "Blacks are not held to the same standard for promotion in my office." "How do we tackle the crime problem?" "Black people are a problem for society." But lurking behind this last

statement is an intriguing bit of rhetorical wordplay. "Society" in this context
stands in direct opposition to "black people," begging the question as to whether
or not African Americans in fact belong to it. Furthermore, in this construction,
"society" has a reverse synecdochic relationship to white America. In essence,
society as the whole stands in for the part of this society that white Americans
represent; the construction of "problem" addresses solely the state of blacks in
society.

THE "NEGRO PROBLEM"

Between me and the other world there is ever an unasked question: unasked by some through
feelings of delicacy; by others through the difficulty of rightly framing it. All, nevertheless, flutter
round it. They approach me in a half-hesitant sort of way, eye me curiously or compassionately, and
then, instead of saying directly, How does it feel to be a problem? they say, I know an excellent
colored man in my town; or, I fought at Mechanicsville; or, Do not these Southern outrages make
your blood boil? At these I smile, or am interested, or reduce the boiling to a simmer, as the occasion
may require. To the real question, How does it feel to be a problem? I answer seldom a word.

—W. E. B. Du Bois, *The Souls of Black Folk*

The analysis of the way black people are seen as a "problem people" as opposed
to people with problems has been presented by a host of African-American
intellectuals, most notably by W. E. B. Du Bois. In 1903, he articulated the
problem of the newly arrived twentieth century as the problem of the color line
or, as he further detailed, the "relation of the darker to the lighter races of men
in Asia and Africa, in America and the islands of the sea." Du Bois's use of the
term "problem" alluded to the "Negro Problem," contemporaneous shorthand
for identifying and collapsing a myriad of issues concerning the place of black
people, a newly emancipated group, who, after centuries of slavery, were historically understood as less than human members of American society. The syntax
of the phrase "Negro Problem" demonstrated a denial of the subjectivity of
black Americans, "Negro" merely qualifying the subject "problem." Making a
syntactic parallel, Du Bois grafted the "problem," or the "Negro Problem," onto
issues associated with the color line, which had received significant social,
political, and juridical attention, most notably with the 1896 *Plessy v. Ferguson*
decision. His joint invocation of the color line and the "Negro" or race problem
suffused what had previously been a glib cipher with the more complex content
of the color line. In essence, in Du Bois's construction, the "problem" or "Negro
Problem" functions as a foil to the color line, which, despite its currency, also
generalized and oversimplified matters of race.

Today, we find ourselves at the turn of another century, still facing issues of
race. However, we are bereft of the facile terminology—such as "Negro Prob-

lem" and "color line"—that once fixed racial issues to a discrete location. The "color line," even with all its limitations, at least at the time provided a crude lingua franca for the discussion of racial issues during the era of racial segregation. One of the hopes of the civil rights movement was the erasure of this color line. However, given the current proliferation of sound bites such as "welfare reform," "school choice," and "the crime problem," it would seem that civil rights victories were incomplete ones at best. The color line was not erased as much as it was rendered invisible. Much has been written on how in recent years racism has been institutionalized and manifests itself more subtly than before. Although the "color line" is now an antiquated phrase—referred to for historical purposes—that has ceased to function as a common descriptor for issues of race relations, the custom to which it refers remains. The change in custom around issues of race continues to lag behind the change in law ushered in with legislation such as the Voting Rights Act of 1965. The invisibility of the color line today affords race the opportunity to operate in a less conspicuous manner than a century ago. Now people may pay less attention to its precise functioning and, as a consequence, may assume that it does not operate at all. This assumption about the obsolescence of race as a social category yields two related consequences. First, it sanctions the proliferation of a kind of political "racially transcendent-speak": "We are first and foremost Americans." "It does not matter if you are black or white." "Judge me not by the color of my skin, but by the content of my character." Second, it renders both charges of racism moot and victims of racism mute and increases the degree to which issues about race relations are inevitably characterized as social "problems." The disconnect between the current spectacle of race and the rhetoric around racial transcendence is predicated on the very invisibility of the color line.

As we approach the new century, arguments that race does not matter anymore are becoming more common, forcing intellectuals who are concerned with issues of race to develop and refine their theoretical apparatus about race as well as gender and sexuality. Our introduction's title, "In Medias Race," is a step toward theorizing the assumption from which the essays in *Race Consciousness* start—that American history, politics, and culture are and have been profoundly "in the midst of race." More significantly, however, these essays demonstrate new ways to present and discuss America's racial self.

START MAKING SENSE

Race Consciousness begins with "Looking B(l)ackward," Robin D. G. Kelley's compelling dystopian vision of black life in the academy at the end of the twenty-first century. Though laced with humor, Kelley's narrative makes serious observations about the interdependency of the academic world with the "real world." Kelley simultaneously celebrates and critiques contemporary approaches to African-American Studies and cautions current and emerging scholars in the field not to forget the work of their intellectual forebears.

The essays in part 1, "Specters of Race: The Culture of America as a Culture of Race," seek to demonstrate the constitutive role played by race in American culture. Although "American culture" has often portrayed itself as racially transcendent, or worse, exclusively white, African-American culture is a fundamental component of "American culture," as Ralph Ellison's literary and jazz criticism and W. E. B. Du Bois's writing on black spirituals have shown. The essays by Gavin Jones and Jeremy Wells identify this sort of cross-cultural exchange in two very different cultural sites: the dialect of the American South and the proto–heavy metal music of rock musician Jimi Hendrix, respectively. Blackness informs American social and political identities differently from cultural identities, however. African-American intellectuals such as James Baldwin and Toni Morrison have cogently identified how ideologies of whiteness are constructed upon and against blackness. Judith Jackson Fossett locates the constructed nature of whiteness and masculinity in the materiality of costumes worn by the Ku Klux Klan as portrayed in the work of turn-of-the-century novelist Thomas Dixon.

Despite the official end of chattel slavery and legally codified segregation, America's history of slavery and colonialism continues to influence the social and material culture as well as the lived experiences of both black and white contemporary Americans. In what ways do the traces of race and history remain? Part 2, "Historical (Re)Visions: Legacies of Slavery and Colonialism," seeks to answer this question with two innovative essays. Monique Guillory presents insightful work on a New Orleans luxury hotel, haunted by its history as the primary site for a racialized system of concubinage known as *plaçage*. The legacies of slavery are also theorized psychoanalytically as experiences of trauma in Bruce Simon's reading of Gayl Jones's novel *Corregidora*.

The social, political, and cultural dimensions of the lives of people of African descent in America remain a fundamental feature of African-American Studies. Such being the case, part 3, "Race(d) Men and Race(d) Women: African-American Cultural Studies," features Margaret Rose Vendryes's consideration of the intersections of race, lynching, and art at an extraordinary 1935 art exhibition. This section also investigates some of the ways race has mattered for black people. Jeffrey A. Tucker's critique of journalist George S. Schuyler's dismissal of race is based in part on an understanding that African Americans use race to identify and empower themselves despite the injustices done to them in race's name. The expression "race man," for example, suggests that black political solidarity depends on a pragmatic understanding and limited acceptance of racial difference. This kind of politicized race consciousness is addressed in Eddie S. Glaude, Jr.'s extensive study of the nationalist impulse concomitant with the spiritual use to which African Americans have put the biblical story of Exodus. John L. Jackson, Jr.'s contribution, on the other hand, illustrates how for black youth in contemporary Brooklyn, racial difference manifests itself as fear and distrust with respect to the surrounding forces of (white) law enforcement and popular media.

Whereas "Race(d) Men and Race(d) Women" focuses on black America's conceptions of racial meaning, the volume's final part, "Cracking the Code: Exposing the Nation's Racial Neuroses," considers white America's reactions to black America in several political contexts. Both Felicia A. Kornbluh's refutation of explanations of the recent ascent of the political Right made by white liberals and white conservatives and Karen Ho and Wende Elizabeth Marshall's critique of politicized constructions of black pathology identify and denounce recent developments in the troubling trend of racial scapegoating in American politics. Paul Kramer's account of the American occupation of the Philippines at the turn of the century identifies the transplantation and iteration of American racisms by the U.S. military within a foreign context. Rusty L. Monhollon closes *Race Consciousness* with a detailed portrait of white reaction to the Black Power movement of the 1960s in Lawrence, Kansas. These essays, each in their own way, attempt to make sense of race at the end of the twentieth century.

ACKNOWLEDGMENTS

Our jobs as editors were made easier through the efforts of many individuals and organizations. First and foremost, we thank our contributors for providing scholarship of excellent quality that literally takes African-American Studies into the new century. The essays in this volume began as presentations at "The 'Negro Problem,' 1895–1995," a graduate student conference in African-American Studies held at Princeton University in March 1995. We thank the panelists, faculty respondents, moderators, participants, and sponsors, who played vital roles in the conference's success.

Astute and generous counsel helped us competently navigate our inaugural journey through the often complex terrain of the publishing world. We thank Arnold Rampersad, in his role as director of the Program in African-American

Studies at Princeton and as our advisor, for having confidence in our abilities and encouraging us without hesitation as we planned our conference and edited this volume. His expert advice has been invaluable. We thank Nell Irvin Painter for her collaboration with Professor Rampersad on the foreword, for her generous support, and for making us contemplate the logistics as well as the labor necessary to complete this project. We thank Wahneema Lubiano for her graciousness and patience as she always made time for us and our ideas, and for being such an inspiring model as organizer of the *Race Matters: Black Americans, U.S. Terrain* conference at Princeton University, April 1994. We thank Diana Fuss for her keen interest in this project and her feedback at every stage of the process.

We thank Robin D. G. Kelley for writing an excellent introduction and for his continuing enthusiasm for this project and generosity to us. We thank Kevin Gaines and Penny Von Eschen for helping us envision the scope of this book during its initial stages and for offering useful feedback on the preface. We also thank Jean Washington, Rene Shepperd, and Hattie Black at the Program in African-American Studies for their unstinting patience and for unfailingly providing access to the program's resources. We also acknowledge the support of members of the Princeton University community including President Harold Shapiro and the Office of the President, Dean John Wilson and the Graduate School, and the staff of Forbes College, especially John Gager, Master at Forbes, for encouraging Judith as she completed this project.

The final assembly of the manuscript was accomplished with the support and assistance of Tom Keenan, Wendy Chun, Doreen Cooper, Gavin Jones, Helen Pallas-Viola, Bruce Simon, Marilyn Walden, and Gloria Jackson Bacon. We thank them for their invaluable help.

Finally, we thank Belinda Redden and Clayton Fossett for believing in us, supporting us, and putting up with us through it all, from the inception of the conference through the publication of this volume.

This book grew from the nurturing environment of the Program in African-American Studies at Princeton University. Ruth J. Simmons, now president of Smith College, mobilized a formidable group of talented intellectuals to advance scholarship in the field when she served as vice provost here. We offer this volume as affirmation of President Simmons's larger vision for the program. With our utmost appreciation, this book is dedicated to her.

JUDITH JACKSON FOSSETT is assistant professor of English and American Studies and Ethnicity at the University of Southern California. Her current project traces the role of the figure of the shadow in American culture.

EDDIE S. GLAUDE, JR., is assistant professor of Religion and Africana Studies at Bowdoin College. He is working on a manuscript about the relation between religion and black nationalism.

MONIQUE GUILLORY is a graduate student in the Department of Comparative Literature at New York University. She is co-editing an anthology entitled *Soul: Black Power, Politics, and Pleasure,* forthcoming from New York University Press.

KAREN HO is a graduate student in the Department of Anthropology at Princeton University.

JOHN L. JACKSON, JR., is a graduate student in the Department of Anthropology at Columbia University. His contribution is an excerpt from a forthcoming larger piece about ethnography in urban America tentatively called *Niggersville.*

GAVIN JONES is a member of the Society of Fellows at Harvard University.

ROBIN D. G. KELLEY is professor of history at New York University. His works include *Hammer and Hoe: Alabama Communists during the Great Depression* and *Race Rebels: Culture, Politics, and the Black Working Class.*

FELICIA A. KORNBLUH is a graduate student in the Department of History at Princeton University. She is an associate fellow of the Institute for Policy Studies in Washington, D.C.

PAUL KRAMER is a graduate student in the Department of History at Princeton University. He is completing a dissertation on the role of anthropology and racial knowledge in the U.S. colonial administration of the Philippines.

WENDE ELIZABETH MARSHALL is a graduate student in the Department of Anthropology at Princeton University.

RUSTY L. MONHOLLON is a graduate student in the Department of History at the University of Kansas. He is currently writing a history of Lawrence, Kansas, in the 1960s.

NELL IRVIN PAINTER is Edwards Professor of History at Princeton University. Her works include *Exodusters: Black Migration to Kansas after Reconstruction; Standing at Armageddon: United States, 1877–1919;* and forthcoming, *Sojourner Truth: A Life, a Symbol.*

ARNOLD RAMPERSAD is Woodrow Wilson Professor of English at Princeton University. His works include *The Art and Imagination of W. E. B. Du Bois; The Life of Langston Hughes,* vols. 1 and 2; *Days of Grace* with Arthur Ashe; and forthcoming, a biography of Jackie Robinson.

BRUCE SIMON is a Charlotte W. Newcombe Fellow in the Department of English at Princeton University. He is completing a dissertation entitled "The Race for Hawthorne."

JEFFREY A. TUCKER is an instructor in the Department of English at the University of New Hampshire. He is currently writing on the works of Samuel R. Delany.

MARGARET ROSE VENDRYES is a graduate student in the Department of Art and Archaeology at Princeton University. She is writing an analysis of the artistic work of the American sculptor Richmond Barthé.

JEREMY WELLS is a graduate student in the Department of English at the University of Michigan.

RACE CONSCIOUSNESS

ROBIN D. G. KELLEY

INTRODUCTION: LOOKING B(L)ACKWARD

AFRICAN-AMERICAN STUDIES IN THE
AGE OF IDENTITY POLITICS

(The tale you are about to read was inspired by Edward Bellamy's utopian socialist novel *Looking Backward,* published in 1887. My apologies to the late Mr. Bellamy for my shameless appropriation of the structure of his fascinating book. The ideas contained in this essay, however, are my own, and I take complete responsibility for all of them— including the most retrograde.

Finally, many of the characters herein are fictitious and are not intended to resemble real persons living or dead. If they do, it is purely coincidental.)

———

"Don't try to speak. If you can hear me, blink your eyes." The voice was faint but distinctive. Obviously a mature, learned man, though in the flood of bright lights he was little more than a brown silhouette.

"Where am I? Who are you?" I asked, trying desperately to gather my bearings and sound intelligible.

"You're at University Hospital. How are you feeling?"

"I feel fine. What am I doing in a hospital? I'm perfectly healthy." It was true; I felt very good, indeed, as if I'd been vacationing in the Caribbean for three solid months. Given my usual pace, it had been a long time since I felt so rested and relaxed.

"The matter is quite complicated," the man replied. As my eyes adjusted to the light, the silhouette leaning over me became visible. He was an elegantly dressed black man, perhaps sixty years of age, with salt-and-pepper hair closely cropped around his ears. He had a kind face, though his expression was one of obvious concern laced with heavy doses of curiosity. "You've just been roused from a deep sleep, or, more properly, a coma. So much I can tell you. Do you recall when you fell asleep?"

"When?" I stammered, confused by the question. "When? Why, just last evening, of course. I was attending a conference on Postraciality at the Crossroads of Signification—I think. I was on my way to a roundtable discussion on *The Bell Curve* but got turned around and couldn't find the room. I don't quite remember. In any case, there were two other sessions that caught my eye: one called What's the "Meta" For?: Narrative, Metanarrative, and Constructing the Sign in Post Modern America, the other titled Deconstruct to Reconstruct, That's All We Do. I chose the latter, found a nice comfortable seat in the back of the room, and proceeded to doze off."

"I understand, Dr. Kelley. But if that's your story, it wasn't last night." As he uttered these eerily familiar words, I was suddenly overcome with anxiety; I felt an asthma attack coming on.

"How do you know my name, uh, Mr. . . . ."

"Legend. Ralph Legend. I'm a part-time instructor at the university and a part-time medical attendant—what they called in your day an 'orderly.' I know a great deal about your day because, like you, I'm a historian. My specialty is the mid- to late twentieth century, which isn't very popular these days since everyone wants to work on the twenty-first—"

"Wait, hold on just a goddamn minute. I'm sure your life story is all that, but I need to know how long I've been sleeping. What day is it?"

"Thursday," he said. "Maybe you'd like to rest just a bit before we—"

"The conference was on a Saturday, so does that mean I've been sleeping for five days?"

"A bit longer than that, I'm afraid."

"More than a month?"

"Longer. Please, Dr. Kelley; you need to preserve your strength. If you calm down I'll tell you. Today is March 3rd ... 2095." Though his words fell somewhere between a whisper and a mumble, the final sentence felt like a gunshot in a dark, soundproof room. Silence stood between us for what felt like fifteen minutes but was probably more like thirty seconds.

"I know this is shocking and awkward, but I don't know how else to tell you. Perhaps you might want to rest a bit before—"

"Hell no," I shouted, surprised at the tone of my own voice and my use of profanity—something I've never been very good at, by the way. "Tell me everything—and I mean everything—right here and now."

"Well, I've been following your case for the past thirty years. For several months back in 1995 you were in the news. The headlines read, 'Promising Young Professor Falls into a Coma during Academic Conference.' Just when you were about to fall out of the media, Charles Murray—you remember him, right?—used you as the basis for his book *The Negro Mind: A Case of National Distraction,* in which he argued that members of racial groups with lower average IQ scores who make it into the ranks of the cognitive elite are incapable of processing so much knowledge. Either they fake their way through their careers, suffer emotional breakdowns or severe nervous disorders, or fall into a coma. Granted, your case was his only evidence, but the man won a Pulitzer nonetheless.

"Anyway, you were eventually brought to the university and placed under observation. I discovered you because I wrote my thesis here at City Community University on race and the rise of the Right at the turn of the century—the twenty-first century. Since nobody wanted to publish the thing and I couldn't get a job, I ended up teaching one course a semester here at CCU and taking odd jobs to make ends meet. When I found out you had been relocated here, I took a position at the hospital so that I might be around if and when you woke up."

I couldn't believe my ears. At first I thought it was some kind of a joke—asleep for a hundred years? Be real! But as I carefully studied the hospital room and took notice of all the new technology, it quickly became clear that things were different. Once I realized it was not a joke, I became angry and resentful. I missed seeing my daughter grow up or my wife's artistic career take off. I never had a chance to say goodbye to anyone in my family, not even my mother. And I never had the pleasure of seeing a book of mine reviewed in the *New York Times* or the *New York Review of Books,* or the *Village Voice,* for that matter. Nevertheless, my melancholy mood was quickly overtaken by curiosity: after all, I am, in essence, a 132-year-old time traveler with a rare opportunity to see the future.

The doctors checked me out and released me that afternoon under Dr.

Legend's supervision. Legend kindly offered to show me around campus. "I read many of your articles and both of your books," he told me, "despite the fact that neither the *Times* nor the *New York Review of Books* reviewed them."

"Don't forget the *Village Voice*," I added, perversely grateful that I'd outlived all those book review editors.

At first I walked slowly and tentatively across the sprawling urban campus; although modern technology preserved my thirty-two-year-old frame, my legs were still weak. Once I got my stride, Dr. Legend started to fill me in.

"A lot has changed since your day," he warned. "Black college students make up about one tenth of one percent of the undergraduate students nationally and an even smaller proportion of the graduate population. With the exception of English, the number of black faculty has dropped to about a fifteenth of what it was a hundred years ago. To make matters worse, the Afro-American Studies program here at City Community, and elsewhere, is now balkanized into several different programs."

Dr. Legend gave me much more than I could absorb. After a few minutes I began to fade out, hearing bits and pieces of his narrative—none of which sounded uplifting or positive. Fifteen minutes later, we entered a tiny gray building in bad need of repair. "This is Asante Hall, the home of the Center for Africological Thought and Practice. The director, Dr. Muhammad Khalid Mansa Musa, usually has office hours about this time. He is pretty well known around these parts, does a lot of media spots, and holds the Distinguished Man of Kemet Chair in Africology. I should add, however, that all black faculty nowadays have chairs except for those of us who teach part-time."

Dr. Musa seemed genuinely pleased to see us. The place was dark and deserted and, besides himself, the only other live body in the building was his part-time secretary. There were no students to be found anywhere.

"I heard on the radio that you had finally been jolted out of your deep sleep," he said as he extended his hand to greet me. "The ancestors work in mysterious ways." Without skipping a beat, he proceeded to tell me about the strength and vision of Africology generally and his program in particular.

"We are out here in the community working with folks who buy our literature religiously. It's these outside funds that keep us going, not the university but the street vendors. Unlike those other Negroes, always talking about difference and diversity within blackness, we know that the man sees only one type—Nigger— and we've been fighting for him to see us as Africans, noble and proud. Any scholars not down for the struggle, not writing about the history or liberation of black people are worthless to us."

"With all due respect, Dr. Musa," I interrupted, "that's a very old debate. The pioneering black scholars practically had no choice but to devote their work to uplifting the race. But is that always the best place for them to be? Aren't there some negative consequences to allowing skin color and ethnic allegiances to drive one's scholarship?" I spoke with hesitation, surprised that people were still talking about such issues but cognizant of the fact that I hadn't a clue as to what transpired over the course of the past century.

"I beg to differ, my brother. You're either with us or against us. If you don't work on some aspect of black life then you're selling out."

"I'm not too sure," I interjected. "I recall seeing something John Hope Franklin wrote a long time ago. An article titled 'The Dilemma of the American Negro Scholar.' I read it in a collection of his essays published a couple years after I finished grad school, but it's older—indeed, it predates Harold Cruse's *Crisis of the Negro Intellectual.*"

"Now you're digging into some old school shit!" blurted Dr. Legend, whose loss of composure surprised all of us. "I'm sorry gentlemen. I don't know what came . . . , uh. Anyway, please continue."

"Thank you. Franklin was pointing out how difficult it was for black scholars to carry the burden of the entire race on their shoulders and how that kept many from pursuing important work in the fields in which they were trained. Do you have a copy of that book around here?"

"Sure, we have everything online or on the ECD system. ECD stands for Extremely Compact Disc. Let me pull it up real quick." The new technology was fascinating. One subway token-sized disc had the capacity to hold an entire university library. In addition to the printed words, we had the benefit of hearing the text read aloud in the author's voice, which had been digitally reconstructed through technology developed by a company called Da Lench Mob Electronics. Dr. Musa highlighted the text in question and pressed the return key. Magically, I was back in my own day listening to the eloquent voice of the dean of black history:

> Imagine, if you can, what it meant to a competent Negro student of Greek literature, W. H. Crogman, to desert his chosen field and write a book entitled *The Progress of a Race.* Think of the frustration of the distinguished Negro physician C. V. Roman, who abandoned his medical research and practice, temporarily at least, to write *The Negro in American Civilization.* What must have been the feeling of the Negro student of English literature, Benjamin Brawley, who forsook his field to write *The Negro Genius* and other works that underscored the intellectual powers of the Negro? How much poorer is the field of the

biological sciences because an extremely able and well-trained Negro scientist, Julian Lewis, felt compelled to spend years of his productive life writing a book entitled *The Biology of the Negro*.[1]

"I see your point, Dr. Kelley, but you completely misunderstand why these scholars made the decisions they did. Nobody held a gun to Benjamin Brawley's head and told him to abandon English lit. He was committed to black freedom and made the proper sacrifice. Besides, where could he have studied Black Studies? Harvard? Howard? Come on, man! He had to invent it first."

"Yes," I retorted, "but don't you think we ought to work in all fields? Perhaps our collective experience gives us a different perspective on science, technology, European literature and art, and so forth? Or maybe our experience *does not* give us any unique perspective on issues related to black people in the United States. After all, you're not suggesting that Africological insights are something we are born with or learn in our families and communities, right? If that were the case, why offer college classes and degrees?"

Dr. Musa, who looked visibly agitated, started to tug on his kente watchband. "You obviously missed a lot while you were sleeping. We're not the naive essentialists we've been made out to be. We insist that culture is learned, it isn't biological. If it were, we'd be out of business. We believe that the best culture, the most liberating culture, existed before the European invasion. We're trying to recover that and reconstruct it for the present generation. That has been our project over the past century plus. And you should know better than anyone that the work we do grows out of real, deep historical scholarship, not guessing games or abstract theorizing. Go back and read the works of William Leo Hansberry or Cheikh Anta Diop or Frank Snowden."

I should have left it alone, but I couldn't. One hundred years is a long time without an argument. "But Dr. Musa," I interjected, "why does every useful thing have to always come out of Africa? What about the important contributions by black nationalist scholars who looked to the black experience in the United States, or the Americas more generally, for resistive and community-sustaining cultural values? I'm thinking about V. P. Franklin's book *Black Self-Determination* or John Langston Gwaltney's *Drylongso*.[2] Where do they fit in the paradigm you're constructing?"

Dr. Musa simply shrugged his shoulders and said, "I'm not familiar with those texts."

"Yea," Dr. Legend added, "they ought to be foundation texts but your predecessors couldn't see the sand for the pyramids. The lefties were no better, though. As soon as black folk start talking about 'us,' 'our people,' 'black aesthetic,' any of that, they start crying essentialism."

"Don't get me wrong," I added, trying to move our discussion to more institutional concerns, "I'm not arguing that the work Africologists do isn't important, politically or otherwise. There are obvious benefits to your approach; in the past black leaders have been able to mobilize folks by invoking a sense of community, a sense of nationhood, and in so doing they have made tremendous strides toward improving their condition and transforming America. But judging from the current situation, you all obviously didn't win. Why do you have such a small office, small staff, and from what I gather, an abysmal enrollment?"

"I admit, we've made mistakes in the past. A century ago we were aware of declining enrollments and the assault on affirmative action, but we didn't have a very good strategy to deal with it. We thought building independent schools and independent institutions within established universities would create a base of support. But not many of our people responded; see, they're brainwashed and we need to set them straight. They need a trip to the East to see our heritage, to understand that we have a long tradition of learning dating back from Egyptian scientists to the Muslim clerics of West Africa. Modern Negroes are just—"

"Now hold on just a second, brother Musa," chimed Dr. Legend. "Don't forget that black enrollment declined because they could no longer get into college; they dismantled all efforts to recruit people of color; used test scores against us; and cut out all financial aid. Now college is the preserve of the white minority."

"What happened to the black colleges?" I inquired, "like Morehouse and Spelman and Morgan State?"

"You really want to know? Some became racially integrated colleges, the rest are behavior adjustment centers."

"Behavior adjustment?" The words struck me as both familiar and absurd. "Yes," Dr. Legend responded, "we'll talk about that later. At any rate, for the past three decades there have been fewer and fewer options for black high school grads. Even trade and technical schools have all but been abolished since there are no more trades to learn. Dr. Musa is right to say that the Africologists tried to establish independent schools for black folks, and it was a good strategy given the circumstances, but few could afford the tuition, and those who could usually got their children into mainstream colleges."

"Running a school costs, you know," added Dr. Musa. "So does running a program—and time is money. I must bid you good day, sirs. Thanks for stopping by." Dr. Musa turned from us and stared coldly out the window. "You are quite fascinating," he murmured, "even if you are possessed with a limited late twentieth-century understanding of the world. I wish you the best of luck readjusting to our society. Tuta o nana."

Dr. Legend gathered me up and together we walked next door to Stuart Hall, where the Program in Antiessentialist Black World Studies was housed. The program was run by committee instead of a single chair—each member representing a different voice, though the faculty was so small that certain individuals had to speak for multiple constituencies. Yet everyone in the family of blackness was represented: Africans, West Indians, black Europeans, Afro-Canadians, black Pacific Islanders, women, men, gays, lesbians, ethnic and cultural hybrids, mulattoes, intellectuals, poor people, middle-class Negroes—you name it. Unfortunately, their vast and inclusive definition of blackness was not accompanied by vast office space. The program had one main office, four tiny faculty offices, and a copying machine that they shared with Africology. The walls were adorned with beautiful artwork and strikingly original posters. My favorite was from a conference titled " 'She's a Bricolage House': Art, Desire, and Black Female Sexuality."

"Dr. Kelley, allow me to introduce you to Dr. Patricia Post; she's on faculty here in the program and holds the RuPaul Chair in Black Culture/Gender Studies." Dr. Post was pleasant, though she looked tired and disheveled. As she explained to us, because of budget cuts, she and her colleagues had to teach overloads in order to cover the range of identities represented by the program. When I asked her whether Dr. Musa's program offered some of these courses, she scoffed. "The Africologists have written off the majority of black folk, and they certainly have no interest in the less flattering and more complicated aspects of black life. Do you know their story? Let me tell you." She leaned toward me and began speaking in a low, conspiratorial tone.

"Those guys might be broke now, but during the turn of the century with the rise of the Gingrich regime, their predecessors, the Afrocentrists, began getting huge government grants. Apparently, their militant defense of two-parent families, their judgments on homosexuality, their attacks on feminism, and their emphasis on tradition earned them support from the 'family values' conservatives. To be fair, not everyone under the banner of Afrocentrism advocated these conservative ideas, and the program directors felt rather uncomfortable taking money from an administration most African Americans opposed. Nevertheless, for a while there they were—as they used to say in the 1980s, 'living large.' "

"Let's be honest," Dr. Legend interrupted. "Only a handful of Afrocentrists benefited back then, and most folks committed to an Afrocentric perspective— and there were many who did not always agree—bolted from those government-funded programs in a hurry. Indeed, the institutions became a shell of their former selves, and once their faculty and student body left or started protesting, the money dried up. The state dropped them like a teenage welfare mother."

As Dr. Legend continued to speak, I recalled my own era, when the kind of scholarship Dr. Post promoted was hot and I, in my own way, was a part of it. "Things weren't so bad for the antiessentialists in the nineties," I pointed out. "We had a real renaissance in Black World Studies: it was the age of diversity within black politics, representations, sexualities; the age when NBA referred to basketball and the New Black Aesthetic; the age of black snap queens and Clarence Thomas; the age when the Whitney Museum could organize an exhibit on black males and display Mapplethorpe's work and not invite hard-core black nationalist artists like the AfroCobra collective; the age of the black British invasion; the age when Paul Gilroy appeared in the *Chronicle of Higher Education,* Isaac Julien appeared on BET's *Our Voices* with Bev, and *The Black Atlantic* found a place on every hip person's bookshelf. It was an age when intellectuals and artists really exploded the cultural straitjacket that blackness had been in the past. Those were exciting times."

For a moment there, I was giddy with nostalgia; that is, until Dr. Post burst my bubble. "You are right; those were relatively good times if you never left the auditorium, conference room, or movie theaters where those issues were being discussed. And don't forget that, while black feminists were the wedge that opened up discussions of diversity within black communities, they were eased on out real quick. Black males became the main subject and black male scholars became the primary voices. The issue of sexuality, for instance, which black women—lesbian and straight—put out on the table, became largely a black male issue. Even the black British invaders—they were men for the most part. OK, except for Hazel Carby . . . but she is but one."

"I see. So what happened after that?" I asked.

"Like every other generation, black folks went out of style. The memoirs and films had become formulaic, and the really creative artists lost their foundation support with the new regime. Moreover, the really cutting edge scholarship became less and less comprehensible to readers beyond a small circle of academics."

"That's true," added Dr. Legend, "but they also messed up by not drawing on and acknowledging earlier intellectual traditions. Sure, they were all into Du Bois and Hurston and the like—the usual suspects—but hardly anyone talked about Albert Murray. In the midst of the Black Power movement of the late 1960s, Murray raised the issue of authenticity before some of the young lions of the 1980s and 1990s had sex for the first time. Dr. Post, can you bring up *The Omni-Americans* on the monitor? Yes, page 97." Suddenly, a simulated voice of Albert Murray began to read:

> Being Black is not enough to make anybody an authority on U.S. Negroes, any more than being white has ever qualified anybody as an

expert on the ways of U.S. white people. It simply does not follow that being white enables a Southern sheriff, for instance, even a fairly literate one, to explain U.S. foreign policy, air power, automation, the atonality of Charles Ives, the imagery of Wallace Stevens, abstract expressionism, or even the love life of Marilyn Monroe.

If it did, then it would also follow that the oldest and blackest Negro around would be the most reliable source of information about Africa, slavery, Reconstruction politics, the pathological effects of oppression, the tactics and strategies of civil rights organizations, the blues, championship sports competition, and the symbolic function of the stud horse principle (and the quest for the earth dark womb!) in interracial sexual relationships.[3]

"See what I'm saying!" shouted Dr. Legend. "You could go back further than that. How can anyone pick up a novel by Wallace Thurman or Countee Cullen or Zora and think black people had to wait till the 1980s to discover there was more than one way to be 'black'? Besides, if students had been steadily reading Benjamin Brawley, W. E. B. Du Bois, Amy Jacques Garvey, C. L. R. James, Eric Williams, Oliver Cox, or even Cedric Robinson, they would not have had to be told by Gilroy and others that black people—as laborers, as thinkers, as bondsmen, as rebels—were central to the rise of the modern West. The difference between the work of your generation, Dr. Kelley, and that of, say, Du Bois and James is that the former pretty much ignored political economy and reduced class to just another identity. It was as if scholars of your age wanted to study the construction of identities without exploring what these identities mean in terms of power and material access. As if identities have some kind of intrinsic meaning irrespective of specific structures of domination."

Dr. Legend's intervention struck a chord in me, evoking more memories of my own age and my own students. The growing interest in the politics of identity had contributed immensely to debates in Black Studies. It has successfully extended our analytical scope to overlooked or trivialized cultural spheres and expanded our understanding of intellectual history. At the same time, the focus on identity sometimes tended to leave discussions of power at the discursive level. Factors such as political economy, labor, and the state were too often missing from treatments of the African diaspora. More significantly, very few scholars of my era—exceptions being Cedric Robinson, John Higginson, Penny Von Eschen, Vincent Harding, Peter Linebaugh, perhaps others—situated black people in the larger world of revolutionary upheaval or paid attention to the role of black labor in both reproducing capitalism and destabilizing economies and regimes.

"You're quite right," I said to Dr. Legend. "In some respects it's liberal pluralism repackaged. While celebrating difference and hybridity, many of those same scholars chastised black people for believing in a core black culture or for insisting that there is such a thing as a single black community. Rather than examine why the notion of a black community continues to carry weight among lots of ordinary people, why appeals to racial solidarity continue to work, most 'antiessentialists' criticize black nationalists for being wrong and for trading in fictions. Not that I'm against criticism, but we need to begin where people are rather than where we'd like them to be."

"I don't disagree with either of you gentlemen," said Dr. Post. "We've learned a lot over the past century and we've made efforts to rectify the problems you've outlined. You, especially, know this, Dr. Legend, since you've taught in our program before. But it's been a hard row. Most of our grad students are still driven by identity politics, and each one seems to always want to speak from his/her standpoint rather than see larger structures and transformations. See for yourself; drop in on Dr. Cannon's graduate seminar on the black body in servitude. In the meantime, I really must run. I have a meeting with the dean about getting our own copying machine."

We all walked out together; Dr. Post scurried down the hall and we headed upstairs to the seminar. Dr. Legend informed me that Dr. Cannon's course was once called "Slavery in the Antebellum South" but students protested to have the name changed. Dr. Cannon, a crusty old historian who fought hard as a young scholar to break down disciplinary boundaries and to "invigorate" his discipline by promoting cultural studies, decided to throw his students off a bit by assigning an ancient text titled *Roll, Jordan, Roll: The World the Slaves Made.* (The students recognized the author as the neoconservative theorist who served as top advisor for the Gingrich administration.) But Dr. Cannon didn't care about the author's politics; he still considered it a masterpiece of scholarly work on slavery—I mean, servitude.

"First of all," announced one of the first-year grads, "the book is too long. He could have said this in 150 pages. More important, the author says almost nothing about sexuality, and when he does he reveals his heterosexist biases. The master's obvious homoerotic desire for the black male body, for example, goes completely unexplored. After all, isn't this why they used chains and whips instead of other forms of punishment? They had other kinds of punitive technologies available to them—why chains and whips?"

"I don't know," added another young voice, "I think he's saying something about the interdependence of the slave and master—the construction of the master's identity is dependent on the slave and vice versa. I'm not too sure about that; they each have autonomous cultures, and within those cultures is a vast array of differences. If we just took the so-called slave community itself, how can we call it a community, given distinctions by age, sex, sexual orientation, division of labor, skin color, etc.? And when we take these factors into account, we can't talk about a uniform 'desire.' Desire is not only socially constructed but can only be understood through the individual psyche, for it manifests itself in a variety of different ways in different people."

"Hold on," interjected the aging professor. "I know this might sound absurd, but bear with me. Maybe the primary reason they enslaved these people was to work on the plantation. Maybe they're interdependent because the master's lifestyle depends on slaves picking cotton which is then sold on the market? Maybe the whips and chains were used to discipline the labor force?"

"What's with the crass economism, Dr. Cannon!? By emphasizing production over reproduction, you are privileging males and thus silencing black women's voices. . . ."

I had heard it all before; it reminded me so much of my own seminars past that I began to feel a bit homesick for 1995. Besides, for all the absurdity embodied in that exchange, from the ridiculously limited psychosexual reading of slavery to Dr. Cannon's unrestrained sarcasm, my students taught me that identity mattered. Scholarly discussions like these not only allowed them to grapple with their own multiple identities, in some respects they succeeded in humanizing the people they studied. By making slaves sexual beings, the discussions made them cease to be just labor-producing profits for the big house. Their interventions, then, were quite useful, so long as they avoided creating hierarchies among different identities and remained true to the historical moment of which they spoke.

Thinking about my students and colleagues made me a little queasy. Dr. Legend escorted me outside into the sunlit courtyard behind Stuart Hall, where I took a minute or two to rest. As it was already late afternoon and we had one last program to visit, we decided to get going as soon as possible. Unlike the Programs in Africology and Antiessentialist Black World Studies, the Urban Underclass Institute had its own building and was located on the other side of campus. Indeed, W. J. Wilson Hall was spectacular—fifteen stories, red brick, huge picture windows in each office, lavish furniture. After the security guards frisked us, we proceeded to the main office on the twelfth floor, where we were greeted by an army of secretaries and assistants.

"Dr. Thomas, there are two gentlemen here to see you. He'll be out in just a moment." A moment passed and out walked a clean-shaven, bespectacled man in his late forties, attired in an elegant tailor-made sharkskin gray suit. Dr. Legend stepped forward to make the formal introductions. "Dr. Kelley, this is the institute's director, Dr. Souless Thomas; Dr. Thomas, meet Dr. Kelley."

"My pleasure, indeed. I read about you in Charles Murray's book. I don't agree with all of his assumptions, but he was a heck of a smart guy."

Suddenly I felt very uncomfortable; I had an overwhelming desire to jump through the large bulletproof picture window behind his desk to see whether it would lead me back to 1995. Dr. Legend probably sensed my discomfort but he did not make any gestures to leave. Instead he flashed a wide grin, letting me know that he found my suffering amusing.

"I have a million questions for you," announced Dr. Thomas. "What was it like in those days? Were you an affirmative action baby? Glad we got rid of that atrocious policy; too many of our people slid by in those days. Did Bill Clinton ever reveal his membership in the Republican Party? Did you ever run into the great thinkers of that era—Steele, Loury, Clarence Pendleton, Alan Keyes, Ken Hamblin? What was Clarence Thomas really like? You know I hold the Clarence Thomas Chair in Economics, right?"

I thought I was going to throw up all over Dr. Thomas's $500 wing tips. He not only brought out the worst in me, but he kept insisting on putting his arm around my shoulder as if we were old friends. I tried hard to be polite.

"I read about those people," I responded, "but never met any of them. Besides, that's all in the past. I'm very curious as to what you all do at the Urban Underclass Institute. When was it founded? Is it mainly a think tank, a research institution? Do you teach classes here?"

"We train some graduate students, but we mainly conduct research on the underclass and develop government policy for dealing with this deviant population. We started out as a group of neoconservative black economists with similar research interests; the group then expanded into a full-fledged institute after we merged with the Department of Criminology and the School of Genetic Engineering. That, my friend, turned out to be a great move; we shifted from econometrics and regressions to applied technology."

"Applied technology? You mean in terms of actually creating jobs? Improving security? Providing better systems of transportation for urban residents? What do you mean?" I asked.

"Oh no!" He chuckled a bit, taken aback by the questions. "Nothing of the sort. By applied technology I'm speaking of behavior modification."

The way the words rolled out of his mouth . . . it was chilling, pure evil. When Dr. Legend first mentioned "behavior modification" centers, I thought he was half-joking, an inside reference to the ways historically black colleges emphasized deportment and manners. Or perhaps I had misunderstood him. Now it was all coming to light.

"You see," Dr. Thomas continued, "as we've been saying all along, what distinguishes the underclass from the rest of society is their behavior. By 'they,' however, I don't mean black people exclusively, though they are still in the majority; the underclass consists of Hispanics as well as whites, especially the growing number of refugees from the European ethnic wars. These people are dysfunctional in every respect—they're violent, nihilistic, grow up in deficient families, and have no desire to do an honest day's work. And before the abolition of welfare, they were addicted to the government dole. Soon after they were cut off, the crime rate skyrocketed. We turned to the most logical solution: since behavior was the problem we needed to figure out a way to change their behavior.

"At first, we tried compulsory national service. We sent young men and women from the inner cities (clearly the most criminal element) to work camps where specially trained staff tried to teach them the ways of civilization. It didn't work; they constantly complained and whined about the way they were treated, their pay, the food, the uniforms, the long hours, the discipline, the armed guards, the barbed wire. We then realized that true behavior modification requires some kind of physiological alteration. The answer was right in front of our eyes, locked away in the primitive simplicity of the frontal lobotomy. So, with the help of engineers and biochemists, we declared chemical warfare on the worst neighborhoods in the country. Through a combination of chemicals and high-frequency radio waves that the human ear cannot detect—you know how those people are; they have a thing for the low frequencies—we've discovered a method of altering the behavior of the poor. For the time being, the system is called Behavior Adjustment Technology or BAT. Within minutes of experiencing BAT, they become kind, patient, forgiving, and passive. And their moral index has risen at least forty points. This method has turned the coldest homeboy into a model citizen—a better gentleman than myself, I might add. Ha, ha, ha! That's a good one. A better gentleman than myself. I must tell my wife that one . . ."

I couldn't believe my ears. My anger turned to utter confusion; I became numb. "So, you've eliminated poverty?" I asked, searching desperately for some silver lining in this dark cloud of human manipulation.

"Eliminated poverty? What? Oh, no, Dr. Kelley. That was never our intent. If we solved the problem of poverty, what would we do for a living? But let's look on the bright side, my friend: they may be poor but they have wonderful dispositions. Right now, BAT is still experimental and has only been used in California. We're poised to implement BAT throughout the rest of the country, but our attorneys advised us to hold off for fear of being sued by the private security industry for taking away their livelihood."

Was this the world we helped create, either by our active participation or our silence? Were we so ill-equipped politically and intellectually as to relinquish our basic right to humanity? What good is Black Studies, Ethnic Studies, Cultural Studies, any sort of humanistic studies in a world where our actions can be altered with the press of a button or a flip of a switch? If this was the fate of humanity, where were our scholars when it was time to respond?

My head began to tighten up, the twelfth floor of Wilson Hall spun madly out of control. A cacophony of ringing cash registers and blood-curdling screams grew louder and louder, becoming so unbearable it brought me to my knees, pulling me beneath the floorboards. Down, down, down I fell, into a vast, enveloping darkness, a pitch-black abyss.

"Robin, time to go. Wake up, it's show time. You don't want to disappoint the students." I knew that voice; it belonged to Wahneema Lubiano. Slowly I opened my eyes, afraid that I'd see nothing but darkness, or worse. To the contrary, I woke from my slumber to find that only a few minutes had passed, not the century of my nightmare. Before me stood the most beautiful sight I'd seen since the birth of my daughter. It was like the final scene in *Brother from Another Planet.* Dozens and dozens of men and women, intellectuals with the brilliance, vision, and a political commitment to create a different future for Black Studies. Alongside Wahneema stood Patricia Williams, Kendall Thomas, Elizabeth Alexander, Nahum Chandler, Tera Hunter, Tricia Rose, Elsa Barkley Brown, Farah Griffin, Craig Watkins—over there, Evelyn Hammonds and Evelyn Brooks Higginbotham, Earl Lewis, Kimberlé Crenshaw, Saidiya Hartmann, Michael Eric Dyson, behind them stood Peter Linebaugh, Penny Von Eschen, Jerma Jackson, Guy Ramsey, George Lipsitz, Michael Awkward, Charles Payne, Joe Trotter, Grant Farred; there's Gina Dent, and Brenda Stevenson, Tiffany Patterson, V. P. Franklin, Michael Hanchard, Jerry Watts, bell hooks, Julius Scott, Kevin Gaines, Hazel Carby, Paul Gilroy, Dwight Andrews, Chana Kai Lee, Linda Reed, David Roediger, Kobena Mercer; outside the ivy walls stood Lisa Jones, James Spady, Greg Tate, Crystal Zook, Arthur Jafa, Joe Wood; poised in the background were the dozens upon dozens of folks who gathered in Princeton to talk about "The Negro Problem"—yea, the grad students bold enough to stand on the shoulders of ancestors and our mentors—Du Bois, Cox, Frazier, Herskovits, Cayton, Drake, Allison Davis, Alain Locke, Charles Wesley, Dorothy Porter, Louise Kennedy, Anna Julia Cooper, John Hope Franklin, Carter Woodson, Baraka, Hurston, Leon Forrest, Gwendolyn Brooks, West, Morrison, Baker, Gates, Arnold Rampersad, Tom Holt, Manning Marable, Mary Berry, Nell Painter, Nellie McKay, Robert Farris Thompson, Nathan Huggins, David Levering Lewis, Anthony Appiah, June Jordan, Hortense Spillers, Stuart Hall, Walter Rodney, ad infinitum. Before me stood an endless sea of faces whose contributions to our work have been invaluable, faces gracious enough to forgive me for not mentioning their names and thoughtful enough to know that I'm running out of space.

As I stand here, on the cusp of yesterday and tomorrow, looking out into the beautiful faces of my colleagues and future colleagues, I feel confident that the future of Black Studies/Afro-American Studies/Africana Studies, whatever we decide to call it, is secure and that there are enough sane, committed, brilliant intellectuals among us to put up a good fight against the right-wing, racist onslaught we now face. They will remain suspicious of liberal pluralism dressed up in postmodern garb, of analyses that completely ignore history or questions of power, of narrow identity politics that presumes people are the sum total of our academic categories, of the tendency to limit our critiques of people's actions to moral chastisement. And I know for a fact that these folks will continue to look b(l)ackward for sources of inspiration and insight, for it is only by looking back that we can make sense of where we are and how we got here. Before we dismiss various schools of thought within this larger matrix we call Black Studies, we need to pay attention to the ancestors and know what they were talking about.

NOTES

This essay was originally presented as the keynote address at "The 'Negro Problem,' 1895–1995," a graduate student conference sponsored by the Afro-American Studies Program, Princeton University, March 3, 1995. This lecture is dedicated to John Hope Franklin, who not only pioneered black studies but wrote one of the seminal essays on Edward Bellamy and the Nationalist movement.

1.   John Hope Franklin, *Race and History: Selected Essays, 1938–1988* (Baton Rouge: Louisiana State University Press, 1989), 299. The essay originally appeared as "The Dilemma of the American Negro Scholar," in *Soon One Morning: New Writing by American Negroes, 1940–1962,* ed. Herbert Hill (New York: Knopf, 1963).

2.   V. P. Franklin, *Black Self-Determination: A Cultural History of African-American Resistance,* 2d ed. (Brooklyn: Lawrence Hill Books, 1992); John Langston Gwaltney, *Drylongso: A Self-Portrait of Black America* (New York: Vintage Books, 1981).

3.   Albert Murray, *The Omni-Americans: Black Experience and American Culture* (1970; New York: Vintage Books, 1983), 97–98.

SPECTERS OF RACE

THE CULTURE OF AMERICA
AS A CULTURE OF RACE

GAVIN JONES

"WHOSE LINE IS IT ANYWAY?"
W. E. B. DU BOIS AND THE LANGUAGE OF THE COLOR-LINE

Between the end of the American Civil War and the beginning of the twentieth century, the understanding of black language became a fundamental part of debates concerning both the subjectivity of African Americans and their cultural influence on the American South and the American nation in general. As we head into a new century these same concerns, in a transfigured form, remain central to the fields of American and African-American Studies. Recent works by Eric Sundquist, Shelley Fishkin, Eric Lott, and Michael North have focused on the language of American culture while pursuing the Ellisonian project of demonstrating the interrelatedness of blackness and whiteness in the United States.[1] By showing how attempts to suppress African America were undercut by a cross-racial exchange of energies that provided—in the words of

Eric Lott—"a channel for the black cultural 'contamination' of the dominant culture" (6–7), each of these works describes America as a "creolized" nation formed by the amalgamation of black and white ethnic traditions. It is in the context of such inquiries into cross-cultural exchange and the role of language within it that I consider W. E. B. Du Bois's *The Souls of Black Folk* (1903). In order to shed new light on a much-discussed work, I relate *Souls* to post–Civil War debates over language and the color-line, debates that frequently used ideas about speech as keys to understanding black culture, and that used these ideas to strengthen or attack the case for racial difference and social segregation. By focusing on the arguments over black language and culture to which *Souls* was to some extent a response, we are able to reevaluate Du Bois's rhetorical strategies and understand how the notion of "double-consciousness"—so often cited as the archetypal threat to black selfhood—was equally problematic for the white community whose color-lines were supposedly its cause.

SPEECH AS A MODEL OF CULTURAL INTERACTION: BLACK LANGUAGE AS THE WHITE MAN'S PROBLEM

The "funny" language of the Gullah-speaking Sea Islanders of the Carolinas, referred to by Du Bois in his chapter "The Sorrow Songs,"[2] was at the center of white interpretations of Southern black speech immediately after the Civil War. William Francis Allen's introduction to *Slave Songs of the United States* (1867),[3] a landmark event in the formal recognition of the musical "creative power" of African-American communities, established the fundamental tensions that would echo throughout subsequent accounts of the black vernacular. The main problem for white observers, especially those from the North like Allen, was the essential difference of this particular variety of black speech, the fact that its "strange words and pronunciations," "frequent abbreviations," and "rhythmical modulations" gave it "an utterly un-English sound" (xxiv). This strangeness was heightened by the fact that Gullah was able to transform the meaning of common words so as to make the English language appear foreign to itself: Allen gives a long list of words whose meanings are "peculiarly" different from "standard" American English, for example *stan'* (which means "look") and *talk* (which means "speak or mean") (xxvii). Rather than seeking an explanation for this unnerving otherness in the retention of African tongues or rhetorical practices, however, Allen turned to the paradoxical belief that Gullah—despite its tremendous ability to signify in a different and original way—was merely the product of "corruption in pronunciation," "extreme simplification in etymology and syntax," and "phonetic decay" (xxv, xxxiii).[4] Rather than being seen as an integral African-American language variety, Gullah was considered (as Du Bois recognized in his use of the ambiguous adjective "funny") at worst comical and at best strange. The paradoxical belief that Gullah was both original *and* derivative, that it behaved like a foreign language but was not actually foreign—a paradox that produced the opinion that Gullah speakers frequently knew not the meaning of their own words[5]—led to the belief that it was an inherently debased "dialect."[6] It was different, in other words, not through foreignness but through inferiority.

Allen's paradoxical position was the result of an inability to account fully for the *difference* of black speech. Although, as we shall see, Allen's recognitions would become part of a predominant movement toward social and linguistic segregation, there was a counterreaction in the South that complicated the idea of a simple division between black and white speech, at the same time as it questioned the idea that black linguistic difference was merely one of corruption or deficiency. Accounts of the Southern dialect of American English before the Civil War, often from visiting Britons like Charles Dickens and the actress Frances Kemble, noted that Southern whites from all class backgrounds learned the grammar and pronunciation of black English and retained the habit throughout their lives, becoming in effect "bidialectal."[7] After the Civil War, these accounts led to the contentious belief that, in the words of James A. Harrison's 1884 essay, "Negro English," "if one happened to be talking to a native with one's eyes shut, it would be impossible to say whether a Negro or a white person were responding."[8] Such observations that the speech of the South was, in the words of another observer, "more largely colored by the language of the negroes than by any other single influence,"[9] were clearly controversial at a time when the white gatekeepers of cultural propriety were drawing the color-line so severely in Southern society. Even more remarkable, however, is the fact that this particular view of language supplemented the recognition of cross-racial dialectal sameness with an acknowledgment of what one observer called "a real negro lingo, having its peculiar and distinguishing characteristics. . . . They exist in the tone of his voice, his manner of speech, his inarticulate interpolations and interjections . . . his frequent use of words in utterly unexpected senses."[10] Accordingly, Harrison's belief in the inability of the unsighted man to tell blacks and whites apart is supplemented by a recognition of an African-American use of slang, "an ingrained part of his being as deep-dyed as his skin" (144), that depends on "the ingenious distortion of words by which new and startling significance is given to common English words (e.g. a *hant* in Negro means *ghost*)" (145). Instead of merely indicating "corruptions" or "mistakes," Harrison lists twenty pages of "Negroisms," together with a thorough explication of the different system of grammar on which black speech depends.

The contentious recognition that the white dialect and the black dialect of the South were virtually identical was thus accompanied by a realization that black language still existed as something *beyond* white language. The white Southerner, it was implied, was using a language that was not completely his or her own, a language that was the product of the black community. In the words of the linguist J. L. Dillard, black English was recognized as "innovative rather than archaic" in that it was more likely to have produced the differences between Northern and Southern white dialect than to have been originally identical with the latter (*Black English,* 191). There was a definite sense, then, in which the linguistic world of the South contained a color-line that did not simply divide "correct" white from "incorrect" black speech, but that marked off a realm of the black vernacular that operated on a level of significance beyond the white community. Movement across this color-line was unidirectional, preventing white access to the full range of black meaning. Because it signified in two separate areas, black language was accordingly perceived as containing an ambiguity, a power of double meaning that often remained strangely untranslatable (as Harrison recognized, the "English equivalents are far from conveying the pungent meaning of the Negro expressions" [175]). This ambiguity corresponds to what modern scholars have termed the "counterlanguage" or "antilanguage" that developed within slave communities: a system of communication, inherited from Africa, that represented and created an alternative level of reality through the use of satirical double meaning.[11]

This double view of black language ("double" in the sense that it was both identical with yet additional to white Southern English) was doubly problematic for the white community. By failing to divide black from white speech completely, it allowed for the subversive notion of cultural intermingling between people of supposedly separate racial groups, while it also allowed for the possibility of a private level of communication among people of African descent, a realm of meaning that drew the color-line *against* the white community. Many white intellectuals in the South responded to this threatening notion by drawing their own linguistic color-lines that echoed Allen's account of black speech as entirely "foreign" to white speech—in that it never intermingled with the white variety—without conceding that the black variety might in fact *be* foreign in its grammar and vocabulary, that it might actually represent an African substratal presence. Allen's belief that Gullah was "foreign" owing to processes of corruption, decay, and simplification entered the assumptions and terminology of much post–Civil War philology. In Maximilian Schele de Vere's 1872 study, *Americanisms: The English of the New World,* for example, black speech is described as "subordinate" to and entirely without influence on the white variety, formed by "ignorance" and "carelessness," and determined by "some difficulty both in their hearing and in their organs of speech."[12] Physical determinism combined with mental denigration to produce the linguistic equivalent of a policy of black inferiority and subjugation. African retentions were not recognized; in fact, the emphasis fell on the idea of an Anglo-Saxon ability to assimilate other cultures and races, an ability that led to Joel Chandler Harris's claim that the dialect of Uncle Remus was simply white English three hundred years out of date and led to the popular "scientific" theory of black linguistic archaism expounded in the 1920s and 1930s by, among others, George Philip Krapp and Cleanth Brooks.[13] African-American language was forced into the Anglophone tradition at the expense of its modernity and integrity: black speech was both out-of-date and imitative, the product of either a backward and innately deficient mind or at best a product of what Du Bois called a "geographical color-line" (153) that saw the isolated nature of many black communities as facilitating the retention of archaic dialectal forms from particular parts of the British Isles.

Owing to the prevailing belief in a direct correlation between language and mental "ability," the understanding of speech played an integral part in the debate over the social and civil distinctions involved in the founding of the color-line in the post-Reconstruction South. The comparative tolerance of black English by wealthy whites before the Civil War, which led to the observation that the color-line had broken down in Southern speech, was destroyed by the new situation, in which poor whites and blacks were thrown into competition, and in which the tracing of white language to black influence was felt as a deep insult. This, combined with the felt need of Southern whites to defend their dialect against Northern assumptions of its inferiority, led to a concerted effort to exorcise evidence of black English and to restore Southern "pride," an effort that resulted in the denial of what Ernest Dunn has called a "genuine Black dialectal experience."[14] This attempt to split Southern speech apart can also be seen at work in the type of dialect literature made popular by Thomas Nelson Page and Joel Chandler Harris after the Civil War. Dialect writing was part of the wider language of the color-line: it was an attempt to encode an essential blackness in the written representation of speech, an attempt to make the lines of writing into color-lines designed to divide and discriminate on the printed page. As William Cecil Elam expressed it in his essay "Lingo in Literature" (1895), while in actual life black speech and white speech were virtually identical, when they were depicted in literature black speech was exaggerated in its "lingual barbarisms" while white speech was "revised according to Noah Webster and Lindley Murray," an act of discrimination that "is not only against the Reconstruction acts and the Civil Rights bill, but is forbidden by the Federal Constitution, as now amended" (286). Dialect writing was another example of what Du Bois called the "power of the cabalistic letters of the white man" (8) against the idea of linguistic and cultural equality, a power that established black speech as an incorrect and alien element within contemporary American English.

The attempt to establish a color-line in the language situation of the South, a color-line that might divide the "complexity" and "correctness" of white language from the African American's "corrupt" meaning and phonetic "decay," was an attempt to counteract the realization that black speech had produced white Southern speech while maintaining the power to resist it. Hence, this imposition of a color-line acted to separate black and white usage not at the point where black language existed in addition to white language, but at a point that marked the differences between these language varieties at every level. It was a color-line that depended on the paradox that black language was essentially different from yet entirely familiar to white language; that it was separate from white language without being unnervingly "other." This debate over language was central to a wider debate over the cultural interaction of races in the South, a debate that revolved around the white fear that the cultural fabric of the South may have been produced by the weaving together of two cultural strands (broadly speaking, the Anglo-American and the African-American) into a new, hybrid mode. It was a fear that the culture of the South, like its language, was a "creolized" amalgamation of two racial traditions. Rather like the problematic of representation identified by Homi Bhabha in the colonial situation—whereby the contact between cultures produces a hybridity that undermines the dominant culture's "univocal grip on meaning" and claims to "authenticity" by leaving the language of colonial authority "open to the trace of the language of the other"[15]—the debate over the racial origins of Southern culture was haunted by the idea that black language had generated the white language of the South while maintaining the power to undermine it.

AMERICANISMS IN *THE SOULS OF BLACK FOLK*

The Souls of Black Folk engages these debates over black speech in several fundamental ways, not least in Du Bois's discussion of the Sorrow Songs in the final chapter. Here, Du Bois remotivates the discourse of white ethnography, appropriating the positive elements within it while avoiding its derisive paradoxes. Du Bois exploits the notion that black language is a signifying alternative, that "things evidently borrowed from the surrounding world undergo characteristic change when they enter the mouth of the slave" (212), *without* suggesting that this "characteristic change" might be the product of linguistic corruption or might lead in the direction of nonsense. Du Bois rescues the recognition of "real poetry and meaning" (210) in black vernacular expression and considers the breakdown in intelligibility between blacks and whites the result of a displacement of African tongues[16] or a white misunderstanding of a "naturally veiled" (209) way of talking. At various points, Du Bois appropriates the common

observation that black speech was somehow "inarticulate" and lacking in grammatical coherence. His description of the small black community in the Tennessee Hills, whose thoughts "when ripe for speech, were spoken in various languages" (57), is an implicit recognition of a key aspect in white accounts of
black language: namely, the significant variety observed between different classes
of speaker and—during Reconstruction and after—within the single speaker as
his or her language came under new forces of transformation.[17] Throughout
Souls Du Bois parodies (or signifies on) the white interpretation of a lisped (66)
and inarticulate (75) black speech in order to provide social causes and cultural
solutions for observations of language behavior that were too often cited as *in
themselves* sufficient cause for racial segregation, just as they were supposed to be
sufficient proof of black mental ineptitude.

The debate over the African-American voice thus forms a theme in *The Souls
of Black Folk* that emphasizes the danger of a lack of individual articulation, the
danger of linguistic division within the black community, and the danger of a
breakdown in intelligibility between blacks and whites, all three of which are
powerfully illustrated in the story "Of the Coming of John." The Southern
village in which this story takes place is described as half-conscious and "inarticulate" because of the cultural division between blacks and whites (189); the black
community becomes unintelligible to itself when the educated black John
returns to speak in "an unknown tongue" (196); and Jennie's powerlessness
when molested by the white John is directly related to her "inarticulate" voice
(201). Just as John teaches the black children in the village not to "chop" their
words (200), Du Bois's story offers a lesson in the need for a coherent language
of interracial *and* intraracial identity.

Transcending this thematic role in the work, the debate over black speech is
profoundly significant to the structures of African-American experience around
which Du Bois builds *The Souls of Black Folk.* The notion of the "Veil," for
example, seems directly related to a color-line that was just as important to
discussions of linguistic division as it was to social segregation. As we have seen
in accounts of Southern speech, in the time of slavery this Veil (a color-line
permeable in one direction only) was a source of black strength, a preservation
of a private cultural world inaccessible to whites, a spiritual refuge, a channel for
rebellious talk. Accordingly, philologists after the Civil War recognized that this
realm of strange meaning and ambiguity was potentially threatening to the white
community. Du Bois transfigures this white perception of black language by
showing how, in the post-Emancipation world, this Veil becomes a threat to the
black community as well. The opacity of the Veil, its tendency to mask the
black self, becomes dangerous in a world where whites control the means of
recording and projecting American culture, because it facilitates the exclusion of

a true image of blackness from mainstream America, thereby condemning the African American to a condition of incomplete self-consciousness.

This condition is developed further by Du Bois in his now famous notion of "double-consciousness":

> this sense of always looking at one's self through the eyes of others, of measuring one's soul by the tape of a world that looks on in amused contempt and pity. One ever feels his two-ness,—an American, a Negro; two souls, two thoughts, two unreconciled strivings; two warring ideals in one dark body, whose dogged strength alone keeps it from being torn asunder.
>
> The history of the American Negro is the history of this strife—this longing to attain self-conscious manhood, to merge his double self into a better and truer self. In this merging he wishes neither of the older selves to be lost. He would not Africanize America, for America has too much to teach the world and Africa. He would not bleach his Negro soul in a flood of white Americanism, for he knows that Negro blood has a message for the world. He simply wishes to make it possible for a man to be both a Negro and an American, without being cursed and spit upon by his fellows, without having the doors of Opportunity closed roughly in his face. (5)

An unusual element in this passage is Du Bois's use of the term *Americanism*— traditionally a linguistic concept for a word, sense, or phrase peculiar to or originating from the United States—which implicitly connects this description of double-consciousness to the debates about language so prominent in late-nineteenth-century America. In this respect, Du Boisian double-consciousness can be read as a critique of the means by which the irony and ambiguity of black counterlanguage function in a world of supposed freedom. In the time of slavery, the "double words" that Du Bois identifies as stemming from the African American's double life (165) would have been manifested in the "naturally veiled and half-articulate" message of the Sorrow Songs (209). In a time of supposed emancipation, these double words manifest themselves in what Du Bois describes (in the chapter "Of the Faith of the Fathers") as the "two-edged weapon of deception and flattery, of cajoling and lying," destructive to the black community through the creation of pretense and hypocrisy, and destructive to the white community through the creation of revolt and radicalism (165–66). The language of ambiguity essential to the slave becomes a language of paradox in a world riven by the color-line.

Yet Du Bois's idea of double-consciousness is not just a critique of blackness.

It is also a critique of whiteness and, more important, a deconstruction of "Americanness." By paying close attention to the terminology of this passage, we arrive at a logical model strikingly similar to the unsettling understanding of the linguistic condition of the South described earlier. The sense of "always looking at one's self through the eyes of others" was also true for a situation where the white community was using a language partly beyond its control, a language that was able to encode insurrectionary sentiment and exist as a rhetoric of resistance beyond its interpretation. The threatening idea of ethnic intermixture implied by such a view is integral to Du Boisian double-consciousness. Instead of opposing the categories of "Negro" and "American," Du Bois qualifies the linguistic concept of "Americanism" by terming it "white Americanism" and opposing it to the condition of being "American" itself, which he locates as one half of the binary strife *within* the soul of the African American: when Du Bois mentions "Africa" and "America" in this passage he is clearly discussing the two older selves of the "American Negro." Just as the Southern dialect of American English was perceived to differ from the vague notion of a "correct," implicitly white speech because of the generative role within it of black language, likewise in Du Bois's description of double-consciousness the category of "American" differs from the lesser category of "white Americanism" because of the role of the "Negro soul" in the former. [18]

Not only does *Souls* declare the need for the black community "to know . . . the power of the cabalistic letters of the white man," but it also suggests the need to "test" this power by questioning the myths and assumptions upon which white culture depends (8). By opposing "American" to "white Americanism" in his description of double-consciousness, Du Bois implies that the truly "American" must by definition contain an element of blackness. This undermines the idea of a color-line in Southern speech that dismissed Americanisms derived from the slaves as, in the words of Schele de Vere, "nothing more than unsuccessful efforts to speak correct English" (150). As common descriptions of the blackness of the Southern dialect contradict myths of racial independence, Du Bois's idea of double-consciousness similarly works against the attempt to apply the notion of the color-line to American culture as a whole. Du Bois's description of double-consciousness is thus a remarkable rhetorical move that appears to placate white fears that "the American Negro . . . would not Africanize America" while it also suggests that an authentic and original American culture must necessarily contain an African element. Any gesture toward the calming of white fears is inherently ironic: the "Negro" would not Africanize America, suggests Du Bois, because he already had. In this way, Du Bois's apparent criticism of black selfhood reflects back on the white world from which the very notion of double-consciousness may have originally been gleaned. [19]

To redress a situation in which black "counter-cries" were frequently lacking in "formal logic" (88), Du Bois manipulates the logical structures of *Souls* to force upon the reader a recognition of the "intellectual communion" (149) that existed between blacks and whites in the pre–Civil War South. It was a communion that was necessary once more, thought Du Bois, if the greater ideals of the American Republic were to be realized in a cross-cultural exchange whereby two "world-races may give to each other those characteristics both so sadly lack" (11). This Ellisonian logic of cultural intermingling is repeated at key points throughout *Souls*[20]—for example, in Du Bois's description of the religion of the poor white as "a plain copy of Negro thought and methods," thereby making "the study of Negro religion . . . not only a vital part of the history of the Negro in America, but no uninteresting part of American history" (157)—yet nowhere is it more obvious than in Du Bois's chapter on the Sorrow Songs. As we have seen, Du Bois's discussion of these songs clearly remotivates the language of white ethnography, the paradoxical language that considered the "originality" and "genuineness" of black music to be—in the words of Allen—"partly composed under the influence of association with the whites, partly actually imitated from their music" (vi). The remotivation of this sentiment appears in Du Bois's description of the four steps involved in the development of the Sorrow Songs:

> The first is African music, the second Afro-American, while the third is a blending of Negro music with the music heard in the foster land. The result is still distinctly Negro and the method of blending original, but the elements are both Negro and Caucasian. One might go further and find a fourth step in this development, where the songs of white America have been distinctively influenced by slave songs or have incorporated whole phrases of Negro melody. (209)

Once more, Du Bois refuses to oppose the categories "Negro" and "American." Instead, he uses the terms "Caucasian" and "white America," which function like "white Americanism" in the earlier description of double-consciousness. Again and again, Du Bois's choice of language refuses to allow the possibility that a genuine Americanness can exist without an element of blackness. The unsettling cultural process that was recognized at work in the Southern dialect after the Civil War is extended by Du Bois to apply to the wider aspects of American culture, creating the possibility that processes of "Afro-Americanization" were at work within the American nation as a whole. Allen's paradox, that black vernacular products are somehow original *and* derivative, is destroyed. According to Du Bois's idea of the stages of the Sorrow Songs, the truly "original" music, the authentically American blending of what Du Bois calls "Negro" and "Caucasian" elements, is "*distinctly Negro*," and the element of "imitation" and "debasement" is discovered in the white community. As Du Bois phrases it in his conclusion to *Souls*, the African-American gifts of story, song, sweat, and Spirit have been actively woven with "the very warp and woof of this nation" (215). The logical conclusion of Du Bois's work is that anyone seeking the ideal segregation of the color-line must find Southern speech, American music, and the cultural originality of the American nation to be distinct problems.

THE LANGUAGE OF THE COLOR-LINE

Du Bois's description of double-consciousness and his account of the Sorrow Songs work against the drawing of the color-line in American culture because they expose how this culture is itself marked by cross-racial exchange. The power of the color-line to divide the South into "two great streams" (148) is perhaps the main target of *The Souls of Black Folk*. According to Du Bois, this color-line was "that central paradox of the South" (80) because, rather than solving the "Negro Problem," it precluded absolutely the very type of race contact necessary for the "effectual progress" of the African American (80); because its singular focus on color thwarted the drawing of lines of crime, incompetency, and vice (152); because it flatly contradicted the beliefs and professions of a supposedly Christian and democratic nation (151); and above all, because it led to the unidirectional Veil, which created the "strange meaning" (1) of being black in America, whereby a native son—to use Richard Wright's phrase—is made to feel a stranger in his own land (5). These paradoxes were central to the language and the logic of political pamphlets written in defense of the color-line by conservative whites in the Reconstruction and post-Reconstruction South, pamphlets that depended on the convenient appearance of a mysterious "race instinct" designed to gloss over a faltering and often self-contradictory mode of reasoning (as George Washington Cable was quick to realize, arguments based on "race instinct" were inherently paradoxical because, if this instinct were to exist, then it would render superfluous the legally codified color-lines that such arguments demanded).[21] An "ethical paradox" (*Souls*, 165) was at the heart of the color-line, just as it was central to attempts to account for the difference of black culture.

It is as a counterforce to such paradox that we should understand the importance of *articulation* (in the sense of "joining together" in addition to "expressing oneself coherently")[22] in *The Souls of Black Folk*. If white solutions to the "Negro Problem" moved in the direction of paradox, then Du Bois's solution moves in the direction of ambiguity. Du Bois's desire to be both a

"Negro" *and* an "American" is an example of this, as is his move to establish the originality of black song in order to reveal how American culture joins together the double meaning of blackness and whiteness. Accordingly, the rhetorical task of *Souls* can be viewed as an attempt to convert the language of paradox, typical of the white politics of the color-line, into an ambiguous language of cultural tolerance—an ambiguous language that was itself part of an African-American oral tradition, rooted in Africa and flourishing in what was widely recognized as the "sole American music" (205).[23]

As Eric Sundquist has shown, this articulation can be seen in the joining of "music" and "text" in *The Souls of Black Folk,* making Du Bois's work an "act of cultural transfiguration that welded African and white American traditions into a distinctly African-American cultural form, as had the spirituals themselves" (481). As a stylistic technique, moreover, this act of articulation can be seen at work in the large degree of hyphenation throughout *Souls:* the formation of compound words out of the hackneyed phrases of the much-debated "Negro Problem." Examples of this hyphenation include the term "color-line" itself, "double-consciousness," "soul-beauty," "soul-life," together with a host of compounds involving the word "race": "race-dislike," "race-sensitiveness," "race-childhood," "race-brotherhood," "race-feeling," "race-prejudice," "world-races," and so forth.[24] This unusual technique had a precedent in what James Harrison described as the "hybridization" characterizing black English, in which different words or word elements are combined to produce a new, composite meaning (145). It can also be seen as an attempt to forge a new language with which to talk about race, a new language of cultural difference that remotivates in subtle ways the existing words and phrases of the white pamphlet literature then dominating Southern politics. (In this sense, Du Bois's famous aphorism, "the problem of the Twentieth Century is the problem of the color-line" (1), can be read as a remotivation of the phrase "the Negro Problem" itself, a remotivation that identifies the "problem" as the paradoxical politics of segregation rather than simply that of racial presence.) This hyphenating technique is the syntactic equivalent of Du Bois's recognition that color and race cannot exist separately from other factors, that they are not in themselves "crimes" (88). The creation of these new words of double meaning has an analogy in Du Bois's call for a new American world of dual significance, a call for America to recognize itself as a hyphenated culture with a twin racial heritage.

It is here that Du Bois's notion of double-consciousness is particularly significant. As a logical structure, it enacts cultural "hyphenation." By locating the true element of paradox not within American culture but within the African American;[25] by locating the true color-line not between black and white society, but at the interface of blackness and a Southern culture that had assimilated that blackness, Du Bois was able to force upon his reader a recognition of a racially hyphenated American nation. Du Bois's rhetorical task was to transform the paradoxical America of the color-line—in which the black community is pulled apart by "the contradiction of double aims" (6)—into a radically ambivalent nation where blackness and whiteness are equally voiced: a nation where two "world-races"—subtly and silently separate "in many matters of deeper human intimacy" (87)—may combine their race-differences in a single cultural situation where unity and difference exist simultaneously. Such ambivalence is not that of the slave who must perpetually juggle two opposing realities and whose language signifies in two separate realms divided by a Veil, nor is it that of a culture in which "American" and "Negro" are opposite terms. Rather, it is the product of a color-line that functions not as a division but as what Du Bois calls a "point of transference where the thoughts and feelings of one race can come into direct contact and sympathy with thoughts and feelings of the other" (149). It is a cultural transference that depends on lines of linguistic "communication," on the "less tangible but highly important forms of intellectual contact and commerce, the interchange of ideas through conversation and conference, through periodicals and libraries" (134). The alternative to this multicultural America, says Du Bois, is a nation that contains the "strange meaning" of blackness (1), a nation whose very language becomes a "writhing," not just "translated into black" (165), but essentially untranslatable into white.

NOTES

1. I refer to Eric J. Sundquist, *To Wake the Nations: Race in the Making of American Literature* (Cambridge: Harvard University Press, 1993); Shelley Fisher Fishkin, *Was Huck Black? Mark Twain and African-American Voices* (New York: Oxford University Press, 1993); Eric Lott, *Love and Theft: Blackface Minstrelsy and the American Working Class* (New York: Oxford University Press, 1993); and Michael North, *The Dialect of Modernism: Race, Language and Twentieth-Century Literature* (New York: Oxford University Press, 1994).

2. W. E. B. Du Bois, *The Souls of Black Folk* (Harmondsworth: Penguin Books, 1989), 205. Further references to this edition appear in the text.

3. W. F. Allen et al., eds., *Slave Songs of the United States* (1867; Salem: Ayer Company, 1971). The written records of white interest in Southern black speech were often the result of military situations provoked by the Civil War. The Port Royal experiment in South Carolina to which Du Bois refers, where Union army officials placed cotton plantations in the hands of former slaves, resulted in the recording of black song that became the basis for *Slave Songs,* the written foundation of white interest in black music, and one of the earliest attempts to account for the grammatical peculiarities of Gullah. Similarly, Thomas Wentworth Higginson's dual account of the spirituals and of black

LIVERPOOL JOHN MOORES UNIVERSITY
LEARNING SERVICES

dialect (also referred to by Du Bois in "The Sorrow Songs") arose from his experience as commander of a black regiment during the Civil War. See Higginson, *Army Life in a Black Regiment* (Boston: Fields, Osgood, 1870).

4. The fact that Allen recognizes only a handful of Africanisms—which, like Du Bois, he calls "strange words"—(for example, *buckra, churray* [spill] and *oona* [you, both singular and plural]) was perhaps inevitable: not enough was known about African languages until the work of Melville Herskovits and Lorenzo Turner in the 1930s and 1940s. See Michael Montgomery, "Africanisms in the American South," in *Africanisms in Afro-American Language Varieties,* ed. Salikoko S. Mufwene (Athens: University of Georgia Press, 1993), 444. Montgomery speculates, however, that subsequent observers of Gullah probably suppressed their knowledge of Africanisms within Southern U.S. English because such a recognition was "too explosive" politically (442–43). For an account of Gullah as a creole language, and a reevaluation of Africanisms within it, see Salikoko Mufwene and Charles Gilman, "How African Is Gullah, and Why?" *American Speech* 62 (1987): 120–39.

5. See Allen, *Slave Songs,* xix. Allen also considers that African Americans enjoy the humor of "clearly nonsensical" phrases (ix).

6. J. L. Dillard has detected this logic in accounts of black speech that deemphasize African survivals. See "Creoles, Cajuns, and Cable with Some Hearn and a Few Assorted Babies," *Caribbean Studies* 3 (1963): 89.

7. In *Black English: Its History and Usage in the United States* (New York: Vintage, 1972), J. L. Dillard considers this to be beyond any real doubt (186). Shelley Fishkin uses many of Dillard's observations in her recent speculation that Mark Twain may have put a form of black speech into the supposedly white mouth of Huck Finn. Fishkin, *Was Huck Black?*

8. In J. L. Dillard, *Perspectives on Black English* (Hague: Mouton, 1975), 143.

9. L. W. Payne, "A Word-List from East Alabama" (1901), in Dillard, *Perspectives,* 169.

10. William Cecil Elam, "Lingo in Literature," *Lippincott's Magazine* 55 (1895): 287. Payne also has "a more or less distinct consciousness of the pure negroisms" (196) in black English.

11. See Marcyliena Morgan, "The Africanness of Counterlanguage among Afro-Americans," in *Africanisms,* ed. Mufwene, 423–33. This is obviously related to the black rhetorical practice of "signifyin' " discussed, more recently, by Henry Louis Gates, Jr. The fullest explications of the ambiguity of black expression at this time were George Washington Cable's two essays "The Dance in Place Congo," *Century* 31 (February 1886): 517–32, and "Creole Slave Songs," *Century* 31 (April 1886): 807–28, which explore black language and music as a satirical form of resistance to the dominant culture.

12. M. Schele de Vere, *Americanisms: The English of the New World* (New York: Charles Scribner, 1872), 148–50.

13. See Michael North, *The Dialect of Modernism,* 21, for Harris's account of

Uncle Remus's English. For discussions of, and reactions to, the notion that black English is an archaic form of English, see R. I. McDavid and V. G. McDavid, "The Relationship of the Speech of American Negroes to the Speech of Whites," *American Speech* 26 (1951): 3–17; in addition to Dillard, *Black English;* and Fishkin, *Was Huck Black?*

14. See Dillard, *Black English,* 211–12; and Ernest F. Dunn, "The Black-Southern White Dialect Controversy: Who Did What to Whom?" in *Black English: A Seminar,* ed. D. S. Harrison and T. Trabasso (Hillsdale: Lawrence Erlbaum Associates, 1976).

15. See Robert J. C. Young's discussion of hybridity, language, and creolization in the context of modern cultural thinkers like Bakhtin and Bhabha, in *Colonial Desire: Hybridity in Theory, Culture and Race* (London: Routledge, 1995), 20–26.

16. Following Thomas Wentworth Higginson's account of black music in *Army Life in a Black Regiment,* Du Bois gives the example of the "Mighty Myo" as "a strange word of an unknown tongue" (209). See Sundquist's chapter on *Souls* for an account of Du Bois's creation of a mildly Afrocentric argument. Sundquist, *To Wake the Nations.*

17. Again, Allen's introduction to *Slave Songs* is an example of this: he maintains that black dialects vary a great deal between plantations (xxiv); that each plantation is divided into many "grades" of speaker (xxiii); and that the language of the individual—just like black song itself—contains endless variation (iv).

18. Following the observations of Robert Stepto on Du Bois's revisions of this passage, Eric Sundquist has also suggested that the doubling of "Negro" and "American" is less important than the "second doubling" of "African" and "American." Sundquist, *To Wake the Nations,* 487. I would argue, however, that there is a third, equally important doubling—between "American" and "white Americanism"—that allows us to see more clearly the implication of cultural intermixture within the notion of double-consciousness.

19. For a detailed analysis of the Romantic and psychological ideas of double-consciousness of which Du Bois may have been aware (most probably from the thought of Ralph Waldo Emerson and William James), see Dickson D. Bruce, "W. E. B. Du Bois and the Idea of Double Consciousness," *American Literature* 64 (1992): 299–309. For a later and more skeptical view of this, see David Levering Lewis, *W. E. B. Du Bois: Biography of a Race, 1868–1919* (New York: Henry Holt, 1993), 96, 282, and 603.

20. In his essay "What America Would Be Like without Blacks" (a title that seems a direct reply to Du Bois's question "Would America have been America without her Negro people?" [*Souls,* 215]), Ellison describes how "most American whites are culturally part Negro American without even realizing it." *Going to the Territory* (New York: Vintage, 1987), 108. Ellison's notion that, in many ways, the American "mainstream" *is* black—a notion central to many recent

works of American studies (Sundquist's *To Wake the Nations* and Fishkin's *Was Huck Black?* are obvious examples) — relates directly to my reading of *The Souls of Black Folk.*

21. For an example of such pamphlet literature, see Henry W. Grady's 1885 essay "In Plain Black and White," reprinted in *Critical Essays on George W. Cable,* ed. Arlin Turner (Boston: G. K. Hall, 1980), 76–87. For Cable's response to the self-contradictory nature of the color-line, see the various essays collected in *The Negro Question: A Selection of Writings on Civil Rights in the South,* ed. Arlin Turner (New York: Norton, 1958).

22. Bruce Simon has pointed out to me the importance of this term throughout *Souls.*

23. Even the most demeaning and dismissive discussions of black cultural products would often recognize that African-American songs were America's only national music. See Schele de Vere, *Americanisms,* 153.

24. It is difficult to say with any certainty whether the extensive use of hyphenation in *The Souls of Black Folk* was the conscious intention of the author. It may, of course, have been an editorial decision made by A. C. McClurg, the original publisher of the work. Indeed, Du Bois's essay "The Relation of the Negroes to the Whites in the South," as it originally appeared in the *Annals of the American Academy of Political and Social Science* (18 [1901]: 121–40) — it eventually became the chapter "Of the Sons of Master and Man" — does not hyphenate the terms "color line," "race prejudice," and so forth. Du Bois's *Atlantic Monthly* essay, "Strivings of the Negro People" (which became the first chapter, "Of Our Spiritual Strivings"), however, *does* employ the unusual hyphenation of "double-consciousness" (80 [1897]: 194), suggesting that this technique was idiosyncratic to Du Bois and therefore the basis of future hyphenation in the final text of *Souls.* The very unusualness of hyphenating terms such as "color line," together with the apparent care Du Bois took with his proofs (according to Lewis, the original essays were "cut, polished, and mounted with a jeweler's precision for the McClurg collection" [*W. E. B. Du Bois,* 278]) makes it difficult to think that Du Bois was not in control of this element of his style.

25. As the Jewish-American novelist and journalist Abraham Cahan realized at around the same time as Du Bois, a view *into* the ambivalence of the ethnic group was essential in making Americans realize that it was not America itself that was divided so much as the ethnic selves who were forced to live between two cultures divided by what Cahan called the "chasm of race." The common theme throughout Cahan's fiction — of the immigrant speaking an ambivalent language that is neither really "American" nor "foreign" — is also true for Du Bois's vision of the cultural no-man's-land inhabited by the black savant: "confronted by the paradox that the knowledge his people needed was a twice-told tale to his white neighbors, while the knowledge which would teach the white world was Greek to his own flesh and blood" (6).

JUDITH JACKSON FOSSETT

(K)NIGHT RIDERS IN (K)NIGHT GOWNS

THE KU KLUX KLAN, RACE, AND CONSTRUCTIONS OF MASCULINITY

> The Klan was the only way to save our civilisation.
> —Thomas Dixon, *The Traitor*

Decked out in his white robe and mask, spewing white supremacist platitudes during a guest appearance on Geraldo Rivera's talk show, the figure of the hypothetical 1990s member of the Ku Klux Klan may still shock an otherwise rational, even liberal American sensibility. But the Klan member who helped orchestrate racial, ethnic, and religious terrorism against thousands of victims during much of the twentieth century (and still continues to do so) now spars rhetorically with a studio audience, flexing his muscles of hate for shock value, for show, and for his limousine ride through New York City. It would seem that the Klan in our modern-day experience has been transformed from aggressive agent of terror into loud purveyor of hate speech from the "fringe" or "margin" of American society. According to this line of thinking, the modern

Klan is inconsequential, a refuge for misbegotten (poor) whites who display a kind of atavism of racism, reverting to outmoded beliefs that, it would seem, flourished decades ago but no longer hold sway. Because the crucial coupling of violence and ritual has been severed, the Klan no longer operates as the organization capable of the lynching, tarring-and-feathering, burning, and raping that composed its central activities as detailed by folklorist Gladys-Marie Fry and others.[1] In other words, the material basis of Klan violence—the lynched and castrated black victim—and its racist rhetoric—hate speech whose brutality is effected through rhetoric—become conflated in contemporary debates. As the material sense of violence embodied in the Klan image is replaced or displaced by its rhetorical cousin, the modern guise of the Klan is emptied of its violent component and, consequently, both rendered nonthreatening and made available for mass media consumption through Geraldo Rivera and his other talk show peers. (It seems profoundly ironic that the material violence effected by the Klan, originally conceived as necessary for the execution of its extralegal function within society, would be contained at the cusp of the twenty-first century. Instead, the legal actions of the police and other agents of the state regularly and consistently do violence to black [male] bodies without cover of sheet or night.)

But even the performance/articulation of white supremacist thought hints at the pervasiveness and power of the ideological foundation of whiteness and exposes its constructedness. The racist rhetoric of this hypothetical talk show guest is mediated and made powerful through his accompanying Klan regalia. The robe and pointed hat/mask, usually sewn from white fabric, provide tangible continuity between the material and rhetorical work of the organization. The garb, in a sense, stands in as a proxy, albeit incomplete, for the group's actual execution of racist violence. And it is precisely this twinned effect of the robe—both its centrality to the effectiveness of Klan rhetoric and its less-than-complete figuration of that rhetoric—that makes visible the seams in the otherwise unadulterated fabric of white American identity. Though the practice of racialized rhetorical violence by the Klan differs from but still faintly echoes its original practices of racialized material terror, the garb—particularly the robe—remains constant. The robe then functions as a covering or disguise that aids in the communication of a certain white supremacist rhetoric. Consideration of the Klan, its violence, and its ritual as manifest in its costumes provides an opportunity to dismantle the scaffolding of the constructedness of race as we remove the robe of the Ku Klux Klan. What hides or lurks underneath the durable monotones of those robes and masks? If, as David Roediger suggests, whiteness is "a particularly brittle and fragile form of social identity," then those robes may cover delicate veneers.[2]

Viewed from a late twentieth-century vantage, the visual and literary logics of whiteness postulated by the author Thomas Dixon in his narrative trilogy of Reconstruction, written at the cusp of the twentieth century, offer a potential ideological source for representations of whiteness generally and the Ku Klux Klan specifically. In *The Leopard's Spots* (1902), *The Clansman* (1905), and *The Traitor* (1907), the operation of whiteness relies on dual factors: the nonvariegated monotone of white and its blinding visual appeal, which render observers awed by the sight.[3] Dixon describes the instigators of the Klan in *The Leopard's Spots* as "dazed" when they marvel at the power of whiteness undergirding the success of the organization (*TLS,* 153). "It was utterly impossible to recognise a man or a horse, so complete was the simple disguise of white sheet which blanketed the horse, fitting closely over his head and ears and falling gracefully over his form toward the ground" (*TLS,* 153). By reducing the operative terms of his narratives to those of strictly white and black, Dixon constructs an almost seamless Manichean racial, gender, and regional economy for the postbellum period. Whites are courageous, civilized, and rational; blacks are depraved, atavistic, and licentious. Southerners, though defeated by war, retain their dignity. Northerners, fervent in their abolitionist views, behave with apoplectic passion when crushing the South. Yet despite Dixon's narrational attempts to the contrary, the strict binaries are not entirely sustainable. Indeed, as Homi Bhabha suggests, the "ambivalence" constitutive of a multiracial, multicultural society, which Dixon seeks to eradicate, unwittingly returns to his texts through the object of the Klan robe.[4] Indeed, as a (literal) material repository of cultural (racial, gender, sexual) ambiguity that Dixon would otherwise deny, the seemingly stable object of the white robe ironically provides a cover for white skin and a vehicle for the expression of whiteness. How and why does the robe's overdetermined status within the racial logic of Dixon's texts put the fashion (both its material and its design) of whiteness on full display?

The Southern racial economy provides the material and backdrop for Dixon's trilogy. Consumed as popular novels and exchanged as Christmas gifts, Dixon's first three novels rode a tidal wave of commercial success, selling more than a million copies combined.[5] Writing in fervent and hostile response to a stage version of Harriet Beecher Stowe's *Uncle Tom's Cabin* that he had attended in 1901, Dixon inaugurated a best-selling literary tradition built on the appeal of earlier plantation literature of Joel Chandler Harris and Thomas Nelson Page and predicated on both a vehement and overt phobia of black Americans and a profound mistrust of women generally and lower-class white women particularly.[6]

The first work of the trilogy, *The Leopard's Spots,* is set in the late 1860s. Throughout the novel (white) Southerners of Hambright work incessantly in an attempt to reassimilate as docile the newly freed and now uppity black population. The need and desire to control blacks even resonates in the symbolism of the town's name. "Hambright" echoes the predicament faced by Dixon's white population—Ham, that is, blacks as the lewd sons of Ham, yoked to the "bright"-ness of the white citizenry. The organized Klan in this text functions as an extension of the white lynch mob, "the damned thousand-legged beast," and provides a natural and unifying progression that leads smoothly to his second novel, *The Clansman,* in which the Ku Klux Klan plays a more prominent role. In *The Clansman,* the organized Klan does indeed restore order and white rule through the lynching and castration of the black rapist Gus Caesar and the comeuppance of the mulatto as figured in the sinister twins of Silas Lynch and Lydia Brown. Dixon even obliterates any lingering reminders of blackness in the narrative. Although introduced in the text as white, upper-class ladies, Marion and her mother carry the racially suggestive surname "Lenoir" and are subsequently violated twice. Raped in their own home by the newly freed slave Gus, the Lenoir women as "the blacks" are summarily expunged from the text after their assault. Even their nominal trace of black, despite its lingual disguise in French, is eradicated with their fatal jump from Lover's Leap. " 'No one must ever know,' " Marion opines. " 'We will hide quickly every trace of the crime. They will think we strolled . . . and fell over the cliff, and *my name will always be sweet and clean*' " (*TC,* 305, emphasis added). As one of Dixon's characters remarks in *The Leopard's Spots,* "there are things worse than death, man!" in an allusion to white female sexual desecration at the hands of a black man. Marion's and her mother's voluntary deaths guarantee that any of the corruption of blackness implied by their name will not corrupt their blood, blood that could have tainted future white generations. In the shadow of Dixon's plan for white control lurk twinned desires for complete dominion over the black race and total obliteration of the mulatto—whether the weird-blooded mulatta, Lydia, or the potentially tainted Marion. "Are you a White Man or a Negro?" functions as Dixon's Manichean litmus test. Finally, notwithstanding Dixon's seemingly diligent efforts to recuperate the figure of Abraham Lincoln as a Southern sympathizer, the president's assassination in (and subsequent removal from) this text provides proof of Lincoln's own liminal regional and political status as *both* Southerner (born in Kentucky, parents from Virginia) and Northerner (reared in Illinois, guardian of the Union), a logistical impossibility given the internal logic of Dixon's narrative.

In sharp contrast to the first two installments of the trilogy, *The Traitor* tells the story of John Graham, Civil War veteran, who in addition to being a dispossessed member of the planter aristocracy, just happens to be the Grand Dragon of the KKK in North Carolina. As the novel opens, the imposition of the "rule of African barbarism," ushered in with the end of chattel slavery, has already been thwarted by the successful efforts of the Klan. Given this ideological freight, issues of race, gender, and sexuality do, in fact, pervade Dixon's texts, in a fashion akin to ghosts. Dixon allows a war-ravaged white male population to channel the mighty male ghosts of the antebellum period, when planters were planters and slaves were slaves, and to restore (white) order through the very portability and removability of the white robe. In essence, the Klan robe functions emblematically with Dixon's larger literary project. Just as order can be restored by the wearing of a white robe, so too can a sense of shared whiteness be established through the mass consumption of his fiction.

In *The Traitor,* the Ku Klux Klan provides "the only way to save [white] civilisation." But what sources of upheaval and chaos occasioned such a collapse in the social fabric of the society Dixon imagines? How and why do his characters find themselves under siege, unable to shore up the sagging foundations of their culture except through the birth of this fascist, racist, white supremacist organization? Perhaps answers lay in the mission and culture of the Klan sketched by Dixon—an all-white, all-male league of honor dedicated to the overturning of "African rule," a kind of crude shorthand for the rise of black political autonomy after the Civil War. But the expression and display of "white male honor" by the Klan in the face of "black barbarism" of newly freed slaves take curious form, a form that offers clues about the true source of this collapse of civilization. Dixon's clan of proud Confederate veterans from North Carolina exercises its power with the significant aid of a host of objects that have since become synonymous with the action and reputation of the Klan:

> They were dressed in the regulation raider's costume of the Klan. The *white flowing ulster-like robe* came within three inches of the floor. A *scarlet belt* circled the waist, from either side of which hung *heavy revolvers* in leather holsters. A *dagger* was attached to the centre of the belt, and the *scarlet-lined white cape* thrown back on the shoulders. . . . On each breast was wrought the emblem of the Invisible Empire, the *scarlet circle,* and in its centre a white cross. *Spiked helmets of white cloth with flowing masks* reached to the cape on each shoulder, completely covering the head and face. With *red gauntlets* to complete their costume, the disguise was absolute. (*TT,* 124–25, emphasis added)

It is only with the "absoluteness of disguise"—here the "white flowing ulster-like robe" as primary cover—that the mission of the Klan can be effected. In other words, the rising tide of unbroken barbarism displayed by blacks can be dissipated only with a concomitant donning of white disguises.

Walter Benn Michaels has argued that the white Klan disguise formed from the white sheet corresponds to "an essentially invisible racial identity, an identity that can't be seen in people's skins, but can be seen in the Klan's sheets." Michaels continues by noting that

> the purpose of the sheets, then, is not to conceal the identities of individual Clansmen for, far from making their visible identities invisible, the sheets make their invisible identities visible. The Klan wear sheets because their bodies aren't as white as their souls, because no *body* can be as white as the soul embodied in the white sheet.[7]

Yet the process by which the white sheet comes to represent Klan garb or, as Michaels describes it, the "white soul" reveals how the robe comes to signify the "mess" of a certain cultural ambivalence about whiteness—here circulating around issues of gender ambiguity—that would seem absent from Dixon's otherwise pristine text. When Dixon describes one of his heroines in *The Traitor* as a "sylph figure robed in white," the power of whiteness unites both a figuration of white womanhood and the embodiment of white male courage as revealed through the Klan robe. But although Dixon's "sylph figure" is actually a woman, her garb is merely a copy of the *male* fashion standard. "My, but you look one of us to-night!" exhorts the Grand Dragon of the Klan to his female companion Susie, "with that sylph figure robed in white standing there ghost-like in the moonlit shadows!" (*TT,* 8). For Dixon's Klansmen, the "sylph" feminine ideal aids in the performance of a certain kind of white masculinity, masculinity mediated by the switch in gendered expectations about clothing. In this light, John Graham as Grand Dragon might more fittingly be named the "Grand Drag Queen," juggling the demands of and desires for both white masculinity and white femininity.[8]

This cultural dilemma as expressed through the choice of costume brings to mind the work of psychoanalyst and critic Frantz Fanon. Donning his anthropological hat, Fanon states that "the way people clothe themselves together with the traditions of dress and finery that custom implies, constitutes the most distinctive form of a society's uniqueness, that is to say the one that is the most immediately perceptible." Continuing, Fanon opines that "it is by their apparel that types of society first become known, whether through written accounts and photographic records or motion pictures."[9] What are the implications of expressions of white male power being mediated through the dress, a cultural vehicle marking femininity? What kind of society would stake its survival on men who dress as women, particularly virginal, "well-bred" ones? As Dixon flattens out the complexities of black political agency during Reconstruction into simplistic "barbarism," barbarism, figured as blackness, can be countered only by whiteness. But whiteness here finds expression not in the actual bodily presence of empowered white male bodies issuing challenge to a postbellum political and cultural order run by blacks, but in the unifying monotones of white robes, robes made of "cheap domestic" cotton, the financial staple of the antebellum South, and whose literary representations resonate with the garb of the most revered Southern women. In the end, how does the donning of white cloth and red gauntlets as a means of remaining racially "white" and culturally "masculine" impact on our sometimes unquestioning notions of the stability of constructions of whiteness and gender?

Dixon's thematics provide a vantage from which to observe constructions of race—in this case, whiteness—at the turn of the century as they encounter destabilizing issues of sexuality, mobility, and class position. I take the paraphernalia of the Klan, its gauntlets, capes, helmets, and especially its robes, as a constellation of iconographic objects in which can be read other meanings of the organization. An encounter with the Klan of Dixon's fiction at one level becomes an encounter with this litany of objects. And it is through a reading of these objects that a host of queries generated by Dixon's texts may be answered: Is whiteness portable? Is it removable? Is it fabricatable? Is it performable? Is masculinity portable? Is it removable? Is it fabricatable? Is it performable? Can whiteness and masculinity be constructed just as a garment is sewn? Can whiteness and masculinity be donned just as a gown is pulled over one's head? If whiteness and masculinity can be put on and taken off just like any other garment, what has happened to the seeming impenetrable quality of whiteness in a culture that privileges it? What can be said of this brand of masculinity that must be mediated through a costume that seems strikingly reminiscent of the garb of Dixon's revered white heroines? In the end, with actual parades of power exercised by white-robed white men, Dixon's narratives unwittingly call into question the authenticity of white male privilege. If authentic whiteness can be derived only from the wearing of white cloth, does that cloth in fact cover or rather hide a real, but ultimately inferior and flawed white skin?

My focus on Klan iconography, particularly as embodied in the object of the Klan robe, comes out of a measured consideration of Thomas Dixon's novel *The Traitor*. It remains crucial to remember that Dixon literally writes the Ku Klux Klan into textual existence. He offers the first sustained literary consideration (over the course of all three novels) of the culture of the first Ku Klux Klan, a vigilante league arising out of white male frustration with and anxiety about the propagation of black political and economic autonomy in the immediate postbellum era. Moreover, the means by which the power of the Klan is displayed is always the visual aesthetics and power of their garb. In this light, consider Dixon's inaugural description of the Klan outfit in *The Clansman:*

> The disguises for man and horse were made of cheap, unbleached domestic. It came straight from the cotton gin and weighed less than three pounds. They were easily folded within a blanket, and kept under the saddle in a crowd without discovery. It required less than two minutes to remove the saddles, place the disguises, and remount. (*TC,* 315–16)

That same "cheap, unbleached domestic" is the processed result of cotton picked by black hands. But following Dixon's own motivated racial logic, the use of cotton as the material out of which whiteness is constructed results in twinned ironies. First, his use of commercial imagery reveals the underbelly of the Southern racial economy in which cotton is picked and processed for its later use as an instrument of terror against those same individuals who harvested it. Second, cotton, as the *matériel* of a more pristine white skin or (k)night gown, is always already a corrupted fabric, having been sown, reaped, and processed by the black hands on which Dixon is otherwise completely fixated. In essence, despite its brighter-than-white appearance in the fields, cotton grown according to American agricultural, racial, and labor practices can *never be white.* This observation brings to mind a similar construction in Ralph Ellison's *Invisible Man* in which the most blindingly white paint, appropriately dubbed "Optic White," is in fact a miscegenated product made whiter only as it is mixed by black hands, hands that add the requisite drops of black paint to ensure its claim as the "Right White."[10] As Harryette Mullen so cogently argues,

> American myth may rely for its potency on the interdependent myths of white purity and white superiority, but the invisible ones whose cultural and genetic contributions to the formation of American identity are covered up by Liberty White [paint], those who function as machines inside the machine, know that no pure product of America, including the linguistic, cultural and genetic heritage of its people, has emerged without being influenced by over three hundred years of multiracial collaboration and conflict.[11]

Dixon's insistence on the unsullied nature of the fabric and simultaneous denial of its lingering racialized quality reveals most distinctly the ways the construction of whiteness is thoroughly mediated by and dependent on images of blackness and black identity.

By the third novel of Dixon's trilogy, *The Traitor,* there is no black presence or threat; the novel instead becomes a meditation on whiteness, a contest between the "good" Klan and the "bad" Klan. John Graham, as Grand Dragon, receives the order from the Grand Wizard to disband the Klan after one final parade through town. In what is to be their final appearance, the night riders cut dashing figures. As these men begin to process, "the white ghostlike figures could now be seen, the draped horse and rider appearing of gigantic size in the shimmering moonlight. . . . The leader of the Klan was now ten feet away, towering tall, white and terrible, with an apparently interminable procession of mounted ghosts behind him" (*TT,* 47–48). Dixon further writes that "the only visible part of the body was the eye. . . . all eyes looked alike in the shadows of these trappings at night. They were simply flashing points of living light with all traces of colour lost in the shadows" (*TT,* 52). After the parade, Graham declares, "Our work is done. We have rescued our state from Negro rule. We dissolve this powerful secret order in time to save you from persecution, exile, imprisonment and death. The National Government is getting ready to strike. When the blow falls, it will be on the vanished shadow of a ghost" (*TT,* 53–54).

But what is so intriguing about Dixon's vision of the end of this empire of the "good" Klan is that its demise is thoroughly mediated by disposal of the costume, reminiscent of the organization's rise from the power of robes made of "cheap, unbleached domestic." To put it differently, disbanding the Klan requires absolute disposal of the robes. But it is the form of disposal that makes visible the constructed nature of whiteness that is of most interest here. Instead of folding up the robes in tissue paper as souvenirs—akin to the treatment of military costume—and placing them in the attic for the grandchildren to play in fifty years later ("Grandpa, were you in the Klan?"), Dixon's Klan burns them in a grave that Dixon describes as "newly opened" (*TT,* 50). An illustration (see figure 1) by C. D. Williams from the 1907 first edition of *The Traitor,* captioned "some of the men were sobbing," depicts this "newly opened" grave. There is a kind of violence done to the robes as they are burned.

> When all had been placed in the grave, John Graham removed his own, reverently placed it with the others, tied two pieces of pine into the form of the fiery cross, lighted its ends, drew the ritual of the Klan from his pocket, set it on fire and held it over the grave while the ashes slowly fell on the folds of the white and scarlet regalia which he also ignited. *Some of the men were sobbing.* (*TT,* 53, emphasis added)

The pronoun "all" functions to represent the actual helmets and robes, but the lack of an antecedent suggests that "all" figures the way the bodies of actual

Figure 1. "Some of the men were sobbing." From Thomas Dixon, Jr., *The Traitor,* illustrations by C. D. Williams (New York: Doubleday, Page, 1907), p. 52a.

white men are also being burned, if only in a symbolic sense. This becomes a scene of mourning because something living—the Klan organization as itself organic—is dying. Additionally, this ceremony repeats the material violence done by the Klan to blacks and other undesirables through the ritualized use of those same props used at a genuine cross-burning and burning-at-the-stake. John Graham attempts to verbalize his feelings as he watches the robes burn: "Boys, I thank you. You have helped me do a painful thing. But it is best" (*TT*, 53). But the "pain" of the "painful thing" underscores the fact that this is not a real funeral pyre. The ritual over the newly dug grave displaces the actual pain experienced by a real victim of Klan violence and instead enacts the performance of corporeal suffering felt by these "sobbing men." It instead recalls Edgar Allan Poe, one of Dixon's Virginia brethren. The robes, like some of Poe's female characters, have been buried alive, and like so many of the Klan's black victims, have been dismembered while breathing. Moreover, the robes as representations of whiteness maintain a combustible quality. As purveyors and reminders of the authority once associated with white male power as displayed in the antebellum era, the robes are explosive and are not containable, not storable.

But although Graham and company have buried the robes, the force and the allure of the robe offer too potent an attraction to poor and renegade elements within the white community. Because of the authority attached to them, in a figurative sense, the robes in fact resurrect themselves from their grave. Indeed, the removal of the robes recalls the process by which serpents shed their skins, only the Klansmen's "new skins" are lovingly sewn by white female hands. Because this molting effect allows the Klansmen to inhabit new white skin whenever the old seems insufficient, much of Dixon's plot is encumbered with requests for the construction of a new robe as proxy for the creation of a new skin. Steve Hoyle, young upstart and rival to John Graham, and his rogue followers foil Graham's attempts to dissolve the Invisible Empire and instead cling to the power they once wielded as Night Riders. "Within two weeks, Steve Hoyle's new Klan was organized and in absolute control of the Piedmont Congressional District. . . . In spite of the utmost vigilance on the part of [Graham's] committees, the new Klan had inaugurated a reign of folly and terror unprecedented in the history of the whole Reconstruction saturnalia" (*T T,* 95–96). The actions of "saturnalia" look suspiciously like the activities commonly thought to be executed by the Klan of historical record.

> They whipped scalawag politicians night after night and drove them
> from the county. They whipped Negroes, young and old, for all sorts
> of wrongdoing, real or fancied, and finally began to regulate the general
> morals of the community. They whipped a rowdy for abusing his wife

and on the same night tarred and feathered a white girl of low origin who lived on the outskirts of town and ran her from the county. (*TT*, 96)

Dixon effectively cordons off the activities of the new Klan as illicit, illegal, immoral, distinct from the actions of the old Klan, which were righteous, sanctioned, necessary.

This novel in effect grapples with the excess of whiteness generated by the Klan in its successful attempt to eradicate black political and cultural threats. The conflict within *The Traitor* between factions of whiteness recalls Michael Rogin's argument that the film *The Birth of a Nation* (which is based on *The Clansman*) portrays a conflict between white actors in white robes and white actors in blackface, effectively dislocating actual blacks. Rogin reminds us that "masks transform some white bodies into a white host and other white bodies into a black mob. Whites in white sheets defeat whites in blackface. The climax of *Birth* does not pit whites against blacks, but some white actors against others."[12] This dislocation is exposed further in the *mise-en-scène* of *The Traitor* itself. In another illustration (see figure 2) from the first edition, captioned "Stella stared at the lifeless form," the "lifeless form" is Stella's father, who has been murdered by renegade forces of the Klan. Unfortunately, because of the uniformity in garb, the killer cannot be located. But although the robe completely masks individual identities—even that of the murderer—it is actually the Klansmen that occupy characters' interest. Stella's attention, despite the intent of the illustration's caption, is riveted not on her dead father, but on the Klansmen and particularly their outfits. The white robe with its scarlet and cross on a white background mirrors both the white man's blood-stained shirt and the woman's dress: the robe becomes an externalization of the category of whiteness. Interestingly enough, this mirroring effect takes place across the face of Aunt Julie, the black mammy figure in the text and illustration.

Mia Bay and Gladys-Marie Fry argue separately that the Klan's robes are not an externalization of whiteness, because blacks recognized the intricate differences between "good" whites and "bad" whites, which meant that in the end, whiteness was not ipso facto a sign of evil.[13] In other words, white robes fail to signify completely as a racial category. However, insofar as Dixon attempts to construct an iconography of white supremacy that is embodied by the Klan, white robes became a signifier of white identity. Rearticulating Michael Rogin's earlier argument about the film *The Birth of a Nation*, I maintain that Dixon's work is not about what black people think, but about what white people think black people think about white people. To these white people, especially to these white men, white robes figure whiteness. And as a consequence, the white

Figure 2. "Stella stared at the lifeless form." From Thomas Dixon, Jr., *The Traitor,* illustrations by C. D. Williams (New York: Doubleday, Page, 1907), p. 134a.

men in Dixon's narrative seem inordinately attached to their Klan iconography, reluctant to part with it.

The Klan's robes function both metonymically and synecdochically. They are metonymic in that they are an externalized form of whiteness through contiguity to white skin, but they are synecdochic in that the robe stands in for white power in its entirety. Moreover, the very portability and removability that initially characterized the robe in *The Traitor* also mark the garment as a kind of prosthetic device, enabling the completion of Southern white male identity, but also always covering the lack or deficiency that necessitates its use. Despite the historical reality of the instability and discontinuity of Klan costumes, Dixon creates a consistent cultural definition of the Klan. Although the KKK wore black, red, and other color combinations, some men, unable to afford the cost of fabric, resorted to wearing their wives' dresses. Depending on the proximity to or distance from home, others wore no disguise at all.[14] By the time the second Klan formed in the 1920s, Dixon's historically specific description of a consistent Klan outfit, written more than a decade earlier, had become in fact the template for a standardized Klan costume. The robe itself both covers an inferior form of postbellum whiteness (a whiteness now diminished by the increasing autonomy of blacks) and permits the (k)night rider to embody physically the mystique of white power that was thought to have flourished before the Civil War. This kind of embodiment is critical to Dixon's project because it enables the white children of the Civil War, denied the chance to fight because of ill-timed birth, to reenact the "lost cause" of Confederate versus Yankee. A biographical note about Dixon, who was born in 1864, may prove illustrative here. While Dixon's mother was pregnant with him, she walked from Virginia to North Carolina. In retrospect, Dixon often fancied himself making the trek with her, albeit from an embryonic state in her womb. In addition to providing Dixon with the means to reenact the defining cultural moment of the South, the white robe of the Klansman also affords whites generally, but white men specifically, the opportunity to fortify their degraded sense of racial identity with the end of the Civil War. To rephrase Dixon's own epigraph to *The Leopard's Spots,* "The Ethiopian cannot change his skin, but the Klansman can."

NOTES

1. See Gladys-Marie Fry, *Night Riders in Black Folk History* (1975; Athens: University of Georgia Press, 1991), esp. pp. 123–35. See also Nancy MacLean, *Behind the Mask of Chivalry: The Making of the Second Ku Klux Klan* (New York: Oxford University Press, 1994); Kathleen Blee, *Women of the Klan: Racism and Gender in the 1920s* (Berkeley: University of California Press, 1991); Wyn Craig Wade, *The Fiery Cross: The Ku Klux Klan in America* (New York: Simon and Schuster, 1987); David M. Chalmers, *Hooded Americanism: The First Century of the Ku Klux Klan, 1865–1965* (Garden City: Doubleday, 1965).

2. David Roediger, *Towards the Abolition of Whiteness* (London: Verso, 1994), p.12. See also idem, *The Wages of Whiteness: Race and the Making of the American Working Class* (London: Verso, 1991).

3. Thomas Dixon, Jr., *The Leopard's Spots: A Romance of the White Man's Burden—1865–1900* (1902; New York: A. Wessels Company, 1906), p. 95 (hereafter cited in the text as *TLS*). Similar rhetoric can be found throughout *The Leopard's Spots* and the second work of the Reconstruction trilogy, *The Clansman: An Historical Romance of the Ku Klux Klan* (1905; Lexington: University of Kentucky Press, 1970) (hereafter cited in the text as *TC*). See also idem, *The Traitor: A Story of the Fall of the Invisible Empire* (New York: Doubleday, Page and Co., 1907), p. 52 (hereafter cited in text as *TT*). My epigraph comes from *The Traitor* as well, p. 58.

4. See Homi Bhabha, "The Other Question," in *The Location of Culture* (New York: Routledge, 1994), pp. 66–84.

5. See Dixon biography, Raymond Allen Cook, *Fire from Flint: The Amazing Careers of Thomas Dixon* (Winston-Salem, Va.: John F. Blair, 1968), for more detailed publication information. *The Leopard's Spots* sold about a hundred

thousand copies in its first month of release; *The Clansman* sold nearly a million copies in the same period.

6. See especially Joel Chandler Harris, *Uncle Remus: His Songs and His Sayings* (1880; New York: Penguin, 1982); and Thomas Nelson Page, *In Ole Virginia; Or, Marse Chan and Other Stories* (1887; Nashville: J. S. Sanders, 1991). For secondary work on the plantation literary tradition, see Louis Rubin, ed., *The History of Southern Literature* (Baton Rouge: Louisiana State University Press, 1988).

7. See Walter Benn Michaels, "The Souls of White Folk," in *Literature and the Body: Essays on Populations and Persons,* ed. Elaine Scarry (Baltimore: Johns Hopkins University Press, 1988), esp. pp. 185–90. Also see idem, "Race into Culture: A Critical Genealogy of Cultural Identity," *Critical Inquiry* 18 (1992): 655–85.

8. I am indebted to Robin D. G. Kelley for this very appropriate wordplay on Grand Dragon. I also envision psychoanalysis as a site of inquiry, specifically work about masquerade and transvestism. Both Dixon's text and his larger intellectual project along with the critical work of psychoanalyst Joan Riviere from the 1920s provide ample opportunity to interrogate constructions of masculinity—white and black—at a site where psychoanalytic and racial discourses meet. Remember that the whiteness of the robe recalls the garb of the white woman for whom whiteness signifies both racial purity and sexual purity. How are white men implicated in the gendered status of white women; of not having the phallus? There is a strand of Riviere's psychoanalytic discourse that is thoroughly mediated by the interaction between gender and race. Specifically, a case account by Riviere, "Womanliness as Masquerade," might provide some insight about how to address this issue of the Klan robe. See Joan Riviere, "Womanliness as Masquerade" (1929), in *Formations of Fantasy,* ed. V. Burgin, J. Donald, and C. Kaplan (New York: Methuen, 1986), esp. pp. 35–39.

9. Frantz Fanon, "Algeria Unveiled," in *A Dying Colonialism* (New York: Grove Press, 1965), p. 35.

10. Ralph Ellison, *Invisible Man* (1952; New York: Vintage, 1972). For an earlier treatment of the construction of whiteness as expressed through the covering of paint, see William Dean Howells, *The Rise of Silas Lapham* (1885; New York: Vintage/Library of America, 1991).

11. Harryette Mullen, "Optic White: Blackness and the Production of Whiteness," *diacritics* 24, no. 2–3, (Summer–Fall 1994), pp. 74–75.

12. Michael Rogin, " 'The Sword Became a Flashing Vision': D. W. Griffith's *The Birth of a Nation,"* *Representations* 9 (Winter 1985), pp. 150–95, esp. 180–81.

13. See Fry, *Night Riders.* See also Mia Bay, *The White Image in the Black Mind: 1830–1925* (forthcoming, New York: Oxford University Press, 1997).

14. See accounts of KKK costumes in Fry, *Night Riders;* Wade, *The Fiery Cross,* esp. pp. 31–53; and Chalmers, *Hooded Americanism.*

4

BLACKNESS 'SCUZED

JIMI HENDRIX'S (IN)VISIBLE LEGACY IN HEAVY METAL

Musicologist Arnold Shaw's *Dictionary of American Pop/Rock* defines Chuck Berry as "the poet laureate of Teenage Rock."[1] It denotes John Lennon as "the most outspoken [Beatle], evincing a sardonic wit that marked many of the songs he . . . wrote in the sixties."[2] It even finds words to define Bob Dylan: a "gifted, influential, and highly publicized" figure whose "lyrics took on the trappings of poetry."[3] But when it comes to Jimi Hendrix, the dictionary does not even attempt a definition—though what it offers instead is more revealing than any definition could hope to be. The entry for Hendrix reads as follows:

> Jimi Hendrix: See "the black Elvis"; Heavy Metal Rock.[4]

This two-pronged cross-reference is interesting for a number of reasons, not the least of which is the implication that Jimi Hendrix resists definition, that his career and his influence are too complex to lend themselves to the sort of lexicography the dictionary feels comfortable employing with the likes of Berry, Lennon, and Dylan—or James Brown, Bruce Springsteen, Muddy Waters, and any number of important figures in American popular music.

Of equal importance are the various lineages the dictionary suggests by positioning Hendrix between Elvis Presley and heavy metal. It sees him as an Elvis revivalist, or the inheritor of the most important early rock 'n' roll, as well as a metal progenitor, or the benefactor to one of rock's more significant later developments. He also represents a sort of midpoint on the phallocentric continuum that constitutes so much of rock history, from Elvis's pelvis to heavy metal's sometime pseudonym—cock rock. Less easily schematized is Hendrix's relationship to the other two in terms of race. There is a clear irony involved in terming Hendrix "the black Elvis" or designating him a black version of a white man who, since the inception of his own career, had been labeled a white version of a black man. There is also some irony in locating Hendrix as a potential source for heavy metal, which is itself an overwhelmingly "white" form of popular discourse, at least in terms of the racial makeup of its performers and its audience.

There is, however, a logic behind the way Shaw's dictionary handles Jimi Hendrix. By cross-referencing him to two other entries, the dictionary, in effect, creates two Hendrixes: the one audible, the other visible. The entry for "Heavy Metal Rock" concentrates on Hendrix's guitar playing and the sonic foundation it established for later metal musicians. After proclaiming Hendrix "the Heavy Metallurgist par excellence," Shaw cites a sound engineer about how Hendrix "destroys at least two speakers whenever he plays," "burns up a lot of tubes because of the great volume," and "ruins a lot of tremolo bars, too."[5] The entry for "the black Elvis," conversely, focuses on the visual aspects of Hendrix's persona.

> "the black Elvis": Perhaps it was the theatricality of his performances and the erotic way he handled his guitar that led critics to refer to Jimi Hendrix (1942–1970) as "the black Elvis." His hyperamplified guitar playing was shaped by an early idolization of Muddy Waters (b. 1915) and by formative stints with James Brown (b. 1928) and Little Richard (b. 1935). The Monterey Pop Festival of 1967, where he burned his guitar onstage to upstage the Who's destruction of their instruments,

made a celebrity of him. In the three short years before his death from a drug overdose, he racked up four Gold albums: *Are You Experienced?, Electric Ladyland, Axis: Bold as Love,* and *Smash Hits.* Violence and eroticism marked his SRO appearances and his music.[6]

One confronts these two versions of Jimi Hendrix in numerous accounts of the artist's life, and the terms are almost always the same. The audible Hendrix, or the Hendrix who anticipates heavy metal, is almost never discussed in terms of race. The visible Hendrix, or the Hendrix for whom race is a consideration, is rarely discussed in terms of his influence on other artists. *The Dictionary of American Pop/Rock* is an extreme but by no means isolated example. It situates Hendrix in an African-American musical context by citing such forebears as Muddy Waters and James Brown, but it does so only in a paragraph about "the theatricality of [Hendrix's] performances." In order to explain Hendrix's impact on his own successors, the dictionary resorts to a separate definition—one that privileges sound over sight and thereby avoids the question of race altogether.

On some level, then, the audible and visible Hendrixes appear incommensurate. The race-transcending guitarist who helped define heavy metal seems somehow nonidentical with the black man who once played backup for Little Richard. This paper attempts to move toward collapsing these distinctions—between the audible and the visible Hendrix, the metallic and the nonmetallic, the raceless and the raced. To do so requires that I address two important and related questions. First, just what is Hendrix's legacy in heavy metal? It begins with the electric guitar, of course, but it goes far beyond that. Hendrix's stage presence—or better yet, his self-rendering as spectacle—accounts for much of his popularity, and it has tremendous influence on the way heavy metal constructs itself in the twenty years after Hendrix's death. But this personage—the "spectacular," or what I have just termed the "visible" Hendrix—is usually the one invoked in discussions of Hendrix's race. How, then, does one account for the invisibility of race in discussions of heavy metal's heredity? The second question I address concerns Hendrix's own ambitions toward racial transcendence during the late 1960s, and how the spectacular becomes implicated in this transcendental desire. Heavy metal might be seen as the arena in which his desire succeeds all too well, for the Hendrix whom metal claims as its forefather transcends race so completely that he ceases to be a raced subject.

Before I engage either of these questions, I ought to first establish some sense of what I mean by "heavy metal." The term has acquired a variety of connotations over the past twenty-five years—from a fast-paced and technically demanding style of music to a form of orchestrated youth rebellion to "nothing more than a bunch of noise," this last definition coming from the music's many detractors as well as its first great fan, rock critic Lester Bangs.[7] I employ the term simply to indicate a style of popular music that has flourished in various guises since about 1970 (the year of Hendrix's death) and that generally involves loud guitars, heavy drumbeats, an ethos that stresses freedom of spirit, and an insistence on the spectacular. These I take to be heavy metal's most basic elements. Bangs endorses a similarly broad definition, as does musicologist Robert Walser, who is one of very few academic writers to give serious attention to metal.[8] Those who tend toward narrower definitions typically focus on heavy metal's reputation for unseemliness: for example, rock historian Robert Pielke, who writes in 1986, "Most evident in heavy metal has been the attitude of negation, with its emphasis on the images of death, Satanism, sexual aberration, dismemberment and the grotesque."[9]

The argument over what constitutes heavy metal has been played out repeatedly over the last two decades, usually with respect to such acts as Bon Jovi or Aerosmith, whose music conforms to the broad definition of heavy metal I endorse, but not to the narrower one Pielke advocates. I do not wish to replay the debate with respect to Hendrix, though it is important to note that almost every history of the genre mentions him as a father figure, and most metal guitarists cite him as a principal influence. Hendrix was never dubbed a metal guitarist during his lifetime, for the term "heavy metal" was not widely used to describe a style of music until after his death.[10] He did, however, become marketed to a metal audience once metal became codified as a genre, much to the chagrin of some of his devotees. Biographer Charles Shaar Murray bemoans the fact when he says he found Hendrix "binned under 'heavy metal'" in a record store in the 1980s ("right up there with greats like Iron Maiden and Guns 'N' Roses," he sneers).[11]

The debate over whether an act qualifies as heavy metal revolves around how "hard" its music is—how amplified its guitars, how thick its sonic texture. What occasions the debate, however, is the fact that such "soft" acts as Bon Jovi can *look* like such "hard" acts as Iron Maiden by adopting the same leather-and-spandex garb, the same long, stringy hair, the same histrionics in concert. In other words, the preliminary qualification for an act to claim the metal moniker is the metal "look"; hence my desire to emphasize the spectacular as a seminal category in the construction of heavy metal. Even Pielke's formulation, which argues the preeminence of "images of death, . . . dismemberment and the grotesque," is remarkable in its attention to the *visual* aspects of an ostensibly *musical* culture. His definition would exclude Hendrix if one were to apply his categories only to Hendrix's lyrics; however, if one considers violence and excess as performed categories—as emblems of heavy metal's penchant toward the spectacular—then the connection to Hendrix becomes clear.

Consider the following reminiscence from Aerosmith lead guitarist Joe Perry, which appears in *Rolling Stone* magazine's 1990 tribute to Hendrix:

> The guitar sounded like a monster coming out of the speakers. . . . Jimi took it from black and white to multicolor. I always think of this old picture of him—I think he was playing backup for King Curtis. He was wearing a suit, and, I don't know, he kind of looked like a geek. A few years later, he was at Monterey, lighting his guitar on fire.[12]

[handwritten margin note: "PASSING"]

From black and white to multicolor: no Hendrix disciple could have expressed Hendrix's desire to transcend in more appropriate terms. The chromatic metaphor serves Perry well in his desire to put into words the aural dimensions of Hendrix's guitar work. The sounds Hendrix produced with an electric guitar were available to musicians of any race because Hendrix had elevated the instrument beyond a quotidian and high-contrast world of black and white to a seamless and psychedelic sound spectrum. Moreover, the fact that Perry calls Hendrix's guitar "a monster" helps explain how Hendrix could be binned alongside Iron Maiden and Guns 'N' Roses once heavy metal had acquired connotations of violence, power, and the occult. Nuno Bettencourt, guitarist for Extreme, makes a similar observation in the same *Rolling Stone* article: "He must have looked like Satan to people, you know? Like, where did he plug in, and who told him to do it?"[13]

Before electric Satan, however, came the geek in the suit and tie who toiled away the early 1960s as a sideman playing tight rhythm-and-blues arrangements for King Curtis and other black artists. This image of Hendrix—the unlikely one that Joe Perry once glimpsed in an "old picture" (no doubt a black and white)—deserves some attention. Before we go further in examining the performer who burned his guitar at Monterey and set the stage, literally, for heavy metal, we should glance at the "geek" who found himself a victim of what Malu Halasa terms "musical apartheid" because he could only find work playing "black" music to "black" audiences.[14] Doing so will provide a better perspective on Hendrix's rebellion against "black and white" and toward "multicolor"—a paradigm shift that would forever conflict with Hendrix's desire to retain his own "blackness" in the face of allegations that he was a hippie-era Uncle Tom. No discussion of heavy metal in the context of race should proceed without an analysis of this sequence of events, for it provides a representative scenario in which heavy metal discovers in "black" musical forms the inspiration it seeks to simultaneously celebrate and efface.[15]

[handwritten margin notes: "did he retain it enough?" and "so heavy metal is built on black musical forms"]

Hendrix began his performance career playing in a high school band around his native Seattle.[16] Shortly thereafter he played to small crowds at various clubs around Fort Campbell, Kentucky, where he was stationed during the early 1960s as part of the U.S. Army's 101st Airborne Division. Even during these early performances, Hendrix acquired a reputation as an outrageous performer who routinely drew more attention to himself than to the lead vocalist. For one thing, he displayed more talent than most of those with whom he performed. For another, he had already begun to play the guitar with his teeth, to gyrate provocatively, to wag his tongue at the audience—in other words, to execute the maneuvers that would prove shocking enough to mass audiences in 1967, much less to small-scale crowds in 1960. The reputation followed him into the mid-1960s, when he began touring what was known as the "chitlin circuit"—a series of clubs and theaters at which black musicians would perform for black audiences segregated from other venues. Among the well-known acts with whom he performed and/or recorded were Little Richard, Sam Cooke, Jackie Wilson, the Supremes, and the Isley Brothers.

But with success came increasing artistic pressures. Hendrix had become known as one of the most adept rhythm-and-blues musicians in the country. Those who knew him more closely realized he was one of the better blues musicians as well, though there was less financial incentive to pursue a career playing straight-up blues. As a result, Hendrix faced a twofold constraint. First, his irrepressible flamboyance annoyed those fellow band members who expected him to remain in the background and bang out a guitar rhythm according to the simple chord progressions of early rock 'n' roll. He was expected to showcase his expertise during the occasional brief solo, but never to detract attention away from the band as a whole. Little Richard, not surprisingly, is reputed to have been particularly incensed at his guitarist's tendency to upstage him, whereas the Isley Brothers were the happiest to have so dynamic a presence join their act. In all cases, however, Hendrix's sideman duties severely limited his own musical expression.

Second, and even more sinister, Hendrix was able to make a living only by playing within conventionally "black" musical forms because of his skin color. Interracial pop groups were uncommon in the early to mid-1960s; interracial audiences, even rarer. Rock 'n' roll was less than a decade old when Hendrix began performing, and though it had permitted much black music—if fewer black artists—to "cross over" the barrier between "race records" and top 40, it did not yet facilitate the sort of transgression that would become routine a decade later. He was committed to playing within this musical idiom, but he also found himself drawn toward jazz, in part because it relied more heavily on freedom of expression, less on the models of exclusion encouraged by radio stations and *Billboard* magazine.

Hendrix would profess throughout his later career that he yearned to live in a race-blind world where jazz paradigms—improvisational leeway, creative collab-oration, and so forth—provided a basis of existence and interaction. "It's a universalist thought," he would say in an interview in 1969, proclaiming himself to be among the prophets of a new age of global harmony. "[I]t's not a black or white thing, or a green and gold thing. . . . There are a few chosen people that are here to help get these people out of this certain sleepiness they are in." [17] Murray rightly calls Hendrix's "entire career . . . a ceaseless struggle against racial and cultural stereotyping." [18] And though Hendrix is quoted as saying, "Race isn't a problem in my world" amid the palpable racial turmoil of 1968—a sentiment for which he was roundly criticized by black nationalists—it would be a mistake to read him as being oblivious to racialized conflicts. [19] Idealistic, perhaps, but never ignorant: Hendrix understood all too intimately the problems that could arise by thinking of races as prohibitive categories. It was this type of thinking that presented Hendrix the boundaries that he had to cross to achieve commercial and artistic success.

His early encounter with sonic essentialism provided him a great deal of the impetus to move to New York in 1964, where he eventually became a regular at Greenwich Village blues clubs. There he was able to attract the mixed-bag audiences that befitted his own musical tastes. More important, his choice of song and his performance style were not dictated to him by a jealous band leader. He could be as unrestrained as he wished because he was the featured attraction, often the only attraction. David Henderson comments on this stage of Hendrix's career by describing the perfection of what he terms "The Show":

> While young white rock 'n' rollers had often managed to copy and cajole the correct changes of black music, they nevertheless failed to present in their stage presentation "The Show." . . . "The Show" was when the artists or band would do some wild, way-out stuff. "The Show" was the height of the performance, . . . this display [that] would often put both the audience and the performer in a transcendental state where improvisation came to the fore and the unexpected took every-body out. . . . [F]or the true followers of black music, it was this transcendental moment everyone waited for. . . . When Hendrix put on a show, he blew minds and terrified the audience. [20]

Hendrix's reputation for "putting on a show" attracted audiences to the Village dives as powerfully as did his renown for superb musicianship. Among the curious was Chas Chandler, former bass player for the British rock band the Animals, who recognized in Hendrix a revolution waiting to happen. Chandler convinced Hendrix to move to England in 1966, persuading him that the openness he had discovered in Greenwich Village would characterize the British pop scene as a whole. There would Hendrix doff once and for all the geeky suit and don the outlandish garb, hook up with drummer Mitch Mitchell and bass player Noel Redding, and forever change Anglo-American popular music by forming the Experience.

Racial boundaries conditioned this move toward a more spectacular stage presence. The early, low-key Hendrix had trouble achieving interracial exposure, and his performance practice was limited by his backup duties. The solo gigs in Greenwich Village's blues clubs attracted a wider audience and encouraged a more dynamic stage presence. He did not fully realize his transcendental ambitions, however, until the trip to England, the release of the instantly successful album *Are You Experienced?* and most important, his return to the United States for the 1967 Monterey Pop Festival. The multiple-act outdoor concert that set the standard for late 1960s music festivals, Monterey would prove to be one of the era's defining moments. And Hendrix would prove to be Monterey's most memorable performer.

American audiences had yet to see the Jimi Hendrix Experience live, though stories of their success in England abounded, and their first single, "Hey Joe," was climbing up the pop charts. Nothing, however, could have prepared them for what they saw. His set was electrifying. It had to be, for he came on stage immediately after the Who had destroyed their instruments in front of the crowd.[21] Renditions of "Foxy Lady," "The Wind Cries Mary," and Bob Dylan's "Like a Rolling Stone" captivated the crowd from the outset, but what made Monterey Hendrix's most important hour on the stage was the finale. "I could sit up here all night and say, 'Thank you, thank you, thank you,'" he tells the audience that had welcomed him back to the United States so enthusiastically. "But, dig, I just can't do that. So what I'm going to do, I'm going to sacrifice something that I really love." Then he turns the guitar upside down, producing the fuzz and feedback that serve as an introduction to "Wild Thing," a song made famous in 1966 by the Troggs. He performs a backwards somersault during one solo, and he inaugurates the final, extended solo by pressing the guitar against an amplifier with his body before placing it on the ground before him. After kneeling on top of it, he plays it by grabbing the strings and "riding" it in a blatantly sexual manner. He then disappears behind an amp, returns with a squeeze bottle of lighter fluid, holds the bottle between his legs and simulates an ejaculation on the guitar, then sets fire to it and summons the flames as if he were invoking evil spirits. He finishes the set by bashing his beloved, now charbroiled Stratocaster, grabbing a new one, and performing what would become his signature anthem, "Purple Haze."

The Monterey performance serves as a metonym for Hendrix's entire career in many accounts, this one not excepted. Extraordinary guitarist sets music world on fire, only to perish in flames of own success at height of his popularity.[22] Historically, mythically, and imagistically, the performance does represent Hendrix's emergence as a dominant cultural force. Heavy metal, only a few years away from forging an identity for itself, would soon derive as much from the sensational and remotely arcane spectacle of Hendrix burning his guitar as from any other single source.

The language writers use to describe the Monterey performance is particularly revealing. David Fricke begins his 1992 *Rolling Stone* tribute to Hendrix by recounting the Stratocaster sacrifice. He calls Hendrix "a consummate psychedelic showman" who was "literally burning his signature into the pages of rock 'n' roll history" by expressing "affection and gratitude" toward the crowd.[23] Murray focuses more on Hendrix's histrionics: Monterey "was Hendrix *playing* in the most literal sense of the word. It was playful, mischievous, exuberant, euphoric, extrovert; an ex-underdog's high-spirited slapstick display of hey-look-what-I-can-do."[24] The most revealing account comes from John Morthland, who tries to capture what it felt like to experience the Experience at that pivotal moment in Hendrix's career:

> [H]e played guitar with his teeth, he played it behind his back. He humped it and caressed it, and finally, to finish off the set, he burned it. He had played exhilarating music throughout, but when it was over, everyone buzzed about nothing but that *show;* it was dramatic, it was galvanizing.[25]

Morthland sums it up perfectly: the "*show*" was primary, the music an "exhilarating" afterthought. "It was dramatic," he said, emphasizing the importance of the theatrics. "It was galvanizing," he concludes, confirming every transcendental ambition Hendrix might have brought to the concert.

Hendrix's performance in particular and Monterey in general thus figure prominently in the mythology of "The Sixties," an era for which massive outdoor concerts have come to symbolize a larger spirit of uninhibited communion. The dynamics of a post-1960s heavy metal concert, though not exactly identical, are not altogether dissimilar. For one thing, heavy metal has had a great deal to do with the survival of the concert as a cultural institution. *Billboard* magazine reported in 1985 that heavy metal "attracts a greater proportion of live audiences than any other contemporary music forms," and heavy metal tours annually crowd the top of the top-grossing concert lists.[26] But the significance of the concert in heavy metal goes further. Deena Weinstein notes "the ubiquity of concert footage" in heavy metal videos, for instance.[27] For

Walser, however, the concert is fundamental to the music itself: "[E]ven when a listener encounters only the album, much of the same framing is presented, as the packaging of the album is designed to evoke the excitement of live performances."[28] The music of a metal album, in other words, does not lay claim to any semiotic autonomy. It instead functions in an evocative space in which the visual perpetually insinuates itself alongside the audible—via lyrics about the concert experience; sound effects that imitate the reverberation of an arena; the abundance of live albums, live tracks on studio albums, crowd noise integrated into studio tracks; and so forth.

It is no accident that heavy metal's 1970s heyday came with the elaborate histrionics of such performers as KISS and Alice Cooper, and that its resurgence in the mid-1980s would coincide with the rise of MTV. One could also go so far as to cite a recent television advertising campaign for Canon cameras, in which the slogan "Image is everything" is touted by tennis star Andre Agassi, who, until quite recently, had styled himself after heavy metal singers. In short, the visual cannot be overemphasized with respect to heavy metal. "The Show," which Henderson claims Hendrix embodied, could no longer be said to elude white performers once heavy metal had made Monterey part of its own heritage of the spectacle. And though Hendrix is not heavy metal's only source of the spectacular, he does provide the music with its most immediate and most profound inspiration. Henderson's emphasis on the "transcendental" capacity of "The Show" thus proves even more accurate than he might have originally intended.

But while Hendrix's dramatic reintroduction of himself to American audiences at Monterey enabled him to transgress racial boundaries and "galvanize" those gathered for the event, it nevertheless bore the imprint of race precisely because it involved this desire for transcendence. Hendrix never quite escaped the "race question" during his career—neither before Monterey, when he struggled against musical apartheid, nor after it, when he found himself the target of both blues musicians and exponents of black nationalism who wanted him to play a "blacker" style of music. Their entreaties provided some of the impetus to form the Band of Gypsys late in his career—an all-black ensemble oriented more toward rhythm-and-blues. Critics have usually seen the Band of Gypsys' one album as the least significant of the recordings Hendrix released during his lifetime, though all wonder what he would have been able to achieve had he lived to record additional music with them. But the need to compromise also motivated some of his best work. Hendrix offers "Voodoo Chile," a song that appears twice on *Electric Ladyland,* first in a style that bespeaks traditional electric blues, and second in a "Slight Reprise" that signals a sonic revolution.

Hendrix's dilemma was how to retain a sense of tradition while simultaneously transgressing it. He had to ensure that "blackness" remained present in his music, but he also had to combat its becoming a totalizing presence. In the sonic medium of the album, Hendrix could realize this goal by exploding a conventional blues riff into a wild guitar phrase. Transcendence was not so easily accomplished in the combined sonic and visual medium of the concert, for the visible Hendrix was undeniably black. But just as sonic excess enabled him to shuttle between blues and psychedelia, visual excess was vital to his self-presentation as a transcendentally available musical artist. One could rephrase Joe Perry's formulation to account for this phenomenon. Hendrix did not take it from black and white to multicolor; he took it from black *to* black and white *via* multicolor.

It is especially important to understand this aspect of Hendrix's legacy now, for Hendrix, though he has never really "left us" since his death in 1970, is even more "with us" at the moment. He has received an extraordinary amount of attention over the past few years for an artist whose recording career ended twenty-five years ago and whose story has been retold many times since then. A traveling museum of Hendrix memorabilia toured the country in 1994, and a permanent museum opened in Seattle in 1995. The recent explosion of Seattle-based "grunge" rock (in some ways the successor to late 1980s Los Angeles–based heavy metal) prompted many to recall that "grunge" was only the second pop/rock revolution to hail from the area. More concretely, the upsurge of interest in Hendrix has culminated in the recent release of a major "new" compilation of Hendrix studio tracks, *Voodoo Soup* (MCA, 1995), as well as a tribute album recorded by other artists, *Stone Free* (Reprise, 1993). Finally, yet another Hendrix biography has been published within the last four years, not to mention a collection of the artist's "lost writings." [29]

At least part of this increased attention may be attributable to media coverage of an ongoing lawsuit involving Hendrix's name and legacy. The suit centers around whether the rights to Hendrix's unreleased recordings belong to Hendrix's father, Al Hendrix, or to his former producer, Alan Douglas. A recent issue of *Guitar World* magazine devoted itself to the controversy. [30] On its cover is a black and white photograph of Hendrix, circa 1968, pasted in front of a psychedelic background. Emblazoned across his body is the title "The Battle for Jimi's Soul: Who Owns Hendrix's Music?" *Guitar World* chronicles the legal dispute well, yet it does not mention another "battle for Jimi's soul" that has waged since his death, one that has, in effect, pitted him against himself—the audible against the visible, the raceless against the raced—by refusing to permit him the hybridity that so influenced his artistic vision.

Given heavy metal's debt to the visible Hendrix—a debt so profound it can be detected in the way metal *music* has been written and produced—the

Hendrix that survives in heavy metal as a principally audible, principally de-raced figure proves unacceptable. True, heavy metal has remained a largely "white" phenomenon for much of its history. Though it has never exactly legislated the exclusion of African Americans, its "musical apartheid" is still powerful enough to render it remarkable that someone such as Living Colour's Vernon Reid should have tried to play within the genre in the late 1980s—or remarkable that someone such as Jimi Hendrix could have helped spawn it. One cannot, however, cite Jimi Hendrix as a (and sometimes as *the*) father of heavy metal without considering the race politics that informed his own work. To ignore race politics is to echo Alvin Lee, a fellow Woodstock performer who once said, "Hendrix wasn't black or white. Hendrix was Hendrix."[31] The argument appears to grant Hendrix a complete and selfsame identity when, in fact, it filches from him the racially ambivalent split subjectivity that shaped his career. Race was, in fact, a serious enough problem in Hendrix's world to occasion his desire for transcendence. Likewise, race remains a problematic component of heavy metal, in part because the genre exalts a black man as its source of inspiration, but more important, because it so often overlooks the fact that its source of inspiration was black.

NOTES

1. Arnold Shaw, *The Dictionary of American Pop/Rock* (New York: Schirmer, 1982, 35).
2. Shaw, *Dictionary,* 214.
3. Shaw, *Dictionary,* 114.
4. Shaw, *Dictionary,* 172. The *New York Times* dubbed Hendrix "the black Elvis" in a February 25, 1968, story about Hendrix's astonishing rise to the top of the rock world. The nickname was much less audacious than the various appellations concocted in London newspapers after the Jimi Hendrix Experience's first shows in late 1966, among them "Mau-Mau," "The Wild Man of Pop," and "The Wild Man from Borneo." For a broader account of Hendrix's initial popular reception, see David Henderson, *'Scuse Me While I Kiss the Sky: The Life of Jimi Hendrix* (New York: Bantam, 1981), 90–93.
5. Shaw, *Dictionary,* 169.
6. Shaw, *Dictionary,* 39. *Smash Hits,* as its name indicates, was not a new studio album but rather a collection of songs from previous albums. Shaw fails to list a fifth Hendrix album released before his death, *Band of Gypsys.* Numerous live recordings, practice sessions, and unreleased studio cuts have been released since then, though controversy has surrounded each one, since none bore the input of Hendrix himself. For a thorough and well-annotated discography of Hendrix recordings, see Charles Shaar Murray, *Crosstown Traffic: Jimi Hendrix and the Rock n' Roll Revolution* (New York: St. Martin's, 1989), 218–21.

7. Lester Bangs, "Heavy Metal," in *The Rolling Stone Illustrated History of Rock 'n' Roll*, ed. Anthony DeCurtis and James Henke (New York: Random House, 1992), 459.

8. Robert Walser, *Running with the Devil: Power, Gender, and Madness in Heavy Metal Music* (Hanover, MA: University Press of New England, 1993) is not only the best study of heavy metal but also among the better cultural studies of any popular music form. To date, the only other book-length academic text devoted to metal is Deena Weinstein, *Heavy Metal: A Cultural Sociology* (New York: Lexington, 1991).

9. Robert Pielke, *You Say You Want a Revolution: Rock Music in American Culture* (Chicago: Nelson-Hall, 1986), 204.

10. Bangs and Dave Marsh popularized the label in the early 1970s while they were writers for *Creem* magazine. Among the prototypical metal bands they celebrated were the Yardbirds, Cream, the Who, and the Jeff Beck Group. Later acts would fit more squarely within the metal idiom: for example, Led Zeppelin, Black Sabbath, Blue Öyster Cult, and Grand Funk Railroad. For an indispensable discussion of metal's "origins," see Walser, *Running with the Devil*, 1–11.

11. Murray, *Crosstown Traffic*, 207. Henderson intimates a similar disdain of heavy metal in the opening paragraphs of his biography, in which he describes a particularly disappointing Hendrix performance as sounding "like some crazy manic metallic shit, bleeding, eating through the amps." Henderson, *'Scuse Me While I Kiss the Sky*, 2.

12. "Hendrix: Twenty Years After," *Rolling Stone* 594 (13 December 1990): 109.

13. "Hendrix: Twenty Years After," 109.

14. Malu Halasa, "Be Black and Rock," *New Statesman Society* 24 (November 1989): 52.

15. Though these issues deserve much broader consideration than I can give here, some of the other ways that race is implicated in the construction of heavy metal are as follows: metal's blues ancestry, especially in light of the fact that both have been depicted as "the devil's music"; metal's laying claim to different forms of "darkness" and "power" during its formative years—an era in which "Black Power" was a well-publicized ideological force whose advocates were fond of depicting "whiteness" as "sterile" and "vacuous"; the scarcity of mixed-race or all-black metal bands—a fact that led Living Colour's Vernon Reid and *Village Voice* music critic Greg Tate to form the Black Rock Coalition in the mid-1980s; and finally, the affinities between metal and rap during the late 1980s, when both became favorite targets of censorship groups, and both increasingly asserted themselves as the "music of the streets."

16. I derive all biographical material from Henderson, *'Scuse Me While I Kiss the Sky;* and Murray, *Crosstown Traffic*. In addition to narrating the story of Hendrix's life, both are quite good at situating Hendrix in an African-American musical context and a late 1960s political one. Henderson's biography prog-

resses along a fairly linear narrative line, while Murray's approaches Hendrix on a more thematic basis, with individual chapters focusing on Hendrix and the blues, Hendrix and jazz, and so forth.

17. Quoted in Michael Fairchild, Album notes to *Stages, 1969* (sound recording), Reprise, 1991.

18. Murray, *Crosstown Traffic,* 2.

19. Quoted in George Goodman, "Jimi Hendrix Experience: Black and White Fusion in the Now Music," *Look* 7 (January 1969): 38.

20. Henderson, *'Scuse Me While I Kiss the Sky,* 77.

21. Legend has it that neither Hendrix nor Who guitarist Pete Townsend wanted to have to follow the other, and that Hendrix lost the coin toss that would decide who had to go second.

22. The most widely available video version of Hendrix's performance at Monterey—*Jimi Plays Monterey,* distributed under the name *Jimi Hendrix: Live at Monterey*—even acts as a sort of biographical film, briefly tracing his career from the rhythm-and-blues stints through Monterey to his death. *Jimi Plays Monterey,* dir. Chris Hegedus, Pennebaker Associates, 1986.

23. David Fricke, "Jimi: The Man and the Music," *Rolling Stone* 623 (6 February 1992): 42.

24. Murray, *Crosstown Traffic,* 194.

25. John Morthland, "Jimi Hendrix," in *Rolling Stone Illustrated History of Rock 'n' Roll,* ed. DeCurtis and Henke, 413.

26. Quoted in Walser, *Running with the Devil,* 17.

27. Weinstein, *Heavy Metal,* 167.

28. Walser, *Running with the Devil,* 51.

29. John McDermott and Eddie Kramer, *Setting the Record Straight,* ed. Mark Lewisohn (New York: Warner Books, 1992); Bill Nitopi, ed., *Jimi Hendrix: Cherokee Mist (The Lost Writings)* (New York: HarperPerennial, 1993).

30. See especially Alan Di Perna, "Axes to Grind," *Guitar World* 15.7 (July 1995): 50–56+.

31. Quoted in Halasa, "Be Black and Rock," 53.

two

HISTORICAL (RE)VISIONS

LEGACIES OF SLAVERY AND COLONIALISM

5

MONIQUE GUILLORY

UNDER ONE ROOF
THE SINS AND SANCTITY OF THE NEW ORLEANS QUADROON BALLS

Somewhere in the oldest part of New Orleans, there is a woman in a fraying ball gown. With the posture of a cigar store Indian, she beckons from the doorway of a nightclub and smiles demurely at passersby. Across the street, in one of many souvenir shops, a menagerie of kerchiefed mammy dolls grin dumbly through the pane. And farther down the street, it does not take long to find a Confederate flag tacked to the back of a pickup truck or hanging ominously from a French Quarter terrace.

The city of New Orleans is saturated with these historic markers. The antebellum gown, the mammy doll, and the flag each bear some historical reference, but the value of their signification ranges from benign to racist, depending on who is reading and interpreting the signs. For millions of tourists who flock to the city each year, such symbols appear harmless and merely add to the historic "flavor" of the town. But for others, these icons are painful reminders of a shameful past the city now flaunts as a tourist attraction.

Few places revel in their colonial past quite like New Orleans. Before officially joining the American Union in 1803, the land known as the Louisiana Territory was colonized within two centuries by both the French and the Spanish and then the French again. Today, this small but cosmopolitan town of no more than five hundred thousand, is called the most European of all American cities—a subtropical never-never land known for its Caribbean flavor, Third World mysticism, and hedonistic allure. Its two most renowned annual events, Mardi Gras and the New Orleans Jazz and Heritage Festival, draw hordes of tourists from around the world; but millions more flock to the city for its promises of Southern hospitality and old world charm:

> Is New Orleans ever to be redeemed from its imprisonment in the exotic mode? Not of course if the national tourism industry—eagerly abetted by the city and state tourism bureaus—or the national literary industry can help it. Whether or not the economic, political and literary colonization of the South as a whole has ended is arguable, but it is obvious that the literary colonization of Louisiana, and certainly New Orleans, continues.[1]

Nestled at the heart of the French Quarter, or Vieux Carré, what is now known as the Bourbon Orleans Hotel represents a fascinating convergence of memory, history, and place. The historic value of the building at 717 Orleans Street revolves around the various ways the property has served the city as well as the volatile debates that surfaced over these uses. Once revered as the Orleans Ballroom, a great space with the best dance floor in the South during the ante- and postbellum periods, the building became infamous as a place where wealthy white Creole and European men met their colored concubines. Politicians and dignitaries graced its halls. Later, an order of colored nuns lived there, transforming it into a convent, for nearly a century beginning in the late 1880s (see figure 1). Called the Bourbon Orleans Hotel since 1966 (see figure 2), the building has had so many incarnations that it stands only as a reminder of what it once was. Guests pay anywhere from $150 to $400 per night to room there, but for all intents and purposes, the Bourbon Orleans's luster is gone.

This essay explores the unique interdependence of history and the Bourbon Orleans Hotel read through a critical reconstruction of the quadroon balls. Dating back to the late eighteenth century, the balls provided an opportunity for mixed-race women to form liaisons with wealthy white men through a system of concubinage known as *plaçage*. Although the balls were held at numerous locations throughout the city and in other parts of the South, among the most legendary sites is the Bourbon Orleans Hotel. But the Bourbon Orleans is also one of the most controversial sites, for it is largely myth and lore, rather than historic evidence, which locate the balls at this particular locale. My intention here is to unravel a dense palimpsest of history imbued in the Bourbon Orleans Hotel through the history of the quadroon balls by considering not only the particular circumstances of the balls as social events but also how history itself evolved around this building and the colored women identified with it for more than two and a half centuries.

Although tourism prompts the hotel to privilege the history of the balls, another crucial aspect of the Bourbon Orleans's past is the eighty years it housed the Sisters of the Holy Family—an order of colored nuns that established itself in this same building where the balls had been held. The nuns had an "organic" connection to the quadroon balls through their foundress, Henriette Delille. Delille (see figure 3) herself was a quadroon who would have been *placée* had she not become a nun. The Sisters of the Holy Family occupied the space from the late 1880s until 1966. By then, the French Quarter had become the thriving center of New Orleans, and the sisters' property, although structurally worn and damaged over the years, was situated in a prime commercial locale. When the sisters failed to raise the money to make the necessary repairs to the crumbling landmark, a four-year battle ensued over what should be done with the building laden with so much history and coveted for its real estate value.

The juxtaposition of these two extremes—the quadroon concubine and the quadroon nun—set the parameters of proscribed sexuality in which this analysis evolves. My critical reading of that sexuality emerges largely out of two theoretical concepts: Joseph Roach's notion of surrogation and an extension of this trope of commodification that I call the commercial. Roach's surrogation, "the symbolic substitution of one commodity for another,"[2] demonstrates the interrelations between the Bourbon Orleans Hotel, its history, and the quadroons—both as concubines and as nuns. Through surrogation, the problematic nature of the quadroon women (who were accepted as neither black nor white and, more importantly, who posed a sexual threat to the cohesion of white family structures) and their concomitant association with the Orleans Ballroom imbued this space that would be known later as a convent and then a luxury hotel with cultural signification that extended through the centuries until the building itself became as contested as the bodies once traded there. Certainly during the time of the balls, locals regarded the dance hall as a den of iniquity. But long after the balls faded from local memory into legends and myths, the building's reputation haunted it into the twentieth century, when people still

Figure 1. Sisters of the Holy Family Convent in 1964, before the zoning controversy. Photo appeared in the *New Orleans Clarion Herald,* April 21, 1966.

fretted over its scandalous past. Roach's notion of surrogation helps illustrate this symbolic transfer of fear and loathing from the bodies of the quadroon women to a building they once inhabited.

A curious irony illuminates the disquieting history of the quadroon balls. These fetes flourish in literal and figurative proximity to the slave auction block. The Bourbon Orleans is situated less than one city block away from Jackson Square. Only the sacred spires of St. Louis Cathedral separate the terraces of the Bourbon Orleans from the spot on the Mississippi River bank once shadowed by the auction block. Here, women much like those adorned and toasted at the balls also paraded in their finest for the favor of a prospective master. But freedom laid the distinctive line between the belles of the balls and the bargains at the slave auction. For although slaveowners had unquestionable sexual access to their female slaves, a quadroon mistress, acquired at a ball in much the same way that a slave was bought, embodied more than guaranteed sexual fulfillment. These women were as cultured, refined, and trained in all the social finery as their European (even more so than American) counterparts. Thus, the fine cedar parquet of the quadroon balls amounted to little more than the rough planks of the auction block—each supporting a financial trade in raced bodies. But even

70

Figure 2. Bourbon Orleans Hotel at its opening in 1966. Photo appeared in the *New Orleans Clarion Herald,* April 21, 1966.

more important perhaps is the role the bodies themselves played in these exchanges. While the slaves were sold on the auction block, and were stripped of all agency and control over their lives, their futures, and their bodies, at the quadroon balls, the market dynamics were decidedly different. For it was not simply that the dance hall symbolically functioned as an auction block for the quadroon mistresses; rather, through their freedom from slavery, their own bodies assumed the charge of the transaction as the women literally enacted the performance of sexual commerce.

This parallel conflation of the dance hall with the auction block and of the quadroon body and the black slave segues into the domain of the commercial,[3] an extension of Roach's commodification. While a discussion of commodified bodies (the slaves, the quadroon mistresses) and history (tourism and the promotion of the Bourbon Orleans Hotel) is quite plausible in this context, I employ the commercial to consider the quadroon bodies, the building, and its history in a socioeconomic domain beyond the commodification of each element. Although the commercial is applicable to all aspects of the history, bodies, and space that are discussed here, it is most clearly illustrated in a photo essay compiled by New Orleans photographer Frank Menthe. "The End of an Era"

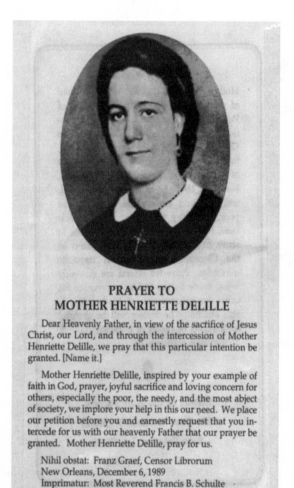

**PRAYER TO
MOTHER HENRIETTE DELILLE**

Dear Heavenly Father, in view of the sacrifice of Jesus
Christ, our Lord, and through the intercession of Mother
Henriette Delille, we pray that this particular intention be
granted. [Name it.]

Mother Henriette Delille, inspired by your example of
faith in God, prayer, joyful sacrifice and loving concern for
others, especially the poor, the needy, and the most abject
of society, we implore your help in this our need. We place
our petition before you and earnestly request that you in-
tercede for us with our heavenly Father that our prayer be
granted. Mother Henriette Delille, pray for us.

Nihil obstat: Franz Graef, Censor Librorum
New Orleans, December 6, 1989
Imprimatur: Most Reverend Francis B. Schulte
Archbishop of New Orleans. December 6, 1989

Figure 3. Prayer card to Sister Henriette Delille, which can be found
in the lobby of the Bourbon Orleans. Efforts to canonize Delille began
in 1984 and are still under way.

features two sets of photos taken two years apart (see figures 4 to 7). The first
set (figs.5 and 6), shot in 1964, documented the final days of the Sisters of the
Holy Family at the Orleans Street convent. Menthe shot the second set of
photos in 1966 to celebrate the grand opening of the Bourbon Orleans Hotel.
In the second set, crystal chandeliers replace natural sunlight, plush carpets cover
wood floors, and other ornate fixtures pointedly illustrate the building's dramatic
conversion from sober convent to luxury hotel. But more striking than these

Figure 4. Dining hall at the Bourbon Orleans Hotel. Photo by Frank Menthe. Appeared in the *New Orleans Clarion Herald,* April 21, 1966.

Figure 5. Young women of color studying at the Holy Family School, St. Mary's Academy. This room became the grand dining hall in the Bourbon Orleans Hotel. Photo by Frank Menthe. Appeared in the *New Orleans Clarion Herald,* April 21, 1966.

physical transformations are the people in the photos—white women costumed in antebellum gowns are posed in exactly the same manner as the nuns were two years before. Setting napkins and dinner plates, they displace young black women who once studied in what became the grand dining hall. While the nuns have a direct, organic connection to the history of the site (through the personal history of their foundress), the white women, used as props to evoke the aura of the balls and the antebellum period, can be no more than superficial stand-ins for this past. Paul Gilroy iterates such uses of history as "history conscripted in the service of the present."[4] Gilroy's notion of history in the service of the present exacts an aspect of the commercial where history is not directly recalled but rather subtly invoked. New Orleans's basic appeal to tourists emanates from nuanced historical allusions—women in antebellum gowns, black waiters in kid gloves doting over white patrons, carriage rides, and Dixieland jazz are all commercial molds of a past that caters to a specific touristic nostalgia.

A HOTEL OF HISTORY, MEMORY, AND MYTH

"Even though history has given high praise to the Orleans Ballroom, [it] is most commonly referred to as the Quadroon Ballroom," states a pamphlet from the concierge desk at the Bourbon Orleans. Despite this definitive claim, some historians doubt that the quadroon balls were ever held at the site that is now the Bourbon Orleans Hotel. But in a zoning controversy that arose shortly before the hotel opened, the history of the building changed according to the interests of different groups. I will elaborate on this debate later, but I mention this now to demonstrate how the "history" of the building—what actually happened or did not happen there during the nineteenth century—is secondary to the myth of the balls that has firmly taken root. This haze of historical ambiguity hovering around the Bourbon Orleans casts it into that social/historic limbo that Michel deCerteau calls "a crack in the system that saturates a place with signification and indeed so reduces them to this signification that it is impossible to breathe in them."[5] The site of the Bourbon Orleans embodies that "crack in the system" because with regard to the nineteenth century and its "systems," the Bourbon Orleans houses a history that the system could not sustain, a socially ordained and socially celebrated mixing of the races. The quadroon women themselves embodied an egregious collapse of social and racial binaries (black/white, slave/free, etc.). This history of transgression would be denied, contorted, and commodified through myths so naturalized in New Orleans culture that if you stand in the Bourbon Orleans today, the signification of the space, rather than the space itself, envelops you.

Certainly the history of the Orleans Ballroom is layered so thick that it is stifling. A mammoth pastel pink building spanning a city block from the

Figures 6 and 7. Nearly two years separate these photographs. Menthe posed the woman in the Bourbon Orleans (fig. 7) "to show the contrast between the old and the new." Photos by Frank Menthe. Appeared in the *New Orleans Clarion Herald*, April 21, 1966.

Figure 7.

debauchery of Bourbon Street to the sanctity of St. Louis Cathedral, the Bourbon Orleans Hotel is a cornerstone of French Quarter monuments. When it opened in 1966, more than five million dollars went into restoring the structure to its original nineteenth-century grandeur. A brochure promoting the new hotel boasted, "In the present restoration, the building has been returned to a faithful likeness of its former self. Descriptions taken from early writings have been used extensively to document the use of rich velvet draperies, ornate crystal chandeliers and other elegant appointments."[6]

In this attempt to restore the structure to a "likeness of its former self," two interesting aspects of the commercial, with regard to the building and its history, emerge. First, there is an obvious selection of what history will be re-created. The decision to return the building to its nineteenth-century essence ignores almost a century of (the more recent) history left by the nuns. This semiotic leap from convent to luxury, postmodern yet antebellum hotel is a commercial move designed not to preserve the rich history of the site, but rather to exploit one aspect of that history that appeals to a specific nostalgia. During the 1960s controversy, an effort was made to save the dilapidated structure; one proposal suggested that a wax museum should be opened at the site to commemorate the works and services of the nuns to the community. This attempt to honor the building's more recent and possibly more "valuable" history was obviously trumped by the more nostalgic structure and commercial strategy of the Bourbon Orleans Hotel. In this homage to a selected history, a second aspect of the commercial surfaces with regard to Fredric Jameson's articulation of the simulacrum—"a transformation of older realities into television images."[7] This application of the simulacrum to the site of the quadroon balls is unique in that the hotel is the actual place where the history occurred. The quadroon balls are not being re-created in an amusement park, restaurant, or night spot; rather, this history is recalled and re-created at the very site where it apparently occurred. The building has become a simulacrum of itself.

The place of the Bourbon Orleans Hotel within the context of New Orleans history underscores the way the city's entire tourist industry revolves around an abstract, intangible sense of "the historic." With relatively few exceptions, tourists file through New Orleans not to visit Civil War battlegrounds, nor to tour the plethora of celebrated historic sites. Rather, the city beckons them with reveries of a past cradled by the Mississippi and tendered by congenial Southern hospitality. But while one can easily designate an EPCOT attraction like that housed at Disneyworld as a simulacrum, people readily believe the illusion of seamless history carefully crafted in New Orleans. Umberto Eco noted during his travels through the Crescent City,

On the way between San Simeon and Sarasota I stopped in New Orleans. I was coming from the recreated New Orleans in Disneyland, and I wanted to check my reactions against the real city which represents a still intact past, because the Vieux Carré is one of the few places that American civilization hasn't remade, flattened, replaced. . . . In New Orleans, history still exists and is tangible, and [it] is not in the grip of a neurosis of a denied past; it passes out memories generously like a great lord; it doesn't have to pursue "the real thing."[8]

Although he does recognize the unique relationship New Orleans shares with its past, Eco fails to see through the illusion of a continuous past that permeates the character of the town. This "great lord" generously passing out memories is no more than the tourist commission serving up slices of selected history greedily consumed by tourists. A candid example of how New Orleans buildings commercialize their history is Café Maspero's Slave Exchange, also found in the French Quarter. The sandwich shop bears this peculiar and disturbing name for a trapdoor, prominently displayed above patrons' heads, that was once used to lower slaves to the auction block. While tourists find this restaurant satisfying with its fare of overstuffed po-boys and its offering of quaint relics from slavery, locals tend to have a more critical attitude toward mixing such history with pleasure and tend to take their meals elsewhere.

So history, even more so than the popularity of food, drinks, music, and fun, is New Orleans's hottest-selling commodity. But there is a difference between the history commodified by the city's place in the national imagination and the nostalgia-driven commercialization that I suggest is embodied in places like the Bourbon Orleans and Maspero's Slave Exchange. The city's air of historic authenticity appears so real primarily because of the actual prevalence of antiquity and ruin in New Orleans's architecture. However, such places in New Orleans are not likely to be found where tourists look for them. As Stewart Brand observed in his recent book, *How Buildings Learn,* when it comes to age and buildings, "It seems there is an ideal degree of aging which is admired. Things should not be new, but neither should they be rotten with age (except in New Orleans, which fosters a cult of decay)."[9] Lafitte's Blacksmith Shop on Bourbon and St. Philip Streets enshrines such a "cult of decay." The foundation is warbled, the lighting dim, and the stone walls damp with the humidity. Lafitte's is the oldest standing structure in New Orleans and looks it, but only a fading plaque near the door marks this distinction. Today it is a popular watering hole for locals, and tourists are lucky to happen upon it through a good tip or guide. Lafitte's Blacksmith Shop, as a historic site, is as much a commodity in the larger scheme of New Orleans tourism as the Bourbon

Orleans. However, unlike the Bourbon Orleans, it is not as self-conscious and self-promoting of its own history. While some efforts have been made to prevent the building from falling completely into ruin, it has not attempted to reconstruct and valorize its own history to save and sell itself.

LES BELLES DAMES

Once a pleasure dome of nineteenth-century New Orleans, when it was known as the Orleans Ballroom, the Bourbon Orleans today still garners symbolic import from the control and regulation of mixed-race, female bodies throughout and after slavery that occurred on the property. Through surrogation, not only were the quadroon women in and of themselves symbolic representations of the horrors of slavery, but they came to represent and be represented by a host of other symbols—from the Sisters of the Holy Family in the late nineteenth century, to the white women dressed in antebellum gowns in Menthe's photos, and finally, to the Orleans Ballroom itself, which changed according to the social constructs of the quadroon women associated with it. Like an aging beauty, it has undergone numerous lifts, nips, and tucks to accommodate its guests while dousing them in historic fantasy.

As we consider the performance of commerce and self-promotion, it is ironic to note that the existence of "tricolor," or mixed-race, balls in New Orleans finds its origins in efforts to save the New Orleans theater. In the 1780s, the New Orleans theater got off to a feeble start, and although many locals enjoyed its productions and operas, its demise seemed imminent on countless occasions. Bernado Coquet and his partner, Jose Boniquet, two important figures in the New Orleans music scene, ran a dance hall patronized by New Orleanians of all classes, castes, and colors. They had been warned by the attorney general that their establishment was coming to be known as "the place where the majority of the slaves of the city gather."[10] Coquet offered to underwrite the theater in exchange for the exclusive rights to hold dances for free persons of color. The balls were to be held every Sunday night and would be increased to two per week during carnival season.[11]

In 1805, Coquet rented his hall to Albert Tessier, who created the concept of "quadroon balls," where two nights per week, dances would be given for free quadroon women and white men only.[12] Tessier has to his credit the first advertisements for the quadroon balls, which he conducted with an air of first-class privilege. Carriages were provided at the door, and rooms could be rented on the premises. Tessier's enterprise proved so successful that several other halls began featuring quadroon dances on selected nights, including the Globe, the Davis Dance Hall, the Salle de Condé, and the Salle de Lafayette.[13]

Characterized by flagrant race mixing (prohibited by New Orleans civil law), the balls are most often recollected in travelers' logs rather than reports from native New Orleanians. To these eager visitors, the balls, and particularly the quadroon women, were quite the rave. Gentlemen were almost always gushingly attentive to the quadroon maidens. One described them as "pretty and often handsome, I have rarely, if ever, met more beautiful women, than one or two of them, that I saw by chance, in the streets. They are much better formed, and have a much more graceful and elegant carriage than Americans in general."[14] Although the quadroon balls cost up to two times more than the proper French balls with white women in attendance,[15] many gentlemen would often steal away from the white balls to socialize with the women of color, "who they prefer to white women because these women demand fewer of those annoying attentions which contradict their tastes for independence."[16]

The principal desire of quadroon women attending these balls was to become *placée* as the mistress of a wealthy gentlemen, usually a young white Creole or a visiting European. Such arrangements became necessary because these quadroon women, by all accounts "white" except legally, found themselves "too much superior to the Negroes, in general to associate with them, and [were] not allowed by law, or the popular prejudice to marry white people."[17] Many of the pairs were as exclusive and lasting as legitimate marriages, and the unions were often celebrated with as much ceremony and rite:

> When the quadroon's admirer became desirous of forming a liaison with her, she usually referred the applicant to her mother. The parent inquired into the circumstance of the suit before regulating the terms of the bargain. In many cases she received fifty dollars a month, during which time the lover had exclusive right to the house. . . . Sometimes the suitor agreed to pay a stated amount, perhaps two thousand dollars, or a sum proportionate to the girl's merits. . . . After the bargain was made, the girl was feted, after which she was probably moved to her newly furnished establishment.[18]

Certainly, there were numerous instances of *plaçage* that occurred independently of the quadroon balls, but regardless of how or where the liaison was made, a quadroon woman usually found herself well cared for if she secured a kind and generous lover. Besides the financial and, to some degree, emotional comfort a suitor provided his quadroon mistress, another interesting aspect of the union was often the question of paternity. While it was uncommon for white American men to claim the offspring slaves bore for them, in many instances of *plaçage*, children, particularly males, were often recognized and named for their European fathers. Consequently, numerous cases were heard in the New Orleans courts in which whites contested and blacks demanded inheritance rights. Although few free people of color won any of these cases, the mere fact that these children were cared for, educated, and acknowledged by their white fathers is notable.[19]

An old Creole saying noted that every young Creole "gallant," when he reached the age of twenty-one, was given a horse and a quadroon girl. This was a widely practiced rite of passage and although many viewed it as a young boy's first dabbling with manhood, many of these relationships lasted until the man married, and some endured even beyond that. Such a lifestyle understandably disrupted the usually genteel families of white Creole lineage to such an extent that one editorial in the 1837 *Argus* urged local Creoles not to frequent the balls. The author indignantly argued that it was a shame for eligible Creole gentlemen to "neglect the white privets to gather black grapes."[20]

In the strongest and most earnest unions, the quadroon mistress had the power to destabilize a Creole family and Creole society in general. One visitor to the city observed that "travelers, Creole (white) residents, everyone forms alliances with these colored women and many have children of them. This license extends also to the rural regions, where the Creoles prefer to live with these women rather than to give a white woman the title of spouse."[21] The writer and historian Grace King called the quadroons "the most insidious and the deadliest foes a community ever possessed."[22] Not only was this by virtue of the Creole men's penchant for these women, but also because it was not uncommon for such strained and volatile relations to erupt in violence. Stephen Longstreet noted how many young Creole men fell in duels protecting the virtue of their mistresses. And then there are more extreme cases of love and war, like the quadroon Pauline, who chained, beat, and starved the legitimate wife and children of her lover. A slave who had pleaded with her to show mercy on the man's family eventually reported her crimes to the authorities. On March 28, 1846, Pauline was hanged before a crowd of five thousand people.[23]

FANCY GIRLS

The complex connections between the practice of *plaçage,* "fancy girl" auctions, and the sexual politics of plantation communities cannot be overstated. The *plaçage* of black women with white lovers could take place only because of the socially determined value of their light skin, the same light skin that commanded a higher price on the slave block, where "light-skinned girls were bid for at prices much higher than those offered for prime field hands. Some adolescent females of mixed race were sold as 'virgins,' obviously discounting the notion that slave women were invariably sought as proven breeders."[24] The movement of such transactions from the slave block to the dance hall made these practices far less public. While anyone, including free blacks, could purchase slaves, only wealthy white men were allowed to attend the balls. Furthermore, despite their popularity among the upper echelon of New Orleans socialites, the balls were covert, underground treasures, and many patrons donned masks in order to protect their identities.[25]

Miscegenation in New Orleans dates as far back as the settling of the Louisiana Territory in 1699. History books indicate that the French Mississippi Company, which was responsible for settling the land, failed to import women to the area for nearly twenty-two years. The scarcity of French women ensured relations with the natives living on the land as well as the slaves who traveled with the company. In 1721, eighty-eight truant girls arrived in New Orleans from La Salpêtrière, a house of detention in Paris. In 1728, a group of more respectable women, *filles à la cassette,* or "casket girls,"[26] were imported from France, and some of them became matriarchs of wealthy Creole families. However, for a vast majority of the settlers, the practice of interracial relations with slaves and native women proved to be the preference, and the arrival of new French women made little difference.[27]

Tracing patterns of miscegenation from the settlement of New Orleans through slavery and the antebellum period, with regard to the quadroon balls, I have wrestled with questions of empowerment and agency for the quadroon women. To what extent were these women able to seize control of their sexuality and their bodies? Although *plaçage* placed quadroons' mothers in the precarious position of sexually exploiting their own daughters, this abomination naturally extended from plantation society, where "if femininity loses its sacredness in slavery then so does motherhood as a female blood rite/right."[28] Indoctrinated by slavery with this understanding of female sexuality, the most a mulatto mother and quadroon daughter could hope to attain in the rigid confines of the black/white world was some semblance of economic independence and social distinction from slaves and other blacks. Stephen Longstreet explicitly describes how such sexual practices were inherited from generation to generation: "The half-white mother told her near-white daughter to latch onto the white massa and make him a slave to her body; to ask for earring [*sic*] and doodads, to hold back a bit and then enflame. It was deadly serious warfare, and the Negro fought it. He slowly saw himself diluted; red hair, blue eyes, different features began to appear in the slave quarter."[29]

Through this strategic commodification of the quadroon body, which I have called the commercial, women of color seized an opportunity beyond the confines of slavery to set the price for their own bodies. Among the best and most noted attributes of the quadroons was not simply their beauty, but also their refinement and mastery of whiteness. In 1832, François Guillemin defended the quadroons before the French consul in New Orleans by arguing that "these women, and many others too, who are not as white as they, have nonetheless by now almost the color and graces of Europe, and have often received impeccable education."[30] Similarly, many other accounts of the quadroon women comment not only on their beauty but also on their carriage, their gaiety, the perfection of their French, and so forth. These qualities characterize the various aspects of the commercial that quadroon women employed to "sell" themselves to prospective suitors. Such practices were directly attacked and undermined by government officials. In 1786, Governor Gustave Miro passed an ordinance that dictated that free women of color must attire and conduct themselves in a manner suited to their inferior social status, which would more easily distinguish them from white women:

> The Negro women must not ape the dress of the white ladies, and by Negro was meant not only those whose color was pronounced but those with only the least taint of African blood, however white and Caucasian their skin might be. They must dress in such a way to be easily distinguished from their pure-white sisters, else they might be mistaken for fine ladies to the discomfiture of those of the opposite sex, who in the latter's ignorance might be unduly drawn to these near-white designing ones.[31]

Such prohibitions were meant to "disenfranchise" the commercial body of the quadroon, the body that not only advertised and sold itself but did so through a performance of whiteness. Furthermore, when Miro's edict required quadroon women to tie their hair up in a kerchief known as a *tignon,* the proud colored women fought back by decorating the plain cloths with ornate beads and plumes. Ironically, many of these women prospered in actual business after they could no longer rely on *plaçage* to support them.[32] Could one dare to suggest that these women learned a sense of business and commerce through the deliberate and contrived promotion of their own bodies?[33]

Quite possibly, the quadroon occupies that liminal space that Judith Butler recognizes as a potentially transgressive site between hegemonic binaries. In her delineation on this idea applied to the sexualization of bodies, she writes, "as a visual fiction, the ego is inevitably a site of meconnaissance; the sexing of the ego by the symbolic seeks to subdue this instability of the ego, understood as an imaginary formation."[34] Similarly, the quadroon body emphasizes the imaginary construction of racial binaries. This idea will also be illustrated in my discussion of the uncanny, but it is evident that the quadroon could fit nowhere in the black/white dichotomy. Ira Berlin explores this phenomenon in Virginia, where there was a similar crisis with miscegenation. " 'There were only two castes, white and black' stormed one Richmond journal. If the legislature wanted to make a third, it should prescribe their status; otherwise, mixed-bloods would soon become governors, judges, jurors, soldiers or lawyers." [35] In New Orleans, "mixed bloods" had already entered the professional world; many free people of color owned businesses and slaves. But quadroon women were invading the pristine domain of the whites' private world, and in their struggle to hold on to their social status and racial superiority, the white Creoles feared that nothing was sacred.

LIFE BEYOND THE BALLS

The quadroon balls thrived until shortly before the Civil War, and with emancipation in 1863, the internal rifts between Louisiana blacks and Creoles began to widen. In the twenty years roughly coincident with the Reconstruction era, the black population of New Orleans doubled, increasing from 25,423 in 1860 to 57,617 in 1880. The white population, while still the majority, rose only by about 14,000.[36] With the emancipation of the slaves and the imminent threat the growing numbers of freed blacks posed to the white establishment, whites sought racial solidarity:

> By the time of the Civil War, sexual relations between whites and blacks were becoming less common in the South, and the social upheaval and the economic devastation brought on by the war did nothing to reverse the trend. Even after the war, when there was a shortage of white men, few white women turned to black men as lovers or husbands. Vigilante groups like the Ku Klux Klan had risen up determined to keep the races apart.[37]

Under such a climate, the quadroon balls steadily dwindled. The Orleans Ballroom continued to be used for social and political gatherings until 1881, when it was donated to the Sisters of the Holy Family. Henriette Delille, the youngest of one of the most established free-colored families in New Orleans, had founded the order in 1842. During the antebellum period, the women of her family shared a long history of *plaçage*, indicated by the fact that she, her sister Cecile, and her brother Jean all had different last names.[38] When Delille was fourteen, her sister was already *placée* with an Austrian man. Delille was soon to have her night at the balls when she surprisingly announced to her family that the quadroons' way of life was a sin and her life's calling was to serve God and teach the poor.[39]

Nearly forty years later, Delille found herself praying and teaching in the same corridors she had denounced as a young woman. Ironically, the order and the school it founded, St. Mary's Academy, historically catered to women of the same racial mixture that typically would have been found at the quadroon balls. A visitor to the school in 1938 noted that "although the convent is for negroes, there are few pure Africans in attendance, if any; for its pupils possess every conceivable mixture of Spanish, French, English and African blood."[40] The order remained on that site until 1964, when the convent became the focus of a citywide debate. Many preservationists argued that the building ought to be returned to its original elegance so that it could be used as a landmark and boost the tourist industry. But most residents in the area sympathized with the nuns and protested the zoning change that would permit the building to become a hotel. The lawyer representing the nuns explained that while the sisters were willing to make the necessary structural repairs to the building, "it must be stressed that the present owners will never restore this building. Their position is that it represents a part of our history for which we cannot be justly proud."[41] On the other side, the preservationists also emphasized that while they did hope to restore the building, "it is the intention of the designers to return the Quadroon Ball Room to its former elegance and beauty, not to 'reproduce' it."[42] The controversy ultimately winded down to a contest between the New Orleans Planning Commission and a private contractor, Wilson Abraham. After the debates persisted for several months, delaying building dates and contract deadlines, an angry Abraham lashed out at the commission and his opponents: "I insist on buying the Holy Family property and I'm going to tear the whole thing down. You can say that glorified house of prostitution won't be there anymore."[43]

The irony of Abraham's referring to the convent as a "glorified house of prostitution" more than a century after the quadroon balls were held on that site reveals a conflation of memory and history that allows a man to speak of a convent and a brothel (of sorts) that used to be there in the same breath. Not only did the history of the site influence how people remembered the space, it also altered their immediate thoughts of that space in the present, a function of memory reminiscent of deCerteau: "It is striking that the places people live in are like the presences of diverse absences. What can be seen designates what is no longer there: 'you see, here there used to be . . .' but it can no longer be seen. Demonstratives indicate the invisible identities of the visible: it is the very definition of a place."[44]

DOUBLE EXPOSURE

In 1788, long before the quadroon balls were firmly rooted in New Orleans culture, 1,500 quadroon women lived in homes supported by white men.[45]

With the continued proliferation of *plaçage* in the nineteenth century, the quadroons posed a very real threat to white Creole families; Anthony Vidler's notion of the uncanny becomes useful when we consider how this force, the aggressive presence of the quadroon women, impacted the private lives of white New Orleanians. Associating the uncanny with haunted houses and the nineteenth-century works of Edgar Allan Poe, Vidler defines the uncanny as "the contrast between a secure homely interior and the fearful invasion of an alien presence; on a psychological level, its play was one of doubling, where the other is, strangely enough, experienced as a replica of the self, all the more fearsome because apparently the same." [46]

Nearly everyone who encountered quadroons and other colored Creole women commented on their beauty as well as their striking whiteness. Thus, the fear, the threat, and the unease the quadroon instilled into white families resonate with Vidler's notion of haunting. Many white women were so driven and possessed by this fear that they started attending the balls themselves to check up on their husbands or even possibly to find husbands. This became such a popular practice that in the 1830s, Mayor Gerrard Culbertson remarked that "at the last ball of that description, there were in the rooms more white ladies than colored ones." [47]

This idea of doubling, of places being inhabited by alien yet familiar bodies, is further illustrated in the photo essay mentioned earlier, by Frank Menthe of the *Clarion Herald,* taken when the Sisters of the Holy Family were vacating the French Quarter site. Menthe photographed the nuns and returned to the site two years later, just around the time of the hotel's long-awaited grand opening. In an attempt to capture the charm of the nineteenth-century Vieux Carré, waitresses and hostesses dressed in antebellum gowns evoking the period. In the two sets of photos, these women are situated precisely in the same spots as the nuns. Menthe said he posed them this way "to show the contrast between the old and the new. I shot the same areas to show how they had been renovated and how they had changed as well as how they didn't change. They tried to maintain the architecture and ambiance of the building. The idea of hiring the women dressed in the ante-bellum gowns was to date it back to the time when the building was in its heyday." [48]

The photos exhibit a sense of historic continuity, but there are drastic differences, in that the two sets of pictures appear to be negative images of one another. Nearly everything that is black in one photo is white in the other—the nuns' black habits are replaced with white gowns, the dark mahogany stairwell has been painted white, and even the black nuns are replaced with white women who are meant to embody the romanticism and exoticism of an age and practice associated with "colored" women. At this time (the mid-1960s), people of color would not be allowed to stay in the Bourbon Orleans Hotel but certainly worked there as domestics and cooks. The only other legitimate way colored women inhabited this space was as nuns—desexed and disenfranchised—their commercial bodies no longer posing a threat to the genteel white home. This again exemplifies Roach's notion of surrogation—the substitution of white bodies for colored ones and, in a sense, one commodity for another. Finally, in the Bourbon Orleans Hotel as it exists today, the commercial body of the quadroon is substituted by the commodified myth of the quadroon balls.

Only a city block separated the quadroon balls from the auction block, but whether against the backdrop of an auctioneer's cry or a French quadrille, there was, nonetheless, the trade of black bodies, all the more valuable when cloaked in white flesh. Beyond the commodification of this body on the auction block, it enters the realm of the commercial. The quadroons were marked by a mastery of whiteness so perfect that when white men had the choice, the quadroon women often beat out the "real" thing. But such dichotomies are precisely what the quadroon body challenged by the fact that it was both white and black. Hence these distinctions between black and white could not be as exclusive as Southern racists wanted them to be. I conclude this analysis with a heavy understanding of its complexity and only hope that I have described the issues with some clarity. Trying to evaluate the history of the Bourbon Orleans with its relation to quadroon women and that connection to the city and its larger history spirals into a multitude of questions about identity, bodies, boundaries, memory, and myth.

Possibly, this project could have been more succinct and facile if it focused on one of the many factors examined in this analysis. But while that might have been more clear, it also would have been incomplete. For how can we consider the history of the Bourbon Orleans without looking at both the quadroon concubines and the quadroon nuns? Similarly, how do we examine these incarnations of the "same" women without a look at Menthe's fascinating photographs? How can we talk about race in New Orleans without attacking it head-on from the auction block and then refracting it through the prism of the quadroon body? As dense and laborious as it may seem, the Bourbon Orleans Hotel garners its historic value from the way it has absorbed and embodied so many other histories—the history of slavery and sexuality, nuns and concubines, a history of infidelity and love, the history of Henriette Delille's devotion to God and the history of Pauline's fatal devotion to a man.

And still, even with so much already in the pot, the delicate strands of this historic web extend beyond the walls of the Bourbon Orleans and the ramparts of the French Quarter. In France, Louisa Lamotte enjoyed a prosperous life without submitting to the sexual servitude of other quadroons like herself. Born in New Orleans, educated in Paris, she became the directress of a girls' school in Abbeyville and was awarded a distinguished teaching honor by the French government. From San Domingue, Ferdinand Séjour Marcou arrived in New Orleans and took Josephine Ferrand as his mistress. Their son, Victor Séjour, a colored Creole, would become one of the most celebrated French playwrights of the nineteenth century, a friend and colleague of Alexandre Dumas. Countless lives, real and imagined, make up the rich myths of the quadroon balls. Calling to us from their troubled history, these ghosts dare us to discover who they really are. In so doing, we run the risk of challenging our own fragile identities.

NOTES

1. Lewis P. Simpson, "New Orleans as a Literary Center," in *Literary New Orleans: Essays and Meditations,* ed. Richard Kennedy (Baton Rouge, 1992), 83.
2. Joseph Roach, "Slave Spectacles and Tragic Octoroons: A Cultural Genealogy of Ante-bellum Performance," *Theater Survey,* November 1992, 33.
3. Though related in some ways, the commercial is not a rearticulation of Marx's commodity fetish, in that the commodity fetish emphasizes the inflated social value and import of various commodities. The commercial, however, seeks to further extend the very notion of the commodity with relation to a specific history and profits turned from the manipulation, exploitation, and reconstruction of that history.
4. Paul Gilroy articulates a similar use of history with regard to R. Kelly's sampling of the 1969 Five Stairsteps' hit, "Ooh Child." Gilroy notes, "His [R. Kelly's] citation of the earlier tune is not motivated by the desire to engage in the archaeology of living intertextual tradition. It works like a stolen sample or a borrowed instrumental riff to index the interperformative relationships that constitute a counter-cultural subculture. He makes the past audible in the here and now, but subserviently; history is conscripted into the service of the present." " 'After the Love Has Gone': Bio-Politics and Etho-Poetics in the Black Public Sphere," *Public Culture* 7 (1994): 53.
5. Michel deCerteau, *The Practice of Everyday Life* (Berkeley, 1984), 106.
6. "Bourbon Orleans: Facts Facts Facts." This was a promotional brochure published by the Kings Hotel Corporation at the height of the zoning controversy in 1966. The brochure was meant to convince residents in the area that the opening of the hotel—and the subsequent zoning changes it entailed—was a worthwhile project.
7. Fredric Jameson, *Postmodernism, or, the Logic of Late Capitalism* (Durham, 1992), 46.
8. Umberto Eco, *Travels in Hyperreality* (San Diego, 1986), 29–31.
9. Stewart Brand, *How Buildings Learn* (New York, 1994), 10.
10. Henry Kmen, *History of Music in New Orleans: The Formative Years, 1791–1841* (Baton Rouge, 1966), 44.

11. Kmen, *History of Music,* 45.

12. Kmen, *History of Music,* 47; Roger A. Fischer, *The Segregation Struggle in Louisiana, 1862–1877* (Chicago, 1974) 17.

13. Kmen, *History of Music,* 47.

14. Frederick Law Olmsted, *A Journey in the Seaboard Slave States, 1853–1854,* vol. 2 (New York, 1904), 594; James Stuart, *Three Years in North America,* vol. 2 (New York, 1833), 203–9; James Silk Buckingham, *The Slave States of America,* vol. 1 (Boston, 1842), 35–38.

15. Lyle Saxon, *Fabulous New Orleans* (New York, 1928), 185. "To take away all semblance of vulgarity, the price of admission is fixed at two dollars so that only persons of the better class can appear there."

16. James Hugo Johnston, *Race Relations in Virginia and Miscegenation in the South, 1776–1860* (Amherst, 1970), 310. Such systems of concubinage were certainly not unique to Louisiana but rather characterized colonial situations in general. In her essay "Making Empire Respectable: The Politics of Race and Sexual Morality in Twentieth Century Colonial Cultures," Ann Stoler explains a similar reaction to these "annoying attentions" in other colonial communities: "Native women were to keep men physically and psychologically fit for work, marginally content, not distracting or urging them out of line, imposing neither the time consuming nor financial responsibilities that European family life was thought to demand." *American Ethnologist* 16, no. 4 (November 1989): 637.

17. Olmstead, *Journey,* 594.

18. Annie Lee West-Stahl, "The Free Negro in Ante-bellum Louisiana," *Louisiana Historical Quarterly* 25 (July 1942): 311.

19. Calvin Dill Wilson, "Black Masters: Side Light on Slavery," *North American Review* 181 (1905): 692. "We are to remember, in connection with the conditions in Louisiana, that a general trait of French and Spanish colonists in all countries has been that they have commonly recognized and provided for the wives taken from among native women, negro, Indian, or any other nationality, and that they have acknowledged and provided for their children; while the Anglo-Saxon, as a rule, leaves these women and children to shift for themselves."

20. *Argus,* October 27, 1837.

21. Herbert Asbury, *The French Quarter: An Informal History of the New Orleans Underworld* (St. Simons Island, GA, 1936), 96.

22. Grace King, *New Orleans* (New York, 1968), 350.

23. Stephen Longstreet, *Sportin' House: New Orleans and the Jazz Story* (Los Angeles, 1965), 111; David Rankin, *The Forgotten People: Free People of Color in New Orleans, 1850–1870* (Baltimore, 1976), 140.

24. Eugene Genovese, *Roll, Jordan, Roll: The World the Slaves Made* (New York, 1972), 416.

25. Fischer, *Segregation Struggle,* 17. "The city council adopted a measure on January 4, 1828, forbidding white men, with or without masks, from attending

dressed or masked balls composed of men and women of color. This ordinance, however, did little to dampen male enthusiasm for the balls. Only sporadic efforts were made to enforce it and the council abandoned its attempts to legislate against mixed amusements for nearly 30 years."

26. These women were so called because the trunks supplied to them by the French government for their journey resembled small caskets.

27. C. C. Robin, *Voyage to Louisiana, 1803–1805*, trans. Stuart Landry, Jr. (New Orleans, 1966), 249.

28. Hortense Spillers, "Mama's Baby, Papa's Maybe: An American Grammar Book," *Diacritics* 17, no. 2 (summer 1987): 65–81. Spillers pulls this from the research of Claude Meillassoux found in Claire C. Robertson and Martin A. Klein, *Women and Slavery in Africa* (Madison, 1983).

29. Longstreet, *Sportin' House*, 109.

30. Alexis de Tocqueville, "Alexis de Tocqueville in New Orleans: January 1–3, 1832," ed. G. W. Pierson, *Franco-American Review*, June 1936, 25–42.

31. Henry Chambers, *History of Louisiana*, vol. 1 (New York, 1925), 342. W. McFadden Duffy, "Ladies of Color," *Roosevelt Review*, September 1938, 48.

32. Asbury, *French Quarter*, 97: "And when the connection was broken, by marriage of the white man or for some other reason, she usually received a competence sufficient to maintain her for the rest of her life or set her up in business. They became modistes or hairdressers, owned slaves whose labors brought them in a comfortable revenue, and in later years had a practical monopoly of the business of operating high class boarding houses for white bachelors."

33. Walter L. Johnson offers an interesting basis for this argument in "Masters and Slaves in the Market: Slavery and the New Orleans Trade, 1804–1864," Ph.D. diss., Princeton University, 1994. Johnson examines the dynamics of the slaving business and demonstrates that without the participation and active involvement of the slaves themselves, the slave trade could not have flourished.

34. Judith Butler, *Bodies That Matter* (New York, 1993), 138.

35. Ira Berlin, *Slaves without Masters: The Free Negro in the Ante-bellum South* (New York, 1974), 365.

36. John Blassingame, *Black New Orleans* (Chicago, 1973), 25.

37. Blassingame, *Black New Orleans*, 26.

38. Harriet Martineau, *Society in America*, vol. 2 (London, 1837), 349.

39. Duffy, "Ladies of Color," 52–53. Marjorie Roehl, "A Young Quadroon Forsakes Society to Serve the Poor," *New Orleans Times-Picayune*, November 9, 1986.

40. Duffy, "Ladies of Color," 54.

41. *New Orleans Times-Picayune*, March 14, 1963.

42. *New Orleans Times-Picayune*, March 11, 1963.

43. *New Orleans Times-Picayune*, March 16, 1963.

44. DeCerteau, *Practice of Everyday Life*, 108.

LIVERPOOL JOHN MOORES UNIVERSITY
LEARNING SERVICES

45. Charles Rousseve, *The Negro in Louisiana: Aspects of His Culture and His Literature* (New Orleans, 1937), 102.

46. Anthony Vidler, *Architectural Uncanny* (Cambridge, 1992), 21.

47. Joe Treagle, *Early New Orleans Society* (New Orleans, 1971), 35.

48. Frank Menthe, interview by author, August 1, 1994.

BRUCE SIMON

TRAUMATIC REPETITION
GAYL JONES'S *CORREGIDORA*

Why the compulsion to repeat the massive story of slavery in the contemporary Afro-American novel, especially so long after the empirical event itself? . . . Contemporary Afro-American writers who tell the story of slavery are increasingly aiming for the same thing: to reposition the stress points of that story with a heavy accent on particular acts of agency within an oppressive and degrading system.
—Deborah E. McDowell, "Negotiating between Tenses"

[S]lavery haunts the literary imagination because its material conditions and social relations are frequently reproduced in fiction as historically dynamic; they continue to influence society long after emancipation. . . . In a formal sense slavery can thus be a most powerful "absent" presence.
—Hazel Carby, "Ideologies of Black Folk"

Is the contemporary compulsion to repeat the haunting story of slavery, as Hazel Carby would have it, testimony to the past's continuing possession of African-American writers, critics, and theorists, in the form of an "ideology of the folk"?[1] Or is it an attempt to master the past, as Deborah McDowell suggests, to recover the traces of agency erased from or misrepresented by the dominant historical record?[2] Is repetition compulsion another form of enslavement or a means of liberation? Or is it completely other? Nowhere are these questions more urgently posed than in Gayl Jones's *Corregidora,* a chilling and powerful historical novel of slavery that is only beginning to be engaged with the necessary critical attentiveness.[3] It is my contention in this essay that *Corregidora* is as much about the structure of traumatic experience as it is about the afterlife of Brazilian slavery and American segregation. Both narrator and novel bear witness to New World history as a history of trauma.

To put forward these claims is to raise the following questions: What does it mean for New World history to be a history of trauma?[4] And what is at stake when we identify catastrophic events, ranging from the forced departure from Africa to the beating of Rodney King, as traumatic?[5] It is to these questions that I now turn.

TRAUMA AND THE LITERARY IMAGINATION

To begin with the basics: Jones's novel seems to span twenty-two years of the life of its protagonist and narrator, Ursa Corregidora—starting in 1947 when she is twenty-five, shortly before she leaves her husband, Mutt, and ending in 1969 when she decides to return to him. Yet *Corregidora* actually spans nine decades and two continents—from pre-Emancipation Brazil to post-segregation Kentucky. The novel opens with a personal catastrophe for Ursa: she loses her unborn child and the capacity to bear children after a fall caused by her possessive husband and a hysterectomy by possibly racist doctors. This personal catastrophe, however, is intimately linked with a familial and historical catastrophe, for in the late nineteenth century the Brazilian slaveowner known as old man Corregidora had first prostituted, then raped and impregnated Ursa's great-grandmother under slavery, and later impregnated their daughter, Ursa's grandmother, some eighteen years after Emancipation. Ursa, having grown up hearing stories of these events from three generations of female forebears, along with injunctions to pass on the memory of the horrors and crimes of slavery to her own descendants, is thus faced with a quite literal identity crisis—the working through of which drives the novel's plot—when she becomes physically unable to "bear witness."

To continue with a question: Why have most readers of *Corregidora* compulsively returned, as it were, to images of haunting and possession? From Claudia Tate's 1979 comment that "Corregidora . . . haunts [Ursa] as if he were still alive," to Melvin Dixon's 1987 view that "Ursa Corregidora learns to assert her will and outrageous voice over the residual history haunting her songs," from Ann duCille's 1993 observation that Ursa is "the last in a long line of black women haunted and emotionally burdened by history," to Madhu Dubey's 1995 claim that Ursa "continues to be haunted by the complex relationships of three generations of her maternal ancestors with their Portuguese slave owner, Corregidora," almost every critic who has written on the novel highlights the haunting power of slavery and history.[6] Despite their divergent and often conflicting readings of the novel, these critics agree that Ursa is haunted, that she is at times possessed by the past. Compare this critical consensus with Cathy

Caruth's exacting definition of trauma: "To be traumatized is precisely to be possessed by an image or event. . . . [Trauma is] a peculiar kind of historical phenomenon . . . in which the overwhelming events of the past repeatedly possess, in intrusive images and thoughts, the one who has lived through them."[7]

Has Ursa, then, been traumatized? If so, we would expect her to suffer

> a response, sometimes delayed, to an overwhelming event or events, which takes the form of repeated, intrusive hallucinations, dreams, thoughts or behaviors stemming from the event, along with numbing that may have begun during or after the experience, and possibly also increased arousal to (and avoidance of) stimulants recalling the event.[8]

Is it not precisely this delayed response that Ursa complains of as she recovers from her hysterectomy early in the novel? Ursa's exasperated complaint—"The shit you can dream. They say it's what you really feel, but it ain't what you really feel"[9]—should be read as a commentary on the narrative structure of *Corregidora,* which foregrounds the way her memories and dreams "repeatedly erupt into her narrative," as Madhu Dubey has recently argued.[10] Dubey recognizes that the italicized portions of the novel interrupt Ursa's narration, that they force themselves upon her, against or irrespective of her wishes. That is, the past literally returns to Ursa in her dreams, in her memories, and, as I will soon argue, in her actions. To Freud, this literal return of the past is an identifying mark of trauma; in *Beyond the Pleasure Principle,* he suggests that the traumatic dreams of World War I veterans pose an enigmatic challenge to his theories of dream-work:

> dreams occurring in traumatic neuroses have the characteristic of repeatedly bringing the patient back into the situation of his accident, a situation from which he wakes up in another fright. This astonishes people far too little. . . . Anyone who accepts it as self-evident that their dreams should put them back at night into the situation that caused them to fall ill has misunderstood the nature of dreams.[11]

According to Cathy Caruth, Freud finds the traumatic dream startling because it cannot be explained in terms of a wish or unconscious meaning but is instead the literal return of the event.[12] The same holds true for Ursa's dreams, as Ursa herself recognizes; the significance of her dreams and hallucinations lies less in their manifest or latent meaning—or even in the workings of condensation and displacement—than in the way they intrude on her telling of her own story.

That is, even as trauma demands testimony, it interrupts the process of testimony; it introduces an imperative to tell and makes that telling impossible.[13] Ursa's singing of the blues testifies to this imperative and this impossibility. Many critics have emphasized how the blues makes life bearable for Ursa by enabling her to contain and control the impact of her catastrophic experiences in a state of creative suspension and productive tension.[14] Yet what Ursa emphasizes about her own blues testimony is her need to sing and her inability to explain this need. The opening sentences of the novel establish the depth of Ursa's need to sing:

> It was 1947 when Mutt and I were married. I was singing in Happy's Café around on Delaware Street. He didn't like for me to sing after we were married because he said that's why he married me so he could support me. I said I didn't just sing to be supported. I said I sang because it was something I had to do, but he never would understand that. (3)

Ursa knows that singing is something she "ha[s] to do"—even in the face of both Mama's and Mutt's censure—but does not understand, or at least cannot articulate, why she feels compelled to sing. Each time she is confronted by disapproval of her singing, she stresses this inexplicable need. To Mutt's question, "*What do blues do for you?*" Ursa replies, "It helps me to explain what I can't explain" (56). To Mama's accusation that she sings "devil's music," Ursa responds, "*[L]et me give witness the only way I can. . . . Yes, if you understood me, Mama, you'd see I was trying to explain it, in blues, without words, the explanation somewhere behind the words. To explain what will always be there*" (54, 66). To herself, she thinks, "I wanted a song that would touch me, touch my life and theirs. A Portuguese song, but not a Portuguese song. A new world song. A song branded with the new world" (59). Ursa's blues testimony is a way of bearing witness to New World history as a history of trauma. But this bearing witness is not a matter of explaining or even understanding what has traumatized her; rather, her singing testifies to the "essential incomprehensibility" of a traumatic event, "the force of its affront to understanding," illustrating that "one does not have to *possess,* or *own* the truth, in order to effectively *bear witness* to it."[15]

If Ursa's dreams and blues testimony suggest that she is one of those survivors of trauma who "become themselves the symptom of a history that they cannot entirely possess,"[16] then her individual dilemma might disclose previously unnoticed dimensions of collective and historical crisis. That is, by examining further the impact of trauma on Ursa's life, we can suggest some answers to the central question of this essay: what does it mean for New World history to be a history of trauma? To do this, we must first reconstruct the events that befell Ursa's great-grandmother in late nineteenth-century Brazil. Only when we understand the repercussions of Great Gram's response to the crimes of the man who once possessed her can we understand how Ursa's trauma is at once individual, collective, and historical.

What is Great Gram's project? In a word, testimony. Her goal is to make plain the sex crimes of the Brazilian elite, as exemplified by her former master, old man Corregidora. As his name suggests,[17] Corregidora was in charge of discipline on his coffee plantation—selecting female slaves to purchase (173), prostituting them to other white men for personal profit (124), preventing them from choosing their own companions, sometimes through torture or murder (125), and finally, through his own sexual practices, "correcting" a race by "marking" it with his "blood" (12). Since this doubly genocidal project was disavowed both after Emancipation in 1888 and in 1891 when the minister of the provisional government of Brazil ordered the archives of slavery burned,[18] Great Gram repeatedly commands her descendants to "pass it down" (9), to "leave evidence" (14), to "make generations" (22), and to "bear witness" (72). As she explains:

> [T]hey didn't want to leave no evidence of what they done—so it couldn't be held against them. And I'm leaving evidence. And you got to leave evidence too. And your children got to leave evidence. And when it come time to hold up the evidence, we got to have evidence to hold up. That's why they burned all the papers, so there wouldn't be no evidence to hold against them. (14)

> They can burn the paper but they can't burn conscious, Ursa. And that's what makes the evidence. And that's what makes the verdict. (22)

> We got to burn out what they put in our minds, like you burn out a wound. Except we got to keep what we need to bear witness. The scar that's left to bear witness. We got to keep it as visible as our blood. (72)

By setting herself in opposition to official Brazilian histories that fail to mention slavery, Great Gram attempts to record the crimes of slavery through the oral transmission of family narratives. Through this passing down of family histories, she hopes to both expose and contest the imposition of ideologies of white supremacy on the Corregidora women.

Yet by the time Ursa begins to hear her family histories, Great Gram's oppositional strategy of passing down such stories has turned into a repetition of slogans either emptied of content or misunderstood. Rather than supplementing Great Gram's case against not just slavery but racism more generally, neither Grandmama nor Mama passes down any narratives of life in the segregated United States. Furthermore, the transmission of Great Gram's narrative is faulty, as in Grandmama's account of Emancipation, which reduces to a statement akin to "I was there," devoid of any sense of outrage or injustice over the official disavowal of slavery (78–79). Even worse is Mama's misuse of legal discourse:

> But you got to make generations, you go on making them anyway. And when the ground and the sky open up to ask them that question that going to be ask. They think it ain't going to be ask, but it's going to be ask. They have the evidence and give the verdict too. They think they hid everything. But they have the evidence and give the verdict too. You said that, Mama. I know I said it, and I'm going to keep saying it. (41)

Rather than concluding with the expected claim to possess evidence of the slaveowners' criminal activities, Mama simply reiterates the fact that *they* control the courts. Instead of accepting Ursa's tentative attempt to correct this error, she fails to realize she has made one in the first place.[19]

My attention to problems of transmission implicitly presents a narrative of decline—from Great Gram's pure oppositionality to Mama's compromised misunderstanding of the testimonial strategy. Yet it is just as plausible to argue that Great Gram herself sowed the seeds of this misunderstanding. While it is certainly accurate to observe that Great Gram's attempt to constitute a truly decolonized black female subjectivity has been reduced to a commitment to making generations—her project of bearing witness has become a project merely of bearing witnesses[20]—this observation, correct as it is, misses the crucial fact that Great Gram was never a figure of pure oppositionality. After all, she stayed at Corregidora's plantation for at least two years, and possibly ten or more, after Emancipation. Furthermore, she seems to follow Corregidora in elevating the capacity to procreate into a standard of moral judgment, as in her dismissal of Corregidora's wife: "*Naw, she couldn't do a damn thing. Naw, she didn't give him nothing but a sick little rabbit that didn't live to be a day old. So then he just stopped doing it. Naw, she couldn't do a damn thing*" (23). Many critics have seconded Tadpole's suggestion that "Procreation . . . could also be a slave-breeder's way of thinking" (22), but Stela Maris Coser, Madhu Dubey, and Sally Robinson have shown how in the context of nineteenth-century Brazil, where prostitution of female slaves was more prevalent than breeding, Great Gram's strategy remained oppositional, even as it was contaminated by white supremacist ideologies of black female sexuality.[21] Still, one might go so far as to argue that the history of her descendants' misunderstandings was overdetermined by Great Gram's crucial conflation of the performativity of testimony with reproduction; by emphasizing the content of her speech over its act, Great Gram makes it possible for her descendants to see her as engaging in a project of memorization, rather than testimony.[22]

What these approaches — exposure of transmission errors, narrative of decline, originary conflation — do not account for, however, is the ambivalence of Great Gram's strategy, the ways hatred and love, aversion and desire are simultaneously at work in her testimony. Dubey and Robinson have carefully analyzed the status of this ambivalence, showing not only that Great Gram's strategy remains oppositional, but also that "the production of ambivalence [i]s a textual strategy" aimed at posing "seriously disquieting questions about the very process of tradition building."[23] That is, the best readings of *Corregidora* are in general agreement that Jones's aim is to stress the necessity of adapting ethico-political strategies to changing places and times, by showing how Great Gram's project, which was oppositional in the 1890s in Brazil, has become counterproductive in the United States of the 1940s and 1950s.[24]

Yet few critics have asked the next logical question: why is it that Great Gram's consciously oppositional strategy of giving testimony repeats some of the very elements of that which she set out to oppose? The best attempts to account for this problem have argued that repetition is the unavoidable risk that Great Gram's strategy of *re*appropriation, *re*motivation, *re*contextualization, *re*inscription, *re*signification, and *re*articulation of master narratives must run.[25] Yet we can push this analysis further, for, in a word, trauma is the reason for Great Gram's repetition compulsion or automatism. Great Gram's repetitious, ritualistic testimony is not only an ethico-political strategy, it is also a means for survival. It is a way of working through her experiences, in order to come to terms with the trauma, not only of enslavement, but also of survival. As Caruth puts it, "for those who undergo trauma, it is not only the moment of the event, but of the passing out of it that is traumatic; . . . *survival itself,* in other words, *can be a crisis.*"[26] Great Gram's insistent repetition of the same stories should be read as an attempt to pursue the accident, to repeatedly leave the site of her captivity. But this is precisely the double bind of trauma: since the act of leaving, of departure, is the central and enigmatic core of trauma, the very narration of that departure can itself be retraumatizing.[27]

We can even locate the precise moment in *Corregidora* when Ursa begins to realize this. While listening to Great Gram, she thinks, "It was as if the words were helping her, as if the words repeated again and again could be a substitute for memory, were somehow more than the memory" (11). Sally Robinson's reading of this moment is exemplary: "Ursa perceives Great Gram's stories as a kind of automatic recitation over which she has no control; her narrative functions independently of her agency. As Ursa gradually comes to realize, Great Gram and Gram *have* no control over their pasts and their discourse."[28] What Robinson does not engage with is the traumatic nature of this automatic repetition. It is no accident that Nadine Fresco's recognition of a pattern to her interviews with Holocaust survivors precisely parallels Jones's presentation of Great Gram's narratives: "The silence was all the more implacable in that it was often concealed behind a screen of words, again, always the same words, an unchanging story, a tale repeated over and over again."[29]

If critics have not emphasized that Great Gram has been traumatized, they also have not noticed that a different kind of traumatic repetition provides an alternative to Great Gram's ritualistic injunctions. Recall that the most explicit and detailed account of Great Gram's relations with old man Corregidora is a five-page monologue toward the end of the novel. Yet this monologue is delivered not by Great Gram, but by Mama—and it derails Mama's telling of her "own private memory" to Ursa.[30] Ursa describes this intrusive interruption precisely in terms of possession: "Mama kept talking until it wasn't her that was talking, but Great Gram. I stared at her because she wasn't Mama now, she was Great Gram talking" (124). When Mama returns to herself, she offers the excuse that she's heard the story so many times she's learned it by heart, but Ursa does not believe her: "It was as if she had *more* than learned it by heart, though. It was as if their memory, the memory of all the Corregidora women, was her memory too, as strong with her as her own private memory, or almost as strong. But now she was Mama again" (129). Ursa thinks that what is "more than learned . . . by heart" is a kind of memory, but the way that Mama has been possessed by Great Gram's testimony in this scene should indicate to us that what has just happened is a traumatic repetition. In Shoshana Felman's terms, Mama has literally become a medium of both Great Gram's testimony and her traumatic experience.[31]

Understanding that Mama has been traumatized by Great Gram's testimony is crucial to reading the controversial ending of the novel, where Ursa returns to—and goes down on—Mutt some twenty-two years after she divorced him. It is precisely this earlier scene of Mama's traumatic repetition to which Ursa refers in the midst of her return to Mutt. In narrating the scene of her return retrospectively, Ursa struggles to describe what was happening as she performed fellatio on Mutt: "It was like I didn't know how much was me and Mutt and how much was Great Gram and Corregidora—like Mama when she had started talking like Great Gram" (184). This "like Mama" here indicates that Ursa as narrator is connecting her own actions in 1969 to the traumatic repetition that she witnessed Mama undergo a few years earlier. Yet Ursa's "like Mama" has been passed over in every reading of the novel; even those critics who read this very passage closely focus on the parallel between Ursa and Great Gram.

Melvin Dixon's arguments typify redemptive readings of the novel, readings that interpret its ending both as a gain of agency for Ursa and as a reconciliation between her and Mutt. According to Dixon, fellatio "places her in control of herself and Mutt." Dixon misreads Ursa's traumatic repetition as a kind of choice, a kind of connection intentionally drawn—or even invented—by her conscious mind, a "metaphorical return" that "allows Ursa to go forward" to reconciliation with her former husband. Although Madhu Dubey implicitly contests Dixon's reading of the ending as redemptive, cathartic, and healing, her reading does not break with his assumption that the return Ursa experiences is strictly metaphorical. While Dubey recognizes that Ursa is not fully in control of herself when she suggests that "maternal discourse so fully permeates the daughter's language of heterosexual love that the daughter ultimately merges into her maternal ancestor," she has no way of explaining why the merging of discourses might lead to a merging of identities.[32]

What these readings miss is the way Ursa's return to Mutt is itself a traumatic repetition—Ursa experiences Great Gram's literal return and possession of her. Where Mama's earlier traumatic reenactment involved a repetition of Great Gram's *testimony,* Ursa's repeats Great Gram's *actions.*[33] It is thus crucial to separate Ursa as character from Ursa as narrator when one reads the final scene of *Corregidora.* We can begin to understand the difficulty of bearing witness to a traumatic history when we focus on Ursa's actions as a narrator—her uncertainty when confronted by her own traumatic repetition, her inability to simply report on or record the experience of returning to Mutt, her need to take recourse in a simile, an analogy, in order to transmit the impact of the experience, and then, only belatedly.

Not only does Gayl Jones show how Ursa, as character and as narrator, bears witness to New World history as a history of trauma, she also makes the interrelation of desire and traumatic repetition a structuring principle of *Corregidora.* Early in the novel, after Ursa has left Mutt and begun seeing Tadpole, the owner of the night club at which she sings, Tadpole asks her, "What do you want, Ursa?" (22). Ursa evades his question in that scene, but, as Dubey points out, the rest of the novel is made up of her attempts to answer it, attempts that are interrupted by eruptions of the past. Nowhere is this clearer than the ending of *Corregidora,* the scene of Ursa's traumatic repetition, which itself is marked by multiple repetitions. Not only does Ursa return to Mutt in this scene, she does so in the very same hotel they had lived in while they were married. Not only does Ursa believe that her performing fellatio on Mutt reiterates Great

Gram's final act before departing from Corregidora's plantation, she also literally cites a question Grandmama had asked several decades (and a mere eleven pages) earlier: "What is it a woman can do to a man that make him hate her so bad he wont to kill her one minute and keep thinking about her and can't get her out of his mind the next?" (173, 184). Not only does Mutt repeat a story about his grandparents he had told Ursa twenty-two years before, he also joins in a classic call-and-response blues dialogue with Ursa at the novel's end.

These multiple repetitions mark a certain kind of closure, one that must be carefully differentiated from other possible endings of the novel. For Jones could have ended *Corregidora* in at least three other ways, all of which would involve the affirmation of some sort of female community: first, with Ursa's return to her hometown in 1961, in order to discover her mother's private memory (104–32); second, with Ursa's second return to her hometown in the late 1960s, this time to share her own private memory with her mother (182); third, with a reconciliation between Ursa and either Cat or Jeffy, both of whom Ursa had rejected soon after leaving Mutt.[34] Instead, surprisingly, Jones ends the novel with a scene of traumatic repetition, Ursa's return to Mutt after what Freud might have called a twenty-two year latency period.

Jones's decision to end *Corregidora* with Ursa's return to Mutt becomes even more surprising when we consider the explicit parallels between Mutt and Corregidora. After all, Mutt was not only responsible for Ursa's fall, his possessive attitudes toward Ursa are also presented as a farcical repetition of slavery's tragic social relations. How else to account for the image of Mutt, consumed by jealousy, dressed in a "Dick Tracy" trench coat, "casing out the joint" for rivals (158)? But this repetition is no joking matter, for there is also a more serious set of parallels. Just as old man Corregidora called Great Gram "Dorita," his "little gold piece" (10, 124), and prostituted her, a shift takes place in Ursa and Mutt's relationship between 1947 and 1948, from Mutt's describing Ursa as a "piece of gold" early in their relationship (60), to a "piece of ass" to be auctioned off or even prostituted when she repeatedly refuses to let him support her (159), and finally to Ursa's critique of men who treat women "like a piece of shit" both before and after Mutt pushes her down the stairs (167).[35] Thus, not only does Jones avoid an affirmation of female community at the end of *Corregidora,* she also suggests that Ursa's return to Mutt is a literal return of the history of slavery.

That is, a return to and of trauma, a traumatic repetition, an ending marked by trauma and an ending that traumatizes. As character, Ursa's attempt to speak and act on her desire is interrupted by a scene of her possession by the past. As narrator, Ursa's attempt to address a listener, to give testimony, to bear witness, is literally interrupted by the end of the novel, an ending that—in its abruptness and compulsive repetitiveness, as well as in its content—suggests that the trauma of slavery is still with us. *Corregidora,* a traumatized and traumatic text, calls on us to testify to a problem of testifying, bear witness to a crisis of witnessing.

SLAVERY AND THE POSSIBILITY OF HISTORY

At first glance, it might appear that my argument sets out to contest and provide an alternative to McDowell's and Carby's. Contrary to McDowell's argument that the contemporary African-American historical novel of slavery aims to "accent . . . particular acts of agency within an oppressive and degrading system," my reading of *Corregidora* emphasizes the ways trauma suspends, supercedes, bypasses, or cancels the agency of Great Gram, Grandmama, Mama, and Ursa. Contrary to Carby's argument that the metaphor of slavery has such a hold on African-American writers, critics, and theorists that it causes a conflation of different modes of production and domination, my arguments about trauma suggest that slavery is "a most powerful 'absent' presence" in much more than a merely "formal sense." And yet, I would argue that my reading is also and at the same time an extension and redirection of their central concerns. My focus on Ursa's actions as narrator highlights the very question of agency that a traumatic repetition seems to foreclose; my focus on Ursa's and Mama's shared traumatic experiences implies that the material, social, and political conditions under which the traumatic repetition returns are of crucial importance.

Still, these comparisons suggest that exclusive attention to what trauma might mean is necessary but insufficient. Let me, then, pose certain supplementary questions to this essay's guiding thread: "What does it mean for New World history to be a history of trauma?" "What does it mean"—to whom, in what conditions, circumstances, contexts? Can it mean differently? "New World history as a history of trauma"—traumatic for whom? What about multiple traumas? What makes one kind of trauma (say, one stemming from slavery) more pressing in a given time and place (say, the contemporary United States) than others? What makes this one more difficult to work through? "Trauma"— what does it mean to transfer to the study of slavery and colonialism a paradigm that is achieving its fullest elaboration only through extensive interviews with Holocaust survivors? Isn't this kind of psychoanalytic reading of the history of slavery politically and intellectually regressive, not to mention idealist? Does it not conflate the analytic scene with the scene of reading? These questions ask, in short, what is at stake in reading the history of slavery as traumatic?[36]

To suggest the direction my answers to these questions might follow, I will consider the final question. For one thing, saying "trauma" helps us respond to conservative attacks on "the language of victimization" or "the claiming of victimhood status," by emphasizing that one does not choose to experience a trauma, but instead is chosen by it. To the kind of nonresponse to claims for justice, like "find me an evil individual perpetrator with malicious intent *and* a completely innocent victim; then, and only then, I'll accept that an injustice has taken place," we could respond that one is not a victim of trauma, one is a survivor of trauma.[37]

Furthermore, saying "trauma" allows us to challenge another cliché to which those who acknowledge the "past injustice" of slavery and segregation often retreat: "all that's past; it's over and done with; put it behind you; forget about it."[38] In return, we should emphasize that trauma is about the literal return—the recurrence and the survival—of a painful, catastrophic event or experience. As Caruth puts it, "the impact of the traumatic event lies precisely in its belatedness, in its refusal to be simply located, in its insistent appearance outside the boundaries of any single place or time."[39] In addition, how and how well survivors live with the painful reenactments of trauma has everything to do with the response of those who were not traumatized. Without some form of recognition and response from others, "a double trauma" takes place. As Tom Keenan explains, "On the one hand there's a cataclysmic event, which produces symptoms and calls for testimony. And then it happens again, when the value of the witness in the testimony is denied, and there's no one to attend or respond—not simply to the event, but to its witness as well."[40] Keenan suggests here that calls to forget a traumatic event or to "put it behind us" can be retraumatizing for the survivors. Such calls also miss the point: rather than being a problem of a too-present, too-pressing memory, trauma is a problem of unclaimed experience and a gap in memory. As Dori Laub puts it, "the trauma survivor who is bearing witness has no prior knowledge, no comprehension, and no memory of what happened." Or as Maurice Blanchot rigorously defines a traumatic event: "infinite infliction which does not reach us in the present, but befalls by linking us to a past without memory." So, if a traumatic event is never present to its survivor, if a traumatic history is not a matter of memory, how can we—or anyone—gain access to it?[41] Might attention to trauma jeopardize the generative turn of such fields as black history, women's history, and labor history to discover, interpret, preserve, and disseminate the traces of what has been ignored, misrepresented, disavowed, repressed, silenced, and obliterated by and in official histories?

As we have seen, Jones's protagonist, narrator, and novel bear witness to New World history as a history of trauma. That is, both narrator and novel bear witness to a traumatic event belatedly, as a way of coming to terms with the fundamental "inaccessibility of its occurrence." Caruth explains the paradox of trauma as follows: "since the traumatic event is not experienced as it occurs, it is fully evident only in connection with another place, and in another time. . . . [T]he history of a trauma, in its inherent belatedness, can only take place through the listening of another." As she concludes, "The attempt to gain access to a traumatic history, then, is also the project of listening beyond the pathology of individual suffering, to the reality of a history that in its crises can only be perceived in unassimilable forms."[42] Even if the project of gaining access to a traumatic experience is impossible, it must still be attempted, with others: "trauma opens up and challenges us to a new kind of listening, the witnessing, precisely, *of impossibility.*"[43]

But this is a lesson that Gayl Jones has already taught us. At one point in the novel, Mutt tells Ursa about his grandfather, who had saved money as a blacksmith and bought land for his family. But, as Mutt continues, "When Mama went into the courthouse to claim the land, somebody had tore one of the pages out the book. . . . Anyway, they ain't nothing you can do when they tear the pages out of the book and they ain't no record of it. They probably burned the pages" (78). Like the burning of the slavery archives in Brazil, Mutt's tale of pages torn out of the book is the central allegory in *Corregidora* for trauma, which destroys both the historical record as traditionally understood and the possibility for its reconstruction. These scenes allegorize not only the destruction of the possibility of referential history, but also the very disavowal of trauma by others that retraumatizes the survivors. In the face of this double trauma, Mutt responds, "they ain't nothing you can do," but Jones's project, like Ursa's blues testimony, rejects fatalism in the face of impossibility. As Jones explains in an interview with Michael Harper, "I don't start with the answers, I start with the telling, and sometimes the answers come out of the telling. . . . That's what we're all looking for—the words and the forms to account for certain things that we feel need to be accounted for."[44] The telling that Jones refers to here must be something other than a simple record, or recording of experience; that telling must take place with a listener, who has an equal share in reclaiming the unclaimable traumatic experience, so that it no longer possesses the one who underwent it. Felman's description of Mallarmé's poetry applies equally to the way Jones's novel attempts to "speak *beyond its means,* to testify— precociously—to the ill-understood effects and to the impact of an accident whose origin cannot precisely be located but whose repercussions, in their very unpredictable and unanticipated nature, still continue to evolve even in the very process of the testimony."[45] Perhaps, then, what *Corregidora* finally does is demonstrate the necessity of reading if we are to gain access to certain kinds of history.[46] *Corregidora* calls on us to learn to listen for and read the address that trauma survivors struggle to—and cannot help but—establish with us, with others.

I close, then, with some questions. What if we were to take seriously Deborah McDowell's invocation of a "compulsion to repeat" at work in and through the contemporary historical novel of slavery? What if we were to take Hazel Carby's wording—that the absent presence of slavery haunts the literary imagination—at its word? What if our readings of the wide range of African-American responses to slavery—antebellum and postbellum slave narratives, sermons, WPA interviews, autobiographies, political writings, poems, short stories, novels, drama, and essays (not to mention music)—were to explicitly engage with and transform recent rethinkings of trauma, testimony, and witnessing? What if, that is, we were to explore the traumatic dimensions of slavery?

NOTES

An earlier version of this paper was presented at " 'The Negro Problem': 1895–1995," a graduate student conference at Princeton University, 3 March 1995. Thanks to the conference participants and its organizers, Judith Jackson Fossett and Jeffrey Tucker; to Arnold Rampersad and Wahneema Lubiano for encouraging me to pursue this project; to Diana Fuss for putting me on the track of trauma; to Ann duCille for pointing me toward important issues and articles; to Mychel Namphy for pushing me to rethink my original take on the blues; to Lawrie Balfour, Wendy Chun, Mike Davis, Diana Fuss, Adam Gussow, Gavin Jones, Thomas Keenan, Tamara Ketabgian, Wahneema Lubiano, Lisa Lynch, Kenneth Mostern, Claudia Tate, and Slavoj Žižek for their careful readings and constructive criticisms of various drafts of this paper; and to Wendy Chun for everything.

1. Hazel Carby, "Ideologies of Black Folk: The Historical Novel of Slavery," in *Slavery and the Literary Imagination,* ed. Deborah E. McDowell and Arnold Rampersad (Baltimore: Johns Hopkins University Press, 1989), 125–26.

2. Deborah E. McDowell, "Negotiating between Tenses: Witnessing Slavery after Freedom—*Dessa Rose,*" in *Slavery and the Literary Imagination,* ed. McDowell and Rampersad, 144, 160. See also idem, *"The Changing Same": Black Women's Literature, Criticism, and Theory* (Bloomington: Indiana University Press, 1995), 141–55.

3. Despite the firestorm of public controversy following the publication of *Corregidora* and *Eva's Man,* and an initial flurry of critical attention, most critics have avoided a close engagement with Jones's works; on this point, see Madhu Dubey, "Gayl Jones and the Matrilineal Metaphor of Tradition," *Signs: Journal of Women in Culture and Society* 20.2 (winter 1995): 245–50. Notable exceptions, whose readings have particularly influenced my own, include Madhu Dubey, *Black Women Novelists and the Nationalist Aesthetic* (Bloomington: Indiana University Press, 1994), 72–88; idem, "Gayl Jones and the Matrilineal Metaphor"; Sally Robinson, *Engendering the Subject: Gender and Self-Representation in Contemporary Women's Fiction* (Albany: State University of New York Press, 1991), 134–87; Stela Maris Coser, *Bridging the Americas: The Literature*

of Paule Marshall, Toni Morrison, and Gayl Jones (Philadelphia: Temple University Press, 1994), 120–63. For analyses of the controversies surrounding black women's novels of the 1970s (and beyond), see Ann duCille, "Phallus(ies) of Interpretation: Toward Engendering the Black Critical 'I,' " *Callaloo* 16.3 (summer 1993): 559–73; McDowell, *"The Changing Same,"* 118–37.

4. In formulating my thesis and my question in this manner, I acknowledge my indebtedness to Cathy Caruth's absolutely critical work on trauma and history; see Cathy Caruth, "Unclaimed Experience: Trauma and the Possibility of History," *Yale French Studies* 79 (1991): 182, 185–92 (special issue, *Literature and the Ethical Question,* ed. Claire Nouvet); Cathy Caruth, "Introduction," *American Imago* 48.1 and 48.4 (spring and winter 1991): 4–7, 9–11 (special issue, *Psychoanalysis, Culture and Trauma,* ed. Cathy Caruth).

5. On trauma and Rodney King, see Avital Ronell, "Video/Television/Rodney King: Twelve Steps beyond the Pleasure Principle," in *Cultures on the Brink: Ideologies of Technology,* ed. Gretchen Bender and Timothy Druckrey (Seattle: Bay Press, 1994), 287, 290–91, 297–303. See also Robert Gooding-Williams, ed., *Reading Rodney King / Reading Urban Uprising* (New York: Routledge, 1993).

6. Claudia Tate, "*Corregidora:* Ursa's Blues Medley," *Black American Literature Forum* 13.4 (1979): 141; Melvin Dixon, *Ride Out the Wilderness: Geography and Identity in Afro-American Literature* (Urbana: University of Illinois Press, 1987), 108, 110, 111; duCille, "Phallus(ies) of Interpretation," 567; Dubey, "Gayl Jones and the Matrilineal Metaphor," 251; see also Melvin Dixon, "Singing a Deep Song: Language as Evidence in the Novels of Gayl Jones," in *Black Women Writers (1950–1980): A Critical Evaluation,* ed. Mari Evans (New York: Anchor Press, 1984), 239; Dubey, *Black Women Novelists,* 74. On haunting and American literature more generally, see Kathleen Brogan, "American Stories of Cultural Haunting: Tales of Heirs and Ethnographers," *College English* 57.2 (February 1995): 149–65.

7. Caruth, "Introduction," 3, 417. See also Dori Laub, "Bearing Witness, Or the Vicissitudes of Listening," in *Testimony: Crises of Witnessing in Literature, Psychoanalysis, and History* (New York: Routledge, 1992), 67; Kai Erikson, "Notes on Trauma and Community," *American Imago* 48.4 (winter 1991): 458.

8. Caruth, "Introduction," 2–3; see also Bessel A. van der Kolk and Onno van der Hart, "The Intrusive Past: The Flexibility of Memory and the Engraving of Trauma," *American Imago* 48.4 (winter 1991): 428–31, 437–38.

9. Gayl Jones, *Corregidora* (1975; Boston: Beacon Press, 1986), 47. Hereafter cited in the text parenthetically.

10. Dubey, "Gayl Jones and the Matrilineal Metaphor," 252–53. In an earlier argument, Dubey makes this point explicitly: "The cyclic, repetitive structure of the matriarchal narrative seems to impede the linear forward movement of the plot. As Ursa tries to recover from her hysterectomy and to create a new

story of her sexual desire, the old story of the Corregidora women inexorably carries her back into the past[,] . . . giv[ing] rise to an acute sense of temporal impasse." Dubey, *Black Women Novelists,* 82.

11. Sigmund Freud, *Beyond the Pleasure Principle* (1920), in *The Standard Edition of the Complete Psychological Works of Sigmund Freud* (hereafter cited as *SE*), ed. and trans. James Strachey, in collaboration with Anna Freud, assisted by Alix Strachey and Alan Tyson (London: Hogarth Press, 1953–74), 18:13. Other relevant passages in Freud's works include *Beyond the Pleasure Principle,* 12–17, 28–33; "Introduction to *Psychoanalysis and the War Neuroses*" (1919), *SE,* 17:206–15; *Moses and Monotheism* (1939), *SE,* 23:66–68, 72–80, 90–102. For brief overviews of Freud's vacillations on trauma, see Caruth, "Introduction," 7–8; van der Kolk and van der Hart, "The Intrusive Past," 433–38.

12. Caruth, "Introduction," 3.

13. On this point, see Dori Laub, "Truth and Testimony: The Process and the Struggle," *American Imago* 48.1 (spring 1991): 77–80, 86, 90; idem, "Bearing Witness," 58, 65, 67–70.

14. Tate, "*Corregidora:* Ursa's Blues Medley," 141; Robinson, *Engendering the Subject,* 160; Dubey, "Gayl Jones and the Matrilineal Metaphor," 263, 264. See also Dixon, *Ride Out the Wilderness,* 113; duCille, "Phallus(ies) of Interpretation," 569; Dubey, *Black Women Novelists,* 84–86.

15. Caruth, "Introduction," 420; Shoshana Felman, "Education and Crisis, Or the Vicissitudes of Teaching," *American Imago* 48.1 (spring 1991): 27. See also Claude Lanzmann, "The Obscenity of Understanding: An Evening with Claude Lanzmann," *American Imago* 48.4 (winter 1991): 473–95.

16. Caruth, "Introduction," 4.

17. For a discussion of old man Corregidora's name, see Dixon, "Singing a Deep Song," 239. I would add to Dixon's discussion of Portuguese that attention to the meaning and connotation of the Spanish verb *corregir* (to mark, grade, correct—in a wider, perhaps Foucauldian sense, to discipline) helps illuminate Corregidora's textual function. In addition, "corregidor" comes up in at least two other contexts: *Der Corregidor* (1896), an opera by German composer Hugo Wolf; and the Philippine island off the Bataan Peninsula, site of a traumatic defeat for the U.S. military in early 1942.

18. Gilberto Freyre, *The Masters and the Slaves: A Study in the Development of Brazilian Civilization,* trans. Samuel Putnam (1933; Berkeley: University of California Press, 1986), 301. Critics generally agree that old man Corregidora is fairly representative of Brazilian slaveowners; at the very least, his practices with regard to female slaves were common (see n. 21, below). For evidence that Jones was reading histories of nineteenth-century Brazil before and during the writing of *Corregidora,* see Roseann P. Bell, "Gayl Jones Takes a Look at *Corregidora*—An Interview," in *Sturdy Black Bridges: Visions of Black Women in Literature,* ed. Roseann P. Bell, Bettye J. Parker, and Beverly Guy-Sheftall (New York: Anchor Press, 1979), 283–84. Coser argues that *Corregidora* should

be read as an intervention in the historiography of slavery (*Bridging the Americas,* 127–28).

19. For an excellent reading of Jones's rearticulation of legal discourses, see Dubey, "Gayl Jones and the Matrilineal Metaphor," 253.

20. See, for example, Jerry W. Ward, Jr., "Escape from Trublem: The Fiction of Gayl Jones," in *Black Women Writers (1950–1980),* ed. Evans, 255; Dubey, "Gayl Jones and the Matrilineal Metaphor," 259–60; Coser, *Bridging the Americas,* 130–32.

21. Coser, *Bridging the Americas,* 132–36; Dubey, "Gayl Jones and the Matrilineal Metaphor," 251, 259–60; Robinson, *Engendering the Subject,* 152–54; see also Freyre, *The Masters and the Slaves,* 454–56. Still, the fact that Great Gram had no other children after gaining her freedom in 1888 suggests that she was not able to follow through on her own strategy.

22. On the performativity of testimony, see Felman, "Education and Crisis," 17–18, 27–28, 34, 54, 64; Caruth, "Introduction," 1–2; Shoshana Felman and Dori Laub, foreword to *Testimony,* by Laub and Felman, xii–xvi, xx; van der Kolk and van der Hart, "The Intrusive Past," 446–51.

23. Robinson, *Engendering the Subject,* 135; Dubey, "Gayl Jones and the Matrilineal Metaphor," 249, 255–58. For more on ambivalence, see Tate, "*Corregidora:* Ursa's Blues Medley," 140, 141; Dixon, "Singing a Deep Song," 241, 243–44; Keith Byerman, *Fingering the Jagged Grain: Tradition and Form in Recent Black Fiction* (Athens: University of Georgia Press, 1985), 178; Dixon, *Ride Out the Wilderness,* 113, 116–17; Coser, *Bridging the Americas,* 141–42. For places where ambivalence is explicitly thematized in the novel, see Jones, *Corregidora,* 102, 131, 184.

24. Or, to borrow from Gayatri Spivak: "what was good in strategy has now become a slogan, and we don't look at the years passing, the situation changing." Gayatri Chakravorty Spivak, *Outside in the Teaching Machine* (New York: Routledge, 1993), 9.

25. This is not to say that such readings downplay the pitfalls of the strategy; see Robinson, *Engendering the Subject,* 152, 160; Dubey, "Gayl Jones and the Matrilineal Metaphor," 252–53. For implicit responses, see Felman, "Education and Crisis," 64; Caruth, "Introduction," 10; Laub, "Truth and Testimony," 85–86, 90.

26. Caruth, "Introduction," 9. See also Sigmund Freud, "Remembering, Repeating, and Working-Through" (1914), *SE,* 12:150–56; Jacques Lacan, *The Four Fundamental Concepts of Psycho-Analysis,* ed. Jacques-Alain Miller, trans. Alan Sheridan (New York: Norton, 1981), 53–64.

27. See Caruth, "Introduction," 10; idem, "Unclaimed Experience," 183, 187, 189–92; Felman, "Education and Crisis," 20–22, 35–37, 56–58.

28. Robinson, *Engendering the Subject,* 152.

29. Cited in Laub, "Bearing Witness," 64.

30. In fact, it is only Ursa's empathic listening to Mama (111, 122–23)—as

opposed to Mutt's silencing of Ursa's testimony and Tadpole's reception of it in silence—that allows space for this kind of traumatic repetition to emerge. See n. 40, below, for various accounts of the responsibilities of the listener, the addressee, during the testimony.

31. Felman, "Education and Crisis," 36.

32. Dixon, *Ride Out the Wilderness*, 112; Dubey, "Gayl Jones and the Matrilineal Metaphor," 257–258. As Dubey recognizes, "The blues voice in *Corregidora* does not express the full, self-present, unified subject affirmed in black nationalist discourse." Dubey, *Black Women Novelists*, 85.

33. For contrasting readings of this scene, see Tate, "*Corregidora:* Ursa's Blues Medley," 141; Dixon, "Singing a Deep Song," 240–41, 244; idem, *Ride Out the Wilderness*, 112, 117; Robinson, *Engendering the Subject*, 156–57, 164–65, 187; duCille, "Phallus(ies) of Interpretation," 568–69; Dubey, *Black Women Novelists*, 80–81; idem, "Gayl Jones and the Matrilineal Metaphor," 250, 258–59, 262–65. For Jones's own comments on the novel's ending, see Bell, "Gayl Jones Takes a Look at *Corregidora*," 285; see also Jones's analysis of blues, repetition, and closure in *Liberating Voices: Oral Tradition in African American Literature* (Cambridge: Harvard University Press, 1991), 38–43, 70–78, 90–98, 151–60.

34. There still has been no detailed reading of sexuality in *Corregidora* that engages with Gay and Lesbian Studies and queer theory. Such a reading might begin by taking up Michael Warner's critique of "repronarratives" ("Fear of a Queer Planet," *Social Text* 29 [1991]: 3–17) and by analyzing Jones's historization of Ursa's homophobia. Ursa first hears of homosexuality from Great Gram, who represents it as something forced on black women, associated with whiteness, marital problems, infertility, insanity, disease, and death (13, 172). Since Ursa feels tainted by whiteness, has experienced marital problems centering on sex and violence, has had to deal with her own infertility, and fears that her dreams might drive her insane, she has a particularly phobic response to Jeffy and Cat. For some perceptive commentary on sexuality and the impossibility of heterosexual desire in Jones's works, see Dubey, *Black Women Novelists*, 76–78, 80–81, 87; idem, "Gayl Jones and the Matrilineal Metaphor," 257–59. See also Gloria Wade-Gayles, *No Crystal Stair: Visions of Race and Sex in Black Women's Fiction* (New York: Pilgrim, 1984), 175; Robinson, *Engendering the Subject*, 165, 183–84; Coser, *Bridging the Americas*, 136–39.

35. On Mutt and Corregidora, see Tate, "*Corregidora:* Ursa's Blues Medley," 141; Robinson, *Engendering the Subject*, 154–56, 160; Dubey, *Black Women Novelists*, 82–83; Coser, *Bridging the Americas*, 126–27.

36. For more eloquent and compelling formulations of these and other questions, see, for example, Theodore Allen, *The Invention of the White Race*, vol. 1, *Racial Oppression and Social Control* (New York: Verso, 1994), 1–24; Judith Butler, *Bodies That Matter: On the Discursive Limits of "Sex"* (New York: Routledge, 1993), 187–222. For oblique responses, see Theodore Adorno, "What Does

Coming to Terms with the Past Mean?" (1959), trans. Timothy Bahti and Geoffrey H. Hartman, in *Bitburg in Moral and Political Perspective,* ed. Geoffrey H. Hartman (Bloomington: Indiana University Press, 1986); Margot Gayle Backus, " 'Looking for That Dead Girl': Incest, Pornography, and the Capitalist Family Romance in *Nightwood, The Years,* and *Tar Baby," American Imago* 51.4 (winter 1994): 421–45; James Snead, "Repetition as a Figure of Black Culture," in *Black Literature and Literary Theory,* ed. Henry Louis Gates, Jr. (New York: Methuen, 1984), 38–57.

37. On these points, see Laub, "Truth and Testimony," 78; Felman, "Education and Crisis," 34–37, 55–56; Caruth, "Introduction," 9–11.

38. Often, this kind of move is combined with a stunning reversal, the assumption that any attention to issues of race or racism is itself the worst form of racism — a betrayal of ideals of "color-blindness." Besides the already classic analyses of this phenomenon by Omi and Winant, Balibar, and Žižek, see Avery Gordon and Christopher Newfield, "White Philosophy," *Critical Inquiry* 20.4 (summer 1994): 737–57. But this move can also go unaccompanied by racism; see, for instance, Mutt's various calls to "forget the past" (99) and "Get their devils off your back. Theirs, not yours" (61). To the immediate link of past and present that trauma imposes, Mutt calls for a clear separation of identities: "we ain't them" (153). Yet when such a move proves impossible for Ursa, Mutt responds with a reproach: "*You Corregidora's, ain't you?*" (61); "you one of them" (154).

39. Caruth, "Introduction," 8. On the temporality of the traumatic event, see Felman and Laub, foreword, xiv–xv; Laub, "Bearing Witness," 57–59, 65; idem, "Truth and Testimony," 84; Caruth, "Introduction," 4–8, 10; Maurice Blanchot, *The Writing of the Disaster,* trans. Ann Smock (Lincoln: University of Nebraska Press, 1986), 6, 7, 14, 17, 28, 89.

40. Cathy Caruth and Thomas Keenan, " 'The AIDS Crisis Is Not Over': A Conversation with Gregg Bordowitz, Douglas Crimp, and Laura Pinsky," *American Imago* 48.4 (winter 1991): 541. On the responsibilities of the listener (the witness to the witness), the establishment of an address, and the necessity of working through the trauma, see in particular Laub, "Bearing Witness," 57–63, 67–73; idem, "Truth and Testimony," 78–82, 84–86, 89–90; Felman, "Education and Crisis," 53, 67–71; Caruth, "Introduction," 10–11, 423; Eric Santner, *Stranded Objects: Mourning, Memory, and Film in Postwar Germany* (Ithaca: Cornell University Press, 1990), 24–26, 28–29; Erikson, "Notes on Trauma and Community," 462–71; van der Kolk and van der Hart, "The Intrusive Past," 446–51.

41. Laub, "Bearing Witness," 58; Blanchot, *The Writing of the Disaster,* 25. Again, I am indebted to Cathy Caruth's posing of this question and the answers she offers (see Caruth, "Introduction," 417–23).

42. Caruth, "Introduction," 7, 10, 423.

43. Caruth, "Introduction," 9. See also Thomas Keenan, "Deconstruction and the Impossibility of Justice," in *Critical Encounters: Reference and Responsibility in*

Deconstructive Writing, ed. Cathy Caruth and Deborah Esch (New Brunswick: Rutgers University Press, 1995), 262–74.

44. Michael Harper, "Gayl Jones: An Interview," in *Chant of Saints,* ed. Michael Harper and Robert Stepto (Urbana: University of Illinois Press, 1979), 353, 366.

45. Felman, "Education and Crisis," 34.

46. On this point, see Ronell, "Video/Television/Rodney King," 299.

RACE(D) MEN AND RACE(D) WOMEN

AFRICAN-AMERICAN CULTURAL STUDIES

7

EDDIE S. GLAUDE, JR.

EXODUS AND THE POLITICS OF NATION

Our language can be seen as an ancient city: a maze of little streets and squares, of old and new houses with additions from various periods; and this surrounded by a multitude of new boroughs with straight regular streets and uniform houses.

—Ludwig Wittgenstein

INTRODUCTION

No other story in the Bible has captured the imagination of African-American Christians the way Exodus has. The story's account of bondage, the trials of the Wilderness, and the final entrance into the Promised Land resonated within the hearts and minds of those who had experienced the hardships of chattel slavery and racial discrimination. Moreover, the story demonstrated the deeds of a God active in history, a "God who lifted up and cast down nations and peoples, a God whose sovereign will was directing all things toward an ultimate end, drawing good out of evil."[1] The Exodus story, in some way or another, helped African-American Christians make sense of their situation and maintain the hope that one day they would be free.

But my interest in Exodus is not so much to provide an account of conceptions of deliverance or liberation in religious terms—even though the story is an example of an act of God. My intention is to explore the political history of Exodus, to describe the ways the story's metaphors became a source for political acts, and the manner in which it was used to explicate the middle passage, enslavement, and quests for emancipation. For Exodus cannot be limited to a sacred text that can be understood only in religious language. The history of the story and its broad application across a disparate field of political engagements suggest that it is also a secular tale, a this-worldly, historical account of resistance and, perhaps, revolution.

SACVAN BERCOVITCH AND THE LANGUAGE OF NATION

Particular attention must be given to the alternative ways a concept of nation is constructed within the ritualized activity of reading, interpreting, and performing the Exodus narrative. Within early African-American politics the idea of nation was used as a means of grounding common interests in an understanding of America's racial hegemonic order. The concept as constructed through analogical readings of the story of Exodus empowered African Americans (although in limited and highly negotiated ways) as they struggled against slavery and racism. And it is at this juncture that broader conceptions of nation in the early Republic provided, to some degree, the vocabularies of African-American constructions of nation: for the story of Exodus is central to the imagining of the American nation. The American Revolution, for example, was viewed by the colonists as a political Exodus. This rhetoric was inherited, in large measure, from colonial New England, from Puritans who imagined their migration from the Old World as an errand to a New Canaan.

According to Sacvan Bercovitch, the idea of errand among the Puritans of New England encompassed the notions of *migration, pilgrimage,* and *progress.* Each of these was an element in an ideological mode of consensus used to fill the needs of a certain social order. Migration suggested not simply the movement from one place to another, but the journey from an Old World to a New Canaan. Migration was prophetic. It signaled the coming of the new millennium in the bounty that was America, for the Puritans' claim of the New World had been sanctioned in the promises of the Bible.

The errand as pilgrimage was broadly conceived as an inward journey, a march through the Wilderness of one's soul to God, or as Bercovitch puts it, "the believer's pilgrimage through the world's wilderness to redemption."[2] This aspect of the errand linked individual action to a broader community of concern. Thus, the concept of pilgrimage promoted individualism without the possibility of anarchy by grounding the community in the private acts of the will and rooting personal identities in social enterprise.[3] Finally, errand as progress referenced the teleology inherent in the biblical story of Exodus. Colonial New England "was movement from sacred past to sacred future, a shifting point between migration and millennium."[4]

By the time of the American Revolution, the idea of errand as migration, pilgrimage, and progress was no longer isolated to the strange musings of a religious community in New England. This biblical typology had melded with republican ideas of government and liberty and aided in the consolidation of a national community. In 1776, Benjamin Franklin and Thomas Jefferson could not imagine the nation apart from the symbols of Exodus. Franklin, for example, suggested that the seal of the United States depict Moses standing with his rod in hand and Pharaoh's army drowning in the Red Sea. Jefferson offered instead the Israelites marching through the Wilderness.

Two major events, according to Bercovitch, expanded this rhetoric beyond the narrow confines of Puritan New England. First, the Great Awakening opened the analogy of America as the New Canaan to any evangelical, North and South, such that between 1740 and 1760 the rhetoric of errand as migration, pilgrimage, and progress was extended to every Protestant American.[5] Second, the French and Indian War expanded this rhetoric even further to mobilize the colonist, evangelical or not, to fight against an outside threat and to fortify civic institutions.

Both of these events involved what Bercovitch sees as a general redefinition of the self. On the one hand, the revivals of the Great Awakening loosened and enlarged the Puritan concept of representative selfhood (as expressed in the concept of errand as pilgrimage) by joining private enterprise with incentives for self-assertion, self-interest, and self-love. On the other hand, the French and Indian War "appealed to conscience and self-interest, only to make these synonymous with Protestant patriotism, and the Protestant cause inseparable from the rising glory of America."[6] In both cases, as in the Puritan use of the rhetoric of errand in New England, revivalism and war were a means to create a social order; they ushered in the first rituals of intercolonial unity by binding "the rights of personal ascent to the rites of social assent."[7]

In the mid-nineteenth century, these symbols of errand were reworked as America's Manifest Destiny. America, the Redeemer Nation, was "popularly conceived as spreading the blessings of democracy, free enterprise, and Protestantism across the continent."[8] The rhetoric of errand laid the foundation for such imperialistic acts: for the story of exodus, its promise of land, and the idea of chosenness justified, to some degree, the conquest and subordination of other people.

In emphasizing the historical developments and transformations in the rhetoric of errand, Bercovitch details what he considers to be a developing ideological mode, the "American ideology." The Great Awakening, for example, not only marked an expansion of a biblical vocabulary to all Anglo-American settlers, but also helped direct the energies of economic growth.[9] The French and Indian War created a kind of Protestant patriotism as it solidified the newly created civic institutions of the colonists. All of this contributed to the rhetoric of the American Revolution.

In their efforts to control the egalitarian impulses unleashed by the Revolution, patriotic Whigs used the ideology of errand as a vehicle for social control. They characterized other revolutions as dangerous, anarchic, or threats to society while describing the American Revolution as the fulfillment of prophecy, the unfolding of a divine plan. According to Bercovitch, the idea of independence within this context gave full sanction to an ideology of consensus. Independence in any other context threatened the stability of society. In the United States, however, the idea of independence "gave a distinctive national shape to the idea of progress."[10] The Puritan rhetoric of errand was transformed, for the American Revolution marked the complete separation of the Old Canaan from the New.[11] And the mechanisms of control that the leaders of the New England faithful created were translated into "a rhetoric of continuing revolution"—what Bercovitch sees as an enduring ideology for a liberal middle-class society.[12]

By ideology Bercovitch means "the ground and texture of consensus—in this case [the United States], the system of ideas inwoven into the cultural symbology through which 'America' continues to provide the terms of identity and cohesion in the United States."[13] This view is extended by what Bercovitch rightly considers self-evident truths:

> that there is no escape from ideology; that so long as human beings remain political animals they will always be bounded in some degree by consensus; and that so long as they are symbol-making animals they will always seek to persuade themselves and others that in some sense, by relative measure if not absolutely, the terms of *their* symbology are objective and true.[14]

Here ideology is understood as necessarily conservative. We are caught within its networks and, in some significant sense, we continuously reproduce its intended meanings.

But Bercovitch suggests that ideology is not merely repressive. For him, ideology works best through voluntary consent, "when the network of ideas through which the culture justifies itself is internalized rather than imposed, and embraced by society at large as a system of belief."[15] The reproduction of ways of living as well as the production of vocabularies for imaginative acts occur within its frame. As Bercovitch notes, ideology serves "to incite the imagination, to unleash the energies of reform, to encourage diversity and accommodate change."[16]

Ideology is not viewed as monolithic. The "American ideology" is, rather, a rhetorical battleground,[17] a context for a variety of conflicts and battles over what it means to be American. But Bercovitch immediately qualifies this view. In the context of the United States, ideology "has achieved a hegemony unequaled elsewhere in the modern world";[18] such that in spite of the contradictory outlooks, upheavals, and discontinuity, the "American ideology" is the best example of ideology's ability to restrict difference and release conflict.

The transformation of the Puritan rhetoric of errand into a rhetoric of continuing revolution is the source of this ideology. The symbology of America contained the act of migration, the progress from theocracy to republic, and the evidence of prophecy in the pilgrimage of the representative American.[19] It represented the complete break from Old Israel and the fulfillment of prophecy with the creation of the New Israel.

> With the Revolution, God has shown that "THE UNITED STATES OF AMERICA are to be His vineyard"—"the principal Seat of [His] glorious kingdom"—wherein the promises of the past "are to be brought to harvest," for "the benefit of the whole world."[20]

One of the main points here is also the most obvious, that Exodus is an important story to the cultural and political beginnings—ideology, if you will—of the nation of the United States, so much so that most political events are captured and understood within its narrative frame. We all know the story. And, in some significant sense, it is our story. We are the New Israelites.

That is, unless you are black. The image of America as the New Canaan is reversed within African-American reenactments of the Exodus story. We are still the New Israelites, but the United States is Egypt and the seat of Pharaoh resides in Washington, D.C. As Vincent Harding notes, "one of the abiding and tragic ironies of our history [is that] the nation's claim to be the New Israel was contradicted by the Old Israel still enslaved in her midst."[21] This contradiction, however, does not diminish the fact that the story of Exodus is, in some respects, a national history. Exodus remains the story and history of a people. Its analogical application within the context of African-American politics in the early nineteenth century (as in its use among white men in the early republic) amounts to nation building,[22] the construction of a corporate identity distinct from yet implicated in broader conceptions of American identity.

For Bercovitch, however, more general uses of the narrative in the United States sidestepped the problem of race. The Enlightenment rhetoric of the "people," although central in other nation-building efforts, was recast within the rhetoric of the continuing revolution. The "people" were distinct from the "chosen people." This distinction allowed for an embrace of the universal impulses implicit in the leveling concept of the people[23] and simultaneously enabled an erasure of the contradiction of that impulse with the presence of slavery and servitude. The contradiction was ameliorated "[t]hrough the rituals of continuing revolution [in which] the middle-class leaders of the republic recast the Declaration to read, 'all propertied, white, Anglo-Saxon males are created equal.' "[24] These men were the chosen people and they were representative Americans—not members of the people.

Although implicit in the story of Exodus is a national ambition in which the Israelites are in search of a definite land base, a place where they can exercise self-determination, the uses of the symbols of Exodus within the American context, according to Bercovitch, are deployed for other ends, most important of which is the construction of cultural continuity or a mode of consensus. The ritualization of Exodus in the United States sought to consolidate a highly stratified society:

> It served . . . as always, to blur . . . discrepancies. . . . It locates the sources of social revitalization and integration. It helps explain how the majority of people kept the faith despite their day-by-day experiences. It reminds us that although the concept of hegemony involves the dialectics of change, the directions of change are in turn crucially affected by the terms of hegemonic constraint. And in this case the effect was demonstrable in the way the rhetoric of consensus molded what was to all appearances the most heterogeneous "people" in the world into the most monolithic of modern cultures.[25]

As seen outside this consensus, however, mid-nineteenth-century America was fraught with differences and conflicts. Racial and ethnic strife and economic disparities were glaring divisions that posed serious threats to U.S. society. Hence the importance of the rhetoric of consensus. It was a way to constrain these differences and conflicts, a means to shackle dissent through this dominant pattern of belief. But unlike his earlier qualifications of what appeared to be a monolithic view of ideology, Bercovitch suggests here that the hegemony of "America" converts dissent into restraint and collapses *all* political expression into an articulation of consensus or simply a debate as to the meaning of America.

Several problems present themselves when we push Bercovitch's arguments. First, although he claims to view ideology as a rhetorical battleground in which sometimes contradictory positions coexist, Bercovitch tends to conclude, more often than not, that ideology compresses dissent and difference into cultural continuity, that its main function in the United States is the production of consensus. On this view, the hegemony of ideology is too strong for cultural dissent to seep beyond its bounds. Thus, in most of his examples cultural and political dissent merely reinscribes onto the social landscape the values against which it supposedly speaks. Second, Bercovitch's view that the leaders of the American nation sidestepped the problems of the Enlightenment rhetoric of the "people" with their ability to define themselves ideologically limits the scope of his analysis. He argues that the "American was not (like the Frenchman or the Latin American) a member of 'the people.' He stood for a mission that was limitless in effect, because it was limited in fact to a 'peculiar' nation." [26] The view that the experiences of African Americans are central to what it means to be American, then, is never taken seriously. These people are part of the "people," maybe, but not members of the *chosen* people. Finally, Bercovitch understands ritual only in terms of forms or strategies of cultural continuity. The ultimate goals of ritual in the context of the United States are the resolution of conflict and the instilling of a dominant ideology. What gets lost in this view is any sense of ritual activity as an arena for the negotiation of power, that is, the negotiation of particular relationships of domination, consent, *and* resistance.

Bercovitch contends, for example, that the ways the symbology of Exodus functioned within mid-nineteenth-century America suggest that the U.S. rhetoric of errand is more cultural than national. Unlike biblical Hebrews, genealogy, geographic boundaries, and a certain form of religious faith were not constitutive elements of the American national community. America was simply an extension of the idea of mission, and its frontiers were open to unlimited expansion. In this case, the primary use of the story was to constrain difference and streamline social conflict.

Each of the problems mentioned earlier can be readily seen in this historical formulation. Bercovitch understands ideology as the means by which a mode of consensus is produced, that is, a system of ideas that provides the terms for identification and national cohesion. The primary function of ideology, then, is the disciplining of dissent and the production of cultural continuity. In mid-nineteenth-century America, for example, the main source of dissent among U.S. renaissance writers was the guiding ideology of the early republic:

It [the ideology of the early republic] had provided an impetus to revolution, a series of rituals of cohesion, and a rationale for the political and social structures of nationhood. As the economy expanded, those structures shifted to accommodate new commercial interests. But the cultural continuities were too strong, too basic, for the ideals themselves to be discarded. They were the foundational truths, after all, of liberal democracy. So the earlier rhetoric persisted, supported by preindustrial traditions and regional agrarian communities that increasingly contrasted with the ways of the Jacksonian marketplace. And on the ground of that opposition, America's classic writers developed a sweeping critique of the dominant culture.[27]

The hegemony of the "American ideology" is so strong that any attempt to engage in social criticism reasserts the hegemony of the ideology. Bercovitch discounts the counterideological, for all social and cultural critique necessarily emanates from a broader system of ideas that provides the terms of dissent; and more important, these critiques cannot "engage in processes of reflection on the values that generate them without at the same time being subsumed by those values."[28] Serious social and cultural criticism is effectively trivialized. Since we cannot escape the "American ideology," what then becomes the point of social criticism?

Also, Bercovitch's suggestion that the U.S. rhetoric of errand is more cultural than national does not seem to me the best way of talking about the uses of Exodus: far better to see Exodus as both national *and* cultural, as a story that provides vocabularies for our beliefs as well as tools for the imagining of our nation. The distinction requires Bercovitch to effectively bracket the problem of slavery and the ideologies that surround the peculiar institution, for national and cultural issues intersect in the early republic's attempt to respond to the pariahs of slavery in an *officially* egalitarian society.

Bercovitch makes this distinction by arguing that the leaders of the American nation sidestepped the Enlightenment rhetoric of the "people." By defining themselves and consolidating power ideologically—through the mobilization and deployment of the rhetoric of continuing revolution—middle-class white males were able to marginalize groups of people and generate, in the process, "a conformist spirit that foreign observers termed a 'tyranny of the majority,'"[29] or what he terms a tyranny of culture.

In Bercovitch's view, the rhetorical deployment of this ideology avoids the pitfalls of the Exodus story and modern nationalism. Again, unlike the biblical Hebrews, genealogy and geography were not constitutive elements of the American national community. Instead, the sacredness of the "continuing errand" was the central vehicle for the national consolidation of the community of the faithful. But surely the presence of enslaved black bodies makes genealogy a central element in the construction of consensus, for the word "white" acquires significance only within the context of America's racial order. The idea of chosenness is racialized, such that members of the chosen people are delineated or distinguished from those who are not chosen. Thus, a sort of genealogical effort usually associated with nationalism is present, even in its conspicuous absence, within the broader ideological move to see the United States as the idea of mission brought up to date.[30]

Moreover, the idea of individual dignity and equality in the United States, so central to the political structure of the nation, cannot be understood apart from an extreme form of servitude. In other words, the meaning of individual dignity and equality in the United States can be grasped only in light of its denial. In Judith Shklar's account, slavery has been the central trope in America's political—and, I would add, cultural—imagination. It constituted, in one sense, a collectivity—propertied, *white,* Anglo-Saxon Protestant males—that understood itself over and against a subjugated other. This vocabulary of exclusion based on notions of "us" and "them," groups of persons as opposed to individuals, is present from the beginning of America's birth. Shklar states,

> What has been continuous is a series of conflicts arising from enduring anti-liberal dispositions that have regularly asserted themselves, often very successfully, against the promise of equal political rights contained in the Declaration of Independence and its successors, the three Civil War amendments. It is because slavery, racism, nativism, and sexism, often institutionalized in exclusionary and discriminatory laws and practices, have been and still are arrayed against the officially accepted claims of equal citizenship that there is a real pattern to be discerned in the tortuous development of American ideas of citizenship. If there is permanence here, it is one of lasting conflicting claims.[31]

The question Shklar raises so skillfully is this: is racial inequality best understood as a violation of American commitment to political equality or is it a fundamental aspect of it? She suggests the latter. From the beginning, the idea of the *racial group,* notwithstanding the peculiar uses of Exodus, has been present (and hegemonic) in the "American" nation.

One of the ironies of Bercovitch's claim of the absence of genealogy and geography is his seemingly naive complicity in the rhetoric of consensus. Although he desires to unmask the operations of the American ideology, Bercovitch, as he would readily admit, is subsumed by its terms, blindnesses, and prejudices. In particular, his analysis of the differences between American nationalism and the nationalisms in the rest of Europe borders on an argument for

American exceptionalism or, at least, repeats the old claim that our nationalism is good (even under critique) and most others are bad. In short, his efforts to distinguish the rhetoric of consensus turn on him. The analyses of French, German, and Russian nationalism, for example, describe the usual bad traits of European nationalism, all of which are absent in America's rhetoric of consensus:

> [U]nder the peculiar circumstances of the new republic—circum-stances that included extraordinary resources of territory, economic abundance, and political leadership, as well as a burgeoning cultural symbology—the system that emerged expressed an increasing harmony between the ideological and experiential dimensions of modern liberal society (moral standards, principles of government, forms of desire, incentives of constraint). Here only, accordingly, of all new nations in 1800, the invocation of the past actually enhanced the values of prog-ress. Here only, of all the hopeful New World republics in 1820, the concept of independence fostered indigenous communal bonds. And here only, of all modernizing Western nations in 1840, the values of newness and of tradition were made to correspond.[32]

On the heels of this sermonic repetition, Bercovitch returns to what makes all of this possible and to that which distinguishes the American nation from others: the fact that this was a culture bound by an extraordinary ideological hegemony, a liberal-symbolic system of thought.[33]

This hegemony, of course, is maintained by a *ritual* of consensus. Bercovitch understands ritual in its broadest sense as the "forms and strategies of cultural continuity." On this view, ritual functions solely as a matter of transmitting shared beliefs or instilling a dominant ideology. Catherine Bell's reconceptualiza-tion of ritual, however, offers a view of ritual as an arena for the negotiation of power. Ritual activity, according to Bell, cannot be limited to the maintenance of American hegemony, for "ritual symbols are too indeterminate and ... flexible to lend themselves to any simple process of instilling fixed ideas."[34] As such, ritual activity entails numerous qualifications of the complexity of Ameri-can microrelations of power.

But for Bercovitch the ritualization of ideology in the United States seems to function only as a mode of consensus. Thus, his analysis tracks those instances where ideology works and maintains the status quo. His view of ritual in effect limits the scope of his analytic tools. Everything becomes ritualized instances of this broader American ideological complex. As Giles Gunn notes,

> What gets lost in this blanket application of ideological categories to social practices is any sense either that ideologies function in different

ways in different circumstances—the gospel of ante-bellum southern evangelicalism to "preach liberty to the captives" meant one thing to white Christians and another to black—or that they are sometimes divided within and against themselves.[35]

For Bercovitch, in his less careful moments, all rhetorical acts of criticism conform to a ritual of consensus in that the issues of debate are restricted, symbolically and substantially, to the meaning of America.[36] His position allows little room for understanding ritual activity as an arena in which resistance *actually* occurs (although in highly limited and mediated ways). As ritualized agents we are merely caught within the coercive webs of our ideological beliefs.

RACE AND THE LANGUAGE OF NATION

An example of the different ways ideology functions in the United States is best illustrated, I believe, in African-American uses of Exodus. In the early nineteenth century, for example, a concept of a black nation, constructed through the use of Exodus symbology, was used in the political rhetoric of many African-American leaders. The existence of this national community was imagined in the image of characters and events found in the Exodus story, such that the national quest of Israel became an analog for the aspirations and aims of African Americans. This imagined community stood as a form of critique of American society for betraying its ideals as well as a means for positive self-identification among blacks. In many ways, it was one of the major forms of resistance to early nineteenth-century claims of African-American inferiority. By analogy, blacks in the United States were the children of God, the chosen people, and a peculiar (perhaps holy) nation; thus, the freedom of the Israelites was linked with the eventual liberation of blacks in the United States.

Although the terms of this dissent drew on a broader rhetoric of chosenness and, even, continuing revolution, they functioned differently in the context of the struggle against slavery and racial discrimination. Unlike the biblical Hebrews and the "white" leaders of the early republic, African Americans in the early nineteenth century were not primarily concerned with using Exodus to mark out the family (blood) ties of fellows or the acquisition of land. The construction of a community of persons with certain moral and civic obligations or duties to that community was more important, for the reality of slavery and the precarious nature of freedom in the United States demanded a moral alertness and vigilance among African Americans of the period.

I do not want to suggest that race was unimportant for African Americans in the early nineteenth century. In some respects, an idea of social solidarity among individuals who happened to be black was impossible without the experiences and relationships of race that these individuals held in common. Even so,

African-American uses of race in the early nineteenth century were not based on any essentialist understanding of the concept. Race language was a tool for grounding a set of common experiences in the struggle against slavery and American racism. Likewise, nation language within this context was a way of grounding these common experiences in an understanding of America's racial hegemonic order. As such, both terms were signs that captured a range of possibilities for African Americans.

From about 1800 to the early 1840s African Americans generally understood nation language in these terms: the sense of peoplehood that emerged as persons drew on biblical typology. This construction of a communal identity did not rely on any biological conception of the racial self (genealogy). Most African Americans of this period did not invest race with any intrinsic value.[37] Race was solely the result of environmental factors and provided no indication of the capacities of individuals or groups of people. Even those who sought to leave the country did so not so much out of a desire to acquire land (geography) for a distinctive people, but rather as an effort to escape the hardships of American life. The early emigrationists, for example, avoided racial and state language.[38]

By the mid-1840s the metaphors of Exodus had sedimented as the predominant political language of African Americans. Over a period of years, the analogy had diffused into the popular consciousness of black America. The ritual employment of bondage, liberation, and nationhood had been elaborated: the middle passage, slavery, and efforts to achieve freedom were now understood within the narrative frame of bondage, the Wilderness, and the Promised Land. Exodus, in effect, was no longer the story of Israel but an account of African-American slavery and eventual deliverance. The narrative was the *taken-for-granted* context for any discussion of slavery and freedom.

Several events led to this broad diffusion of the symbology of Exodus throughout early nineteenth-century black America. Here I want to note briefly the historical events and transformations, specifically the Second Great Awakening, the development of independent black churches, and the forming of the first "race" newspaper, that deepened, in my view, the vocabularies of Exodus in black political rhetoric in the beginning of the nineteenth century.

The Great Awakening between 1740 and 1760 extended the metaphors of Exodus to any evangelical in the North and South. This included African Americans who embraced Christian doctrine, for the evangelical revivals of this period were attended by white and black alike. More important, however, the revivals between 1770 and 1820—the Second Great Awakening—yielded a more extensive embrace of Christian doctrine within black populations, North and South, and thus a broader expansion of the symbology of Exodus among African Americans:

> The emotionalism of the revivals encouraged the outward expression of religious feeling. . . . The analogy between African and evangelical styles of worship enabled the slaves [and free] to reinterpret the new religion by reference to the old, and so made this brand of Christianity seem less foreign than that of the more liturgically sedate Church of England.[39]

The familiarity of worship in these revivals coupled with an initial condemnation of slavery among Baptists and Methodists led to an unprecedented number of conversions to Christianity among blacks. The frequent use of the Exodus story in these revivals only furthered its entrenchment within a developing black political culture.

Within these evangelical movements, churches were conceptualized as societies of people who were capable of changing their own lives. As such, revivalism, to some degree, provided its participants with the means to assert control over their lives, and for those who were lost, to regain some sense of direction.[40] Within the context of American slavery and racial discrimination, this view in the hands of blacks proved significant in the development of a corporate identity and a political culture. Particularly, the "willingness of evangelical churches to license black men to exhort and preach" resulted in black preachers pastoring to their own and laid the foundations for independent black churches, institutions that were the heart of free black communities:

> In all denominations, the black churches formed the institutional core for the development of free black communities. Moreover, they gave black Christians the opportunity to articulate publicly their own vision of Christianity, which stood in eloquent testimony to the existence of two Christian Americas.[41]

These institutions provided African Americans with a formal basis to assert a cultural and communal identity, and one of the main vocabularies for its expression was found in the symbology of Exodus. The metaphors of Exodus were combined with the rhetoric of the American Revolution, such that ideas of freedom and liberty constituted powerful rhetorical tools in the struggle to end slavery and racial discrimination.

Although independent black churches emerged in the South before 1800 and influenced the social and cultural lives of black slaves, my focus is primarily on the development of independent black churches in the North. For example, the African Methodist Episcopal (A.M.E.) Church, founded in 1816 after a series of conflicts with white Methodists in Philadelphia, played a crucial role in the process of political and social self-definition among African Americans. The achievement of institutional independence and the effort toward ecclesiastical self-definition among black Methodists carried over into the political sphere and marked the "first effective stride toward freedom among African Americans."[42]

The efforts of black Methodists were understood not as evidence of doctrinal differences among Methodists but as a commentary on the ubiquity of racism in American society:

> Unlike most sectarian movements, the initial impetus for black spiritual and ecclesiastical independence was not grounded in religious doctrine or polity, but in the offensiveness of racial segregation in the churches and the alarming inconsistencies between the teachings and the expression of the faith. It was readily apparent that the white church had become a principal instrument of the political and social policies undergirding slavery and the attendant degradation of the human spirit. Against this the black Christians quietly rebelled, and the Black Church emerged as the symbol and the substance of their rebellion.[43]

In many ways, independent black churches were the main sites for debate over the problems facing black communities and the crucial vehicles for the construction of a national sense of identity. The fact that their struggles for institutional independence emerged out of struggles against racism in general connected their specific achievements with broader quests for freedom and liberty.

Between 1770 and 1820 African Americans in the North, as evidenced in their participation in the Second Great Awakening and the formation of independent black churches, imbibed the symbology of Exodus primarily through religious experiences. It is during this period that a distinctive sense of group consciousness evolved or took shape among Northern blacks, situating independent black churches at the center of a developing black political culture. For the establishment of black churches and benevolent societies gave the race its first organized voice.[44]

In the late 1820s, however, the formation of the first black newspaper gave added impetus to the national formation of African Americans. Samuel E. Cornish, a Presbyterian clergyman, and John Russwurm, a graduate of Bowdoin College, founded the *Freedom's Journal*. The newspaper intended to address the problems faced by blacks in the North as well as tackle misrepresentations of their community by whites. Their goal was

> to make our Journal a medium of intercourse between our brethren in the different states of this great confederacy; that through the columns an expression of our sentiments, on many interesting subjects which

concern us, may be offered to the publick; that plans which apparently are beneficial may be candidly discussed and properly weighed; if worthy, received our cordial approbation; if not, our marked disapprobation.[45]

This effort also included serious attention to those who were in bondage. Cornish and Russwurm viewed blacks in the South as kindred souls and offered the columns in the *Freedom's Journal* to promote sympathy and action for those held in slavery.

What is interesting about Cornish and Russwurm's effort is not the success of the *Freedom's Journal* (the newspaper was short-lived), but rather the possibility of an imagined community the convention of the newspaper enables. The editors intended the newspaper to be a vehicle for debate and conversation among fellows about the problems of the race. They included in the paper various events from different parts of the country and the world. What connected these events to each other? What allowed their juxtaposition?

Following Benedict Anderson, I argue that the inclusion of a variety of events in the newspaper does not merely demonstrate the sheer capriciousness of the editors, but instead shows that the linkage between these events is imagined.[46] This imagined linkage derives from two related sources: calendrical coincidence and the relationship between the newspaper and the market. The idea of calendrical time allows the events to be discussed simultaneously. The date at the top of the newspaper suggests a commonality between the events and the steady progression of modern time.[47] Events are continuously happening in the world. Even as the newspaper prints accounts of the problems of racism and slavery in the United States on a set date in the year, these occurrences continue even when the paper no longer reports about them. "The novelistic format of the newspaper assures [us] that somewhere out there the 'character' . . . moves along quietly, awaiting its next appearance in the plot."[48]

The newspapers' relationship to the market calls our attention to the fact that newspapers are, in Anderson's words, extreme forms of the book. They are books sold on a colossal scale. The mass production of the newspaper then enables the mass consumption of the events organized within the newspaper:

> The significance of this mass ceremony—Hegel observed that newspapers serve modern man as a substitute for morning prayers—is paradoxical. It is performed in silent privacy, in the lair of the skull. Yet each communicant is well aware that the ceremony he performs is being replicated simultaneously by thousands (or millions) of others of whose existence he is confident, yet of whose identity he has not the slightest

notion. Furthermore, this ceremony is incessantly repeated at daily or half-daily intervals throughout the calendar. What more vivid figure for the secular, historically clocked, imagined community can be envisioned?[49]

The daily consumption of the newspaper produces a genuine sense of community among fellows who would otherwise know little about one another.

The "race" newspaper aided in the broad diffusion of the symbology of Exodus among African Americans. The paper printed sermons, political treatises, debates over emigration, and even festivals that used the story's metaphors as rhetorical devices to struggle against racial discrimination in the North and the institution of slavery in the South. For example, reprinted sermons that drew on the symbology of Exodus—emphasizing the narrative structure of the story and its movement from beginning to end—spoke of freedom promised in Canaan and deployed the image of Egypt to caution against moral and civic backsliding. The mass consumption of these columns by literate African Americans allowed for a fellowship in anonymity and a participation, psychical or physical, in the ritualization of the Exodus story. This effect of the newspaper along with the events of the Second Great Awakening and the formation of independent black churches laid the foundation for the use of nation language in early nineteenth-century black political culture.

But the 1840s marked the beginnings of a decisive shift in the political language of African Americans. The discordant waves of Jacksonian democracy that had already made their way into black enclaves in the North joined with the new science of race.[50] Environmental and biblical accounts of racial differences were now under constant attack. As a result of the seemingly concrete findings of phrenology and ethnology, African Americans were seen as intrinsically different and, for some, inherently lacking in certain moral and mental capacities. Although African Americans responded to these findings with their own ethnological and biblical accounts,[51] many assumed the validity of a portion of the claim: race has intrinsic value.

The different ways the language of race was embraced affected the use of the word "nation." The idea of nation among African Americans in the early nineteenth century was mainly rhetorical.[52] The word was not used to indicate something that actually existed in the world, a sort of nonmoral, descriptive statement about a thing that could either be true or false. Instead, nation language was a means of grounding a set of common experiences and relationships in an effort to combat American racism. And the broader cultural pattern of Exodus symbology in the United States provided the vocabulary for understanding and negotiating America's racial hegemonic order. The idea of a black nation, then, was achieved by dramatic reenactment of the deliverance of the nation of Israel and, subsequently, a kind of inversion of America's imagined community—the New Israel contained the Old.

African Americans' rhetorical use of nation in the early nineteenth century was ambiguous or "fuzzy." "It did not claim to represent or exhaust all the layers of selfhood of its members . . . [nor] . . . did [it] require its members to ask how many of them were in the world."[53] The concept was used only for "practical purposes of social interaction."[54] Remember that race, during this period, has no intrinsic value; it is only a name for environmental effects and a means for mobilizing persons (with a variety of allegiances) to struggle against American racism.

However, the concept of nation in mid-nineteenth-century black America was rhetorical and nonrhetorical. Early conceptions of the national community—ideas generated through the reading and ritualization of the story of Exodus—stood alongside nonrhetorical accounts of nationality and the new racial science. Indeed, nation *was* defined in terms of genealogy and geography. No longer was the term simply used to ground a set of common experiences and relationships in an understanding of America's racial order. Instead, race and nation joined to signal an objective entity, that which, if it did not *already* exist, *should* exist in the world.

But the use of the Exodus story among African Americans survived the pull of racial science, perhaps because the metaphors of the story lent themselves to a wide range of analyses and uses. Political arguments that used rhetorical forms such as the Jeremiad and Ethiopianism were possible to carry on inside the structures of Exodus:

> Within the frame of the Exodus story one can plausibly emphasize the mighty arm of God or the slow march of the people, the land of milk and honey or the holy nation, the purging of the counterrevolutionaries or the schooling of the new generation. One can describe Egyptian bondage in terms of corruption or tyranny or exploitation. One can defend the authority of the Levites or of the tribal elders or of the rulers of tens and fifties. I would only suggest that these alternatives are themselves paradigmatic; they are *our* alternatives.[55]

The decisive shift in nation language in the mid-nineteenth century, then, was not *so* decisive. We still have at work this overarching narrative, an interpretative horizon that assumed a concept of nation or peoplehood. And any understanding of African-American uses of nation in the nineteenth century must begin here: with the African-American version of the Exodus story.

NOTES

1. Albert Raboteau, "Exodus and the American Israel," in *African-American Christianity: Essays in History,* ed. Paul E. Johnson (Berkeley: University of California Press), p. 1.
2. Sacvan Bercovitch, *The Rites of Assent: Transformation in the Symbolic Construction of America* (New York: Routledge, 1993), p. 33.
3. Ibid., pp. 33–34.
4. Ibid., p. 34.
5. Ibid., p. 35.
6. Ibid., p. 36.
7. Ibid. It was also during this period, according to Bercovitch, that a transformation in the role of the founding fathers (the Puritans, not Washington, Jefferson, etc.) occurred. They were now the stuff of legend, characters in a story of cultural beginnings. The backdrop of this change was the revision of the Puritan errand: exodus was now the property of all Anglo-American settlers and heralded "one city on a hill." The foundation was then laid for America's civil religion.
8. David Howard-Pitney, *The Afro-American Jeremiad: Appeals for Justice in America* (Philadelphia: Temple University Press, 1990), p. 11.
9. Bercovitch, p. 37.
10. Ibid., p. 38.
11. Bercovitch states that "[w]ith the revolution, the Puritan vision flowered into the myth of America. For errand itself was rooted in biblical myth. However eccentric their interpretations, the Puritans had relied on the authority of scripture. . . . The Revolutionary Whigs took the justification, rather than the tradition behind it, as their authority. No matter how piously they invoked scripture they were appealing not to a Christian tradition, but to the series of recent events through which they defined the American experience" (p. 39).
12. Ibid., p. 40.
13. Ibid., p. 355.
14. Ibid., p. 356.
15. Ibid., p. 355.
16. Ibid.
17. Ibid.
18. Ibid.
19. Ibid., p. 39.
20. Ibid.
21. Vincent Harding, "The Uses of the Afro-American Past," in *The Religious Situation, 1969,* ed. Donald R. Cutter (Boston: Beacon, 1969), pp. 829–40. Also quoted in Raboteau, p. 9.
22. I am using "nation building" ironically. When most commentators use the

phrase, they are actually referring to the building of viable states. My usage here avoids such terminological confusion. Nations and states are simply not identical. See Walker Connor, "A Nation Is a Nation, Is a State, Is an Ethnic Group, Is a . . . ," in *Nationalism,* ed. John Hutchinson and Anthony D. Smith (Oxford: Oxford University Press, 1994), pp. 36–46.

23. One of the distinguishing aspects of this concept of the "people" is that the source of individual identity is located within it. The people is seen as the bearer of sovereignty, the central object of loyalty, and the basis of collective solidarity. And, for some, this process marks the beginning of modern nationalism, in which its distinctive modern meaning emerges in England in the sixteenth century, when the word "nation" "was applied to the population of the country and made synonymous with the word 'people.'" See Liah Greenfeld, *Nationalism: Five Roads to Modernity* (Cambridge: Harvard University Press, 1991), p. 6. See also Guido Zernatto, "Nation: The History of a Word," *Review of Politics* 6 (1944), pp. 352–66.

24. Bercovitch, p. 44.

25. Ibid., pp. 46–47.

26. Ibid., p. 43.

27. Ibid., p. 364.

28. Giles Gunn, *Thinking across the American Grain* (Chicago: University of Chicago Press, 1992), p. 30.

29. Bercovitch, p. 44.

30. Also, the fact that the frontier was occupied by Native Americans, and that borders were established that separated or divided distinct peoples, situates the so-called *absence* of geographical concerns as a *presence* in the construction of American nationhood. Bercovitch states, "ante-bellum Americans recognized such differences—their frontier separated them from the Indians—. . .they could hardly accept the restriction as permanent. This was God's country, was it not? So they effected a decisive shift in the meaning of frontier, from barrier to threshold. Even as they spoke of their frontier as a meeting ground between two civilizations, Christian and pagan, they redefined it, in an inversion characteristic of myth-making imagination, to mean a figural outpost, the outskirts of the advancing kingdom of God" (51). Bercovitch's point turns on itself. The fact that the meaning of frontier was revised suggests the importance of geography in the construction of the nation, even within the context of the myth itself.

31. Judith Shklar, *American Citizenship: The Quest for Inclusion* (Cambridge: Harvard University Press, 1991), pp. 13–14. Shklar convincingly demonstrates that the concept of freedom is understood in relation to slavery.

32. Bercovitch, p. 45.

33. Ibid., p. 46.

34. Catherine Bell, *Ritual Theory, Ritual Practice* (New York: Oxford University Press, 1992), p. 221.

35. Gunn, p. 31.

36. Bercovitch, p. 49.

37. See Gary B. Nash, *Race and Revolution* (Madison: Madison House, 1990), pp. 57–91.

38. See Wilson Moses, *The Golden Age of Black Nationalism, 1850–1925* (New York: Oxford University Press, 1978).

39. Raboteau, p. 4.

40. Sylvia R. Frey, *Water from the Rock: Black Resistance in a Revolutionary Age* (Princeton: Princeton University Press, 1991), p. 250.

41. Raboteau, p. 8.

42. C. Eric Lincoln and Lawrence Mamiya, *The Black Church in the African-American Experience* (Durham: Duke University Press, 1990), p. 47.

43. Ibid.

44. Jane H. Pease and William H. Pease, *They Who Would Be Free: Blacks' Search for Freedom, 1830–1861* (New York: Atheneum, 1974), p. 17.

45. *Freedom's Journal*, 1827, in *Black Nationalism in America*, ed. John H. Bracey, Jr., August Meier, and Elliot Rudwick (New York: Bobbs-Merrill, 1970), p. 26.

46. Benedict Anderson, *Imagined Communities: Reflections on the Origins and Spread of Nationalism* (London: Verso, 1993), p. 33.

47. I am well aware of the criticism of Anderson's conception of modern time. I do not have the space to account for my peculiar reading of African-American conceptions of modern time, which relies heavily on a rereading of Anderson's formulation.

48. Anderson, p. 33.

49. Ibid., p. 35.

50. I am thinking about the works of Charles Caldwell, *Thoughts on the Original Unity of the Human Race* (1830), and George Calvert's work on phrenology in 1832. Samuel George Morton, *Crania Americana* (1839) and his follower Josiah Nott also come to mind. The important point is that by the "late 1840s the racial question was at the heart of scholarly discussion in the United States. . . . The concept of racial inequality had clearly carried the day . . . [and] the most general disagreement with Nott and Morton was not that they divided the world into superior and inferior races, but that in adopting polygenesis as the original reason for racial differences, they had challenged the Mosaic account of creation." Reginald Horsman, *Race and Manifest Destiny: The Origins of American Racial Anglo-Saxonism* (Cambridge: Harvard University Press, 1981), p. 133.

51. James McCune Smith, *The Destiny of the People of Color, A Lecture Delivered before the Philomathean Society and Hamilton Lyceum in January 1841* (New York: n.p., 1843), p. 9; idem, *A Dissertation on the Influence of Climate on Longevity* (New York: Office of the Merchant's Magazine, 1846); Frederick Douglass, "The Claims of the Negro Ethnologically Considered," speech delivered to the Philozetian and Phi Delta Societies of Western Reserve College in

Hudson, Ohio, July 12, 1854, in *The Frederick Douglass Papers,* series 1, *Speeches, Debates, and Interviews,* vol. 2 (1847–54), ed. John W. Blassingame (New Haven: Yale University Press, 1982), p. 505.

52. This distinction is similar to Kenneth Burke's discussion of semantic and poetic meaning in *The Philosophy of Literary Form,* 3d ed. (Berkeley: University of California Press, 1973 [1941,1967]), pp. 138–67.

53. Partha Chatterjee, *The Nation and Its Fragments* (Princeton: Princeton University Press, 1993), p. 223.

54. Ibid.

55. Michael Walzer, *Exodus and Revolution* (New York: Basic, 1985), p. 135.

8

JEFFREY A. TUCKER

"CAN SCIENCE SUCCEED
WHERE THE CIVIL WAR FAILED?"

GEORGE S. SCHUYLER AND RACE

The last two decades have seen much attention paid to a peculiar phenomenon in African-American culture and politics that has frequently been
referred to as the "new black conservatism." The critical attention paid to the
publication of works such as economist Thomas Sowell's *Economics and Politics
of Race* (1983), cultural critic Shelby Steele's *Content of Our Character* (1990),
law professor Stephen Carter's *Reflections of an Affirmative Action Baby* (1991),
as well as other works by law professor Randall Kennedy and cultural critic
Stanley Crouch, have put black conservatism on the intellectual map. And the
1991 appointment of Clarence Thomas to the U.S. Supreme Court has even
given black conservatism a juridical site of political influence.[1] Ronald Suresh
Roberts aptly labels this group of black conservatives the "Tough Love Crowd"

because of their tendency to defend their attacks on traditional liberal black leadership and programs such as affirmative action by claiming to have only the best interests of black America in mind.[2] Although their viability as representatives of the interests and values of most African Americans has been dismissed by most,[3] the racial logic they demonstrate has become popular with conservatives of all colors as well as with liberals who are desperate for a way around the difficult racial issues facing the country. This logic promotes the faulty notion that awareness of and attention paid to racial difference cause racial strife and division; and it justifies itself by making claims to a rational, scientific, and supposedly nonpartisan objectivity. Roberts cites Stephen Carter's self-described endeavors "to describe history with a sort of certainty that natural scientists bring to the task of describing the physical world," thereby gaining access to what Carter calls the "essential truth."[4] Roberts notes Shelby Steele's similar tactic of employing the jargon of clinical psychology to achieve what the back cover of *The Content of Our Character* calls "the perfect voice of reason in a sea of hate."[5] Roberts correctly concludes that the "Tough Love Crowd" is attracted to claims of objectivity and "truth" because they lack a real constituency—among either blacks or whites—and need some sort of tool to help them gain credibility and "stay aboard the progressive project."[6]

But is the "*new* black conservatism" really new? Although Cornel West's insightful critique "Assessing Black Neoconservatism" cites 1975—the publication date of Sowell's *Race and Economics*—as the beginning of black conservatism's emergence onto the national political stage, West is quick to point out that conservative political thought among African Americans predated Sowell's book by decades.[7] The claims of Sowell, Kennedy, Thomas, Steele, and others merely echo those of one of the most important, if least recognized, figures in the history of African-American letters, George S. Schuyler. An analysis of Schuyler's career reveals how Schuyler's racial theories anticipated those of the black neocons, and illustrates the logical limits and political inadequacies of such theories.

It was about a century ago, on February 25, 1895, that George Samuel Schuyler, the most widely read black journalist of the 1930s, was born in Providence, Rhode Island. Schuyler grew up comfortably in Syracuse, New York, in a solidly middle-class family. "My folks boasted of having been free as far as any of them could or wanted to remember," Schuyler remembers in his autobiography, "and looked down upon those who had been in servitude."[8] His father, the head chef at a local hotel, died when Schuyler was very young. His mother remarried a delivery driver who moved the family to a more rural area. Schuyler's mother had only an eighth grade education, but was a remarkably intellectual woman who passed on a love of writing and reading to her son.[9]

Schuyler's journalistic career began in New York City in 1923, when he began working as a jack-of-all-trades for the *Messenger* (1917–28), the monthly black periodical edited by A. Philip Randolph and Chandler Owen. He soon became the *Messenger*'s office manager and a contributing editor shortly thereafter. Schuyler disdained the serious tone characteristic of most black journals of the time and took it upon himself to inject a sense of humor into the scene.[10] In his column "Shafts and Darts," Schuyler demonstrated a talent for the sharpest sort of satire. Langston Hughes once called Schuyler's column the best thing in the *Messenger*,[11] and in 1926 drama critic Theophilus Lewis went so far as to (over)state that aside from Jean Toomer, Schuyler was the only African American producing "genuine literature" in prose form.[12] A year later Schuyler began writing "Views and Reviews," a regular column for the *Pittsburgh Courier*, at that time the second largest black weekly newspaper in the country, and began what would be a forty-year-long association with the journal, during which he would also write numerous editorials and short stories. Schuyler's brand of humor was hugely popular, earning him both comparisons to and the admiration of H. L. Mencken, with whom Schuyler became a friend and correspondent.[13] Schuyler published articles in Mencken's *American Mercury*, as well as many other journals, such as the *Nation, Negro Digest*, and the *Crisis*, at which he also worked as business manager from 1937 to 1944. Although Schuyler said of his career, "I was all the time a newspaperman and was not an artiste,"[14] he managed to write numerous works of fiction, including the 1931 novel *Black No More* and a set of serialized fiction he originally published in the *Courier*—under the pseudonym Samuel I. Brooks—that are available to us today in the collection entitled *Black Empire* (1936–38), a fantasy about the exploits of a secret black organization that invades Liberia in order to conquer and unite Africa, turning the continent into a formidable world power. Schuyler also published over four hundred other, often weekly written pieces of short or serialized fiction in the *Courier*,[15] an output that dwarfs even that of Charles Dickens.[16] Topping off Schuyler's career are an autobiography, *Black and Conservative* (1966), and several other nonfiction books. Considering this tremendous body of work and his popularity during the 1930s, it is not surprising that Schuyler has been called "America's finest and most prominent black journalist of the early twentieth century."[17]

But Schuyler has also been identified as perhaps the most politically conservative black man in American history. Despite the fact that he began his journalistic career with the *Messenger*, "the first Socialist magazine edited by and for blacks in America,"[18] and began his intellectual career as a "card-carrying" member of the Socialist Party,[19] it is safe to say that throughout the rest of his life, Schuyler was obsessed with battling communism.[20] Specifically, he believed that the Communist Party was conspiring to pit black Americans against whites, supposedly so that the Comintern could succeed at some sort of secret, nefarious scheme.[21] According to Schuyler, the International Labor Defense's involvement in the 1931 "Scottsboro Boys" case displayed "all the earmarks of a Communist plot."[22] With regard to the civil rights movement, Schuyler criticized the marches on Washington as "mob demonstrations . . . part of the Red techniques of agitation, infiltration, and subversion."[23] He inflicted the sharpest critique on black leaders and intellectuals with ties to the Communist Party, such as W. E. B. Du Bois[24] and George Padmore, whom he labeled "a Red Uncle Tom."[25] In 1964 he contended that the Reverend Dr. Martin Luther King, Jr. was unworthy of his Nobel Peace Prize because the protest methods King used were, according to Schuyler, anything but "nonviolent."[26] That year Schuyler started writing for the John Birch Society's *American Opinions,* and three years later in 1967, he ran unsuccessfully against Adam Clayton Powell for New York's Eighteenth Congressional District seat.[27] Schuyler even supported the 1964 presidential campaign of Barry Goldwater despite, or perhaps because of, the latter's opposition to the Civil Rights Act. Schuyler also called Malcolm X a "pixilated criminal," comparing the slain black leader to Benedict Arnold.[28] Given *these* facts, it is not surprising that in his autobiography Schuyler can call Joseph R. McCarthy "a well-intentioned politician" and "a great American."[29]

Over the course of his career, Schuyler's increasingly conservative views narrowed his audience and forced the *Courier* to gradually distance itself from him. Although Schuyler continued to receive accolades from organizations like the John Birch Society and the New York Conservative Party, fewer and fewer black Americans agreed with or were interested in what he had to say, especially during and after the civil rights movement. Schuyler died in 1977, isolated from the rest of black America and all but forgotten in his profession.

George Schuyler's story is that of a black American intellectual figure deserving of scholarly attention, if not admiration.[30] The little existing academic criticism on Schuyler generally comes to either or both of two conclusions about his life and work. The most common of these is that he is consistently inconsistent. In *Black Writers of the Thirties* (1973), James O. Young cites one of Schuyler's "Views and Reviews" columns in which he criticizes *Amos 'n' Andy* for its disparaging representations of African Americans, and a later column in which Schuyler claimed that "such types as they portrayed were as common as gonococcus."[31] Historian John Henrik Clarke said, "I used to tell people that George got up in the morning, waited to see which way the world was turning, then struck out in the opposite direction."[32] Literary critics such as Ann Rayson have concluded that Schuyler's tendency to contradict himself suggests that he was less interested in maintaining an ideological stance than in maintaining his marketable reputation as the most controversial, and therefore most widely read, black journalist around.[33]

The other most frequent portrayal of Schuyler, one not incompatible with the first, is that of a black man at war with himself. Noting the broad ideological range of the journals Schuyler wrote for (the *Messenger,* the *Courier,* the *Crisis,* the *Nation, Reader's Digest,* the John Birch *Review of the News,* etc.), Henry Louis Gates, Jr., sees Schuyler as an example of the deleterious effects on the black psyche of the "double consciousness" W. E. B. Du Bois identified in *The Souls of Black Folk* (1903).[34] According to Gates, Schuyler was unable to reconcile the political conservatism that would dominate his work during the 1960s and 1970s with the 1930s-style radical black nationalist persona of his sometimes nom de plume, Samuel I. Brooks. "In the end," Gates says, "what defeated Schuyler's grand promise as an intellectual was his failure to negotiate between these two antipodal personas, between the sanguinary nationalism of Brooks and the reactionary venom of his own later writings."[35] For Gates, Schuyler serves as a tragic reminder of Toni Morrison's accurate observation in *Playing in the Dark* that "the trauma of racism is . . . for the victim, the severe fragmentation of the self."[36]

These portraits of Schuyler are arguably valid and instructive; however, by portraying Schuyler only as a victim of 'race,'[37] Gates's portrait deactivates Schuyler's agency.[38] As "victim," Schuyler seems less accountable for his always provocative but frequently fallacious, insupportable, and ultimately dangerous claims.[39] Ronald Suresh Roberts is skeptical of critiques that simply chalk up black conservatism to "some kind of deep psychic bitterness," because they draw attention away from the claims of black conservatives, claims that white conservatives have made without being subjected to "armchair psychoanalysis."[40] Although Schuyler's consistent inconsistency may suggest that discerning any coherent argument on his part is an impossibility, literary critic James O. Young is correct in stating that a view of Schuyler's career in total reveals certain patterns of his thought.[41]

The most significant of these patterns is Schuyler's faulty theories about the way 'race' works in modern American society. Schuyler is perhaps the only African-American writer who could conclude an autobiography with the statement "At best, 'race' is a superstition."[42] In Schuyler's case, such a claim did not indicate a lack of awareness of white racial hatred toward black America. Rather, for Schuyler, the way to combat white supremacy was to throw out the concept of 'race' altogether. This strategy finds its clearest articulation in a 1944 essay that Schuyler provocatively titled "The Caucasian Problem," which argues that there never has been a "Negro Problem," because it was not "Negroes" who brought Africans across the Atlantic to be slaves in America, or who created Jim

Crow laws or championed white supremacy. Instead, the country suffers from a "Caucasian problem."[43] This argument is typical of Schuyler's wit, but much of the essay dwells on a slightly different topic: the scientific bankruptcy of 'race,' its meaninglessness as a category in the context of the natural sciences. The essay correctly states that 'race' "began as an anthropological fiction and has become a sociological fact," but it demonstrates no awareness of 'race' beyond this scientific bankruptcy.[44] Schuyler's overemphasis on a narrowly defined scientific ideal stemmed from his faith in scientific rationality's ability to overcome racial antagonisms, a faith that informed his creation in the early 1940s of the Association for Tolerance in America, an organization whose mission was "to recondition the white masses by scientific propaganda."[45] Through radio announcements, billboard advertisements, and printed pamphlets, Schuyler's organization highlighted black participation in the war effort, militated against associations of blackness with "public discourtesy, boorishness, uncleanliness, obscene language, garish display and drunkenness,"[46] and tried to convince white America "that national unity is dependent upon national brotherhood; that real democracy is impossible without fraternity; that liberty cannot be realized without equal opportunity and freedom of choice."[47] The organization had limited but significant success; however, after eleven months the ATA folded. Still, the power of scientific reason to combat racism was one of the few subjects on which Schuyler wrote seriously. For example, "The Caucasian Problem" concludes with the following admonition:

> If there is sincerity and determination in the hearts of the mighty, there is still time to make a new world where tolerance, understanding, mutual respect and justice will prevail to a greater degree than men have ever dared dream. True, this means a complete about face on the part of the white world, but this is only right since the race problem is of its own making. The alternative here and abroad is conflict and chaos. We shall have to make a choice very soon.[48]

This genuinely moving conclusion, however, does not sufficiently compensate for serious problems with the uses to which Schuyler put his racial theory. Schuyler used the claim that 'race' is merely a socially constructed illusion to critique black race leaders as frequently as white supremacists. In his foreword to *Black No More,* James A. Miller states that in Schuyler's mind, anyone who asserted differences between blacks and whites "was yielding to the arguments of racists."[49] For example, Schuyler labeled W. E. B. Du Bois's calls for black cultural, political, and economic solidarity in the mid-1930s "a complete surrender to segregation and therefore acceptable to every Klansman, Fascist, and

Nazi."[50] "The Caucasian Problem" identifies "the study of African history and civilization, the fostering of Negro business, the support and growth of the Negro press, the power of the Negro church, and the general development of anti-white thinking" as manifestations of "a racial chauvinism countering that of the whites which has dangerously deepened the gulf between the two peoples who are actually one people."[51] The cultural logic of this theory was expressed in the essay Schuyler is perhaps most famous for, "The Negro-Art Hokum," which appeared in the June 1926 issue of the *Nation* with Langston Hughes's essay "The Negro Artist and the Racial Mountain," which identifies and encourages a unique, specifically black American literary aesthetic. Schuyler, on the other hand, argues that whites contributed to jazz as much as blacks, that black visual art is indebted solely to its fundamental European influences, that "the Aframerican is merely a lampblacked Anglo-Saxon," and that "aside from his color . . . your American Negro is just plain American."[52]

Schuyler's racial theories are also demonstrated in two engaging works of fiction, *Black No More* and *Black Empire,* both of which propose creative solutions to the "Negro Problem." Schuyler described *Black No More* as "a satire on the American race question . . . the first, I believe, to treat the subject with levity."[53] The Schuyler authority Michael Peplow calls it a "savage attack on both whites and blacks obsessed with color," including both white supremacists and blacks who use cosmetics to lighten their skin tone.[54] Schuyler's novel tells the story of Max Disher, a black Harlemite who falls in love at first sight of a beautiful white woman. Unfortunately for Max, she promptly and sharply rejects his advances. This incident helps Max decide to volunteer to be the first customer of Dr. Junius Crookman's "Black No More, Inc." Dr. Crookman, who has concluded that the only ways to solve the "Negro Problem" are for blacks to "get out, get white, or get along,"[55] has decided to solve America's race problem by developing an electrically stimulated, biochemical process that turns black people white. The treatment is a success; Max emerges from the office looking Caucasian, and in "the greatest migration of Negroes in the history of the country,"[56] black Americans leave their hair-straighteners and skin-whiteners behind for the Black No More agencies that start to pop up across the country. Soon, blacks everywhere are turning white. However, instead of solving the nation's racial problems, Black No More, Inc., creates chaos. The company troubles black race leaders Santop Licorice and Dr. Shakespeare Agamemnon Beard—caricatures of Marcus Garvey and W. E. B. Du Bois, respectively—who worry that with so many black people turning white, they will soon lose a valuable source of income. Whites, from the U.S. attorney general to the white supremacist Knights of Nordica—a spoof of the Ku Klux Klan—are thrown into confusion and worry over this turn of events, especially after a "white" woman, who is revealed to be a Black No More customer, gives birth to a black child. As a result, the obsession with protecting white womanhood from the imagined sexual threat of black men increases. Manual labor in the South shrinks as the black labor pool there heads northward for Black No More agencies, leaving working-class whites, who (quite reasonably) demand better wages and work conditions, to take their places. Both Beard's "National Social Equality League" (the NAACP) and the white supremacist Knights of Nordica do all they can to put Black No More, Inc., out of business, but the company just keeps raking in the green. Ultimately, Max Disher uses his new complexion to go to the South, where he tricks the leader of the Knights of Nordica and marries his daughter, the white woman who refused his advances back in Harlem.

The novel's subtitle, *An Account of the Strange and Wonderful Workings of Science in the Land of the Free, A.D. 1933–1940,* suggests the important role Schuyler's particular understanding of the scientific plays in the novel and the role scientific rationality plays in Schuyler's thinking. The novel is designed to emphasize the scientific meaninglessness of 'race' and the arbitrariness of color consciousness. When it is discovered that the Black No More process produces a skin color that is a few shades lighter than that of the average "authentic" white person, black is suddenly beautiful, and Americans of all complexions rush to spend their money on tanning services and formulas in an effort to look darker. When white researchers try to determine the "bloodlines" of every American citizen in order to determine who is "really" white, they discover to their astonishment that more than half of the white population has some trace of "black blood." These facts influence the novel's significantly violent and darkly ironic penultimate scene, in which a mob in Mississippi lynches the Democratic vice presidential candidate, a white man whose "tainted" racial heritage has been made public, and his assistant.

Black No More may appear to be what critic John M. Reilly calls an "antiutopia," a novel that features scientific deconstructions of 'race' but places little faith in humanity's ability to use that knowledge to create a better society, thereby challenging the feasibility of utopian thought.[57] However, it is important to realize that the satiric and utopian impulses are not mutually exclusive. A satire is by definition a humorous critique intended to change behavior or thinking.[58] More significantly, Schuyler's satire is not aimed at the transformative potential of science itself, but is instead tightly focused on specific white supremacist and black 'race' organizations. The novel's parodies of Du Bois and Garvey are perfect examples. The NAACP is ridiculed as a not-so-notfor-profit organization of cigar- and pipe-smoking black Europhiles and "white (men) of remote Negro ancestry"[59] who are both out of touch with and eyed suspiciously by the people whose interests they are supposed to assert and defend. The NSEL's president, Dr. Beard, is a portrayal of Du Bois as the haughty, hyperformal editor of the *Dilemma*.[60] Most damningly, Schuyler portrays this "champion of the darker races"[61] as a hypocrite, especially with regard to color consciousness and his ethnic heritage:

> Like most Negro leaders, he deified the black woman but abstained from employing aught save octoroons. He talked at white banquets about "we of the black race" and admitted in books that he was part-French, part-Russian, part-Indian and part-Negro. He bitterly denounced the Nordics for debauching Negro women while taking care to hire comely yellow stenographers with weak resistance. In a real way, he loved his people. In time of peace he was a Pink Socialist but when the clouds of war gathered he bivouacked at the feet of Mars.[62]

Black No More's caricature of Marcus Garvey is no gentler. Through the character Santop Licorice, Garvey is portrayed as a moneygrubbing polygamist obsessed with his own importance and whose Back-to-Africa society is having an increasingly difficult time getting blacks to invest in its Royal Black Steamship Company, thanks to Black No More, Inc. "Why should anybody in the Negro race want to go back to Africa at a cost of five hundred dollars for passage," Schuyler's narrator asks, "when they could stay in America and get white for fifty dollars?"[63] The "racial chauvinism" that these figures represent to Schuyler, not science, is his principal target. Perhaps science cannot "succeed where the Civil War had failed,"[64] but according to Schuyler, that is only because of what he sees as the reprehensible insistence on 'race' by the race leaders, such as Du Bois and Garvey, that his novel sharply satirizes.

Whereas *Black No More* was a slap in the face of America's race and color consciousness, the collection available as *Black Empire* presents a crafty, covert derision of Pan-Africanist sentiments. Written with the military conflict between Italy and Ethiopia in mind, *Black Empire* originally appeared as two titles of weekly serialized fiction in the *Pittsburgh Courier*. "The Black Internationale: A Story of Black Genius against the World" was published in thirty-three chapters from July to September 1937. "Black Empire: An Imaginative Story of a Great New Civilization in Modern Africa" was published in twenty-nine chapters between October 1937 and April 1938. *Black Empire* introduces readers to a secret black international organization led by the ruthless Dr. Henry Belsidus, a Manhattan physician whom Gates aptly describes as "Du Bois, Booker T. Washington, George Washington Carver, and Marcus Garvey rolled into one fascist superman."[65] Through means as remarkable for their ruthlessness as for their technological advancement, the Black Internationale invades Liberia. Once the Internationale establishes its headquarters there, it sets out to unite all African nations and turns the continent into a military powerhouse. These series were enormously popular in the late 1930s, so much so that a reader wrote the *Courier* asking for specifics as to where in Africa and when the fictional Dr. Belsidus was engaged in his struggle, as if he were an actual person.[66]

Black Empire displays the features of the pulp science fiction that was being published at the time, such as cliffhanger endings, improbable rescues, and numerous elements of the macabre and fantastic. For example, the Black Internationale disposes of enemy spies by dumping them into pits of acid. The Empire fights off attacks by European forces with planes that are hidden in futuristic underground hangars. These planes are used to drop cages full of disease-infested rats on Europe. Members of the Black Internationale communicate among themselves via what we would recognize today as fax machines and eat food grown through advanced hydroponics. And the final European assault on Africa is thwarted by the Black Internationale's combination particle beam/death ray. Other elements reflect the influence of scientific rationalist thought, such as the advanced meatless diet prepared without cooking, with which the Black Internationale nourishes itself. According to John A. Williams, Schuyler was probably reading science fiction as well as many of the popular science magazines that were available during his story's creation.[67]

As a black nationalist fantasy that extends the "Back-to-Africa" sentiment attributed to Marcus Garvey and his Universal Negro Improvement Association (UNIA) to an imaginary conclusion, *Black Empire* initially makes Schuyler look like the type of "race man" that he satirized in *Black No More.* In the afterword to *Black Empire,* Robert A. Hill and R. Kent Rasmussen claim that although Schuyler held ultraconservative views during the 1940s, "during the thirties he was definitely a radical, . . . an activist and a militant advocate of civil rights."[68] Hill and Rasmussen also note Schuyler's numerous attacks on European imperialism in Africa, with which *Black Empire* is completely in step.[69] However, having established satire as Schuyler's favorite rhetorical mode, we can read *Black Empire* in a different way. Schuyler despised Garvey, going so far as to compare him to Hitler.[70] It is also important to remember that Schuyler wrote these stories as Samuel I. Brooks, a name he used on a number of occasions for short or serialized fiction. In a letter to *Courier* colleague P. L. Prattis, Schuyler expressed his opinion of his alter ego's work and of Garveyite nationalism:

> I have been greatly amused by the public enthusiasm for "The Black Internationale" which is hokum and hack work of the purest vein. I deliberately set out to crowd as much race chauvinism and sheer

improbability into it as my fertile imagination could conjure. The result vindicates my low opinion of the human race.[71]

This communiqué suggests that Schuyler wrote *Black Empire* to critique and exploit Pan-Africanist sentiments among many of the *Courier*'s readership. In a 1936 letter to Ira F. Lewis, the *Courier*'s general manager, Schuyler proposed a series of stories set in the West Indies to boost circulation:

> The Ethiopian war is over. The news value of Joe Louis is certainly not going to be what it was, at least not for a long time. So, what have you? Is there anything in prospect or on the horizon that will bring in fifteen or twenty-five thousand circulation? If there is I don't see it. Do you?[72]

The proposal was unsuccessful, but it shows that Schuyler and, most likely, the *Courier*'s management as well were chiefly interested in selling more papers. Therefore, what Hill and Rasmussen suggest tentatively deserves confident assertion, that "the *Black Empire* may have been a cynical joke that Schuyler played on his readers."[73] Schuyler's writing as Samuel I. Brooks is not so much the Jekyll/Hyde transformation of a soul divided against itself as it is the carefully crafted maneuver of an intellectual bent on debunking 'race' in all its manifestations.

Schuyler, like the aforementioned black neocons, was attracted to a narrowly defined scientific ideal. Like his black neocon descendants, Schuyler overinvests in the notion of scientific objectivity, that science is a transparent medium providing clear access to truth. However, Donna Haraway, perhaps the single most important contemporary writer on science as culture, states that "official ideologies about objectivity and scientific method are particularly bad guides to how scientific knowledge is actually *made*."[74] All forms of knowledge claims, most certainly and especially scientific ones, are social constructions, according to Haraway.[75] "*Science is rhetoric*";[76] its statements about the world no less shaped by historical forces and personal and political interests than any other discourse. Perhaps even more important, statements about reality, even if projected from some impossibly positionless space, have political impact. Haraway is quick to remind readers of the important role responsible scientific inquiry plays in providing necessary information about the world, and warns against an over-the-top constructionism that yields nothing but unproductive cynicism.[77] But her work primarily serves to force revisions of our conceptions of the scientific from a detached, objective field that operates above the fray of political struggles, to a contested discursive terrain where the uses put to claims about the world have very real effects on people's lives.

The writings of black neoconservatives are not the only proof that Schuyler's racial theories have survived to manifest themselves in the contemporary era. The February 13, 1995, issue of *Newsweek* features a cover story entitled "What Color Is Black? Science, Politics and Racial Identity," which claims that "the familiar din of black-white antagonism seems increasingly out of date," due to increases in interracial marriage,[78] immigration, and "partly because diversity is suddenly hip."[79] The article's trump card is a report on the "surprising new lessons" revealing that the concept of 'race' has no scientific value.[80] This same issue of *Newsweek* features an article entitled "The End of Affirmative Action."[81]

The scientific bankruptcy of 'race' also informs contemporary philosopher Kwame Anthony Appiah's well-intentioned but problematic critique of appeals to black racial consciousness in W. E. B. Du Bois's "Conservation of Races" (1897) and discussion of Pan-Africanism in Du Bois's *Dusk of Dawn* (1940). Appiah is aware that for Du Bois, 'race' is less "biological" than "sociohistorical" and that Du Bois is attempting "a revaluation of the Negro race in the face of the sciences of racial inferiority," a conception of 'race' that understands "that the white and Negro races are related not as superior to inferior but as complementaries."[82] However, Appiah sees Du Bois's simultaneous "reliance on and repudiation of race" as "curious," and labels "impossible" Du Bois's attempt to revise the hierarchical structure of racial difference so as "to give 'race' a 'horizontal' reading."[83] Appiah's critique does not stoop to the levels of Schuyler's tactics of name-calling and caricature, nor is it motivated by the same political interests. However, both Appiah and Schuyler base their arguments on the emptiness of 'race' as a scientific signifier, from which Appiah concludes that 'race' is an unnecessary evil:

> The truth is that there are no races: there is nothing in the world that can do all we ask race to do for us. As we have seen, even the biologist's notion has only limited uses, and the notion that Du Bois required, and that underlies the more hateful racisms of the modern era, refers to nothing in the world at all. The evil that is done is done by the concept and by easy—yet impossible—assumptions as to its application.[84]

These arguments, like Schuyler's, ignore the role 'race' plays as a building block around which political and cultural identities are created. It is in this sense that Lucius Outlaw describes race consciousness as a "black cultural common sense."[85] Outlaw reminds his readers of "the lived experiences of *real* persons whose experiences are forged in life worlds in part constituted by self-understandings that are in large measure 'racial,' no matter how 'scientifically' inadequate."[86] 'Race' inflects African-American identities in crucial ways: politically,

ulturally. Because it is such an important part of many black Ameri-
ntities, 'race' refuses to vanish in a puff of logic when faced with its
onstructedness. It is also a mistake to assign equal value to different
iations of 'race.' Michael Omi and Howard Winant's *Racial Formation in
United States* (1986) argues that "racial meanings" are "politically contested."[87] Different articulations of 'race' have different meanings. The type of
work that an articulation of 'race' does depends much on its source. For
example, the ends to which the NAACP has historically put 'race'—as a tool
that organizes and mobilizes black Americans politically—are not the same as
those of the KKK.

'Race' is indeed a mirage scientifically speaking, and a construct socially,
culturally, politically, and ideologically; but making this claim does not elide its
power to shape human lives in a very real way. Schuyler's life and career are
instructive not only of the psychic toll of 'race,' but also of the ways arguments
like Schuyler's, which assume that 'race' just does not matter anymore, dovetail
all too easily into harmful conservative political agendas. Racism is more than
just the imposition of unfair differences—differences of access to material and
political resources, opportunity to use those resources, and quality of life—it is
also the unfair disregard of constitutive differences—cultural specificity, group
history, political position. The recognition of constitutive differences, not their
denial, serves as a tool for black empowerment, and is in turn a key step
toward America's realization of what Du Bois called the "ideal of human
brotherhood."[88]

NOTES

1. Ronald Suresh Roberts, *Clarence Thomas and the Tough Love Crowd* (New York: New York University Press, 1995), xi.
2. Roberts, xi, 3.
3. See Cornel West, "Assessing Black Neoconservatism," in *Prophetic Fragments* (Trenton: Africa World Press, 1988), 55–63. West correctly states that although "black liberalism is in a deep crisis" (55), black neoconservatives do not offer a satisfactory political alternative. "Black liberalism indeed is inadequate," West says, "but black conservatism is unacceptable" (59).
4. Quoted in Roberts, 5.
5. Quoted in Roberts, 6.
6. Roberts, 17–18.
7. West, 55.
8. George S. Schuyler, *Black and Conservative* (New Rochelle, NY: Arlington House, 1966), 3–4.
9. Schuyler, *Black and Conservative*, 13.
10. Nickieann Fleener, "George S. Schuyler," *Dictionary of Literary Biography*, vol.

29, *American Newspaper Journalists, 1926–1950,* ed. Perry J. Ashley (Detroit: Bruccoli Clark/Gale Research Co., 1984), 316.

11. Theodore Kornweibel, Jr., *No Crystal Stair: Black Life and the "Messenger," 1917–1928* (Westport, CT: Greenwood, 1975), 122.

12. Kornweibel, 117–18.

13. Fleener, 316.

14. Richard A. Long, "An Interview with George S. Schuyler," *Black World* 25.4 (1976): 69.

15. Robert A. Hill and R. Kent Rasmussen, afterword to *Black Empire,* by George S. Schuyler (Boston: Northeastern University Press, 1991), 259–60.

16. John A. Williams, foreword to *Black Empire,* by Schuyler, xi.

17. Hill and Rasmussen, 262.

18. Kornweibel, 222.

19. Schuyler may have joined the Socialist Party because it was the only intellectual game in town. However, he spends much of his autobiography criticizing socialists for their lack of humor. See Schuyler, *Black and Conservative,* 113–16.

20. Fleener, 316.

21. Schuyler, *Black and Conservative,* 187.

22. Schuyler, *Black and Conservative,* 187. The "Scottsboro Boys" case was perhaps the biggest legal case of the 1930s. It involved nine young black men who were indicted unfairly on charges of raping two white women. One of the women later reversed her testimony. See Dan T. Carter, *Scottsboro: A Tragedy of the American South* (Baton Rouge: Louisiana State University Press, 1969).

23. Schuyler, *Black and Conservative,* 341.

24. Fleener, 318.

25. Schuyler, *Black and Conservative,* 147. Schuyler had also praised Padmore's "How Britain Rules Africa" as a masterpiece. See Henry Louis Gates, Jr., "A Fragmented Man: George Schuyler and the Claims of Race," review of *Black Empire,* by George S. Schuyler, *New York Times Book Review,* September 20, 1992, 31, 42–43.

26. Fleener, 321.

27. Fleener, 321.

28. Quoted in Gates, 31.

29. Schuyler, *Black and Conservative,* 330.

30. With the recent growth of academic interest in science fiction, particularly that by black writers such as Octavia Butler and Samuel Delany, it is important to recognize Schuyler's *Black No More* and *Black Empire* as the first published examples of speculative fiction by an African American.

31. Quoted in James O. Young, *Black Writers of the Thirties* (Baton Rouge: Louisiana State University Press, 1973), 84.

32. Quoted in Fleener, 322.

33. Ann Rayson, "George Schuyler: Paradox among 'Assimilationist' Writers," *Black American Literature Forum* 12.3 (1978): 105.
34. Gates, 31.
35. Gates, 43.
36. Gates, 43.
37. I have used single quotation marks to refer to 'race' as a concept.
38. Schuyler would have hated a description of him as a "victim" of anything. Like many black intellectuals of the 1920s and 1930s, Schuyler was concerned with representations of blackness both among African Americans and to white America. Throughout his career Schuyler militated against representations that he believed pathologized blackness. For example, his autobiography describes black New Yorkers in the 1930s as "proud to be what they were, with no evidence of the inferiority complex and racial self-hate that the current crop of psychologists think they ought to have" (*Black and Conservative,* 139). He spoke of his daughter Philippa, a child prodigy who wrote piano compositions at age four, as representative of Harlem youth (*Black and Conservative,* 235). In 1934 Schuyler wrote a study of Harlem schools that attempted to emphasize the high quality of the schools and the scholarly achievements of their black students (Fleener, 317).
39. Gates's assessment of Schuyler appears in a *New York Times Book Review* article that seeks primarily to introduce Schuyler to a public unfamiliar to him and to situate the author within the field of Afro-American Studies. However, the article does not hold Schuyler accountable for his theories on 'race,' and abstains from a critique of those theories.
40. Roberts, 4.
41. Young, 84.
42. Schuyler, *Black and Conservative,* 352.
43. George S. Schuyler, "The Caucasian Problem," in *What the Negro Wants,* ed. Rayford W. Logan (Chapel Hill: University of North Carolina Press, 1944), 281.
44. Schuyler, "The Caucasian Problem," 297.
45. Schuyler, *Black and Conservative,* 259.
46. Schuyler, *Black and Conservative,* 263.
47. Schuyler, *Black and Conservative,* 259.
48. Schuyler, "The Caucasian Problem," 298. In typically self-contradictory fashion, Schuyler states the following in *Black and Conservative:*

> Once we accept the fact that there is, and always will be, a color caste system in the United States, and stop crying about it, we can concentrate on how best to survive and prosper within that system. This is not defeatism but realism. It is tragic and pointless to wage war against the more numerous and more powerful white majority, and so jeopardize what advantages we possess. (121–22)

Schuyler's conclusion in the same autobiography, "At best, 'race' is a super-stition," demonstrates how easily a political project that seeks to erase 'race' falls prey to an agenda that maintains, or at best resigns itself to, 'race'-based social and political inequalities.

49. James A. Miller, foreword to *Black No More,* by George Schuyler (1931; Boston: Northeastern University Press, 1989), 4.

50. Schuyler, *Black and Conservative,* 227.

51. Schuyler, "The Caucasian Problem," 296–97. James O. Young notes that Schuyler's critiques of black racial consciousness would not keep him from criticizing African Americans for what he felt was insufficient support of Ethiopia during the 1935 crisis with Italy. See Young, 90.

52. George Schuyler, "The Negro-Art Hokum" (1926), in *Voices from the Harlem Renaissance,* ed. Nathan Irvin Huggins (New York: Oxford University Press, 1976), 310.

53. Schuyler, *Black and Conservative,* 170.

54. Michael Peplow, "The Black Picaro in Schuyler's *Black No More*," *Crisis* 83.1 (January 1978): 7–8.

55. Schuyler, *Black No More,* 27.

56. Schuyler, *Black No More,* 87.

57. John M. Reilly, "The Black Anti-Utopia," *Black American Literature Forum* 12.3 (1978): 107.

58. M. H. Abrams observes, "Satire has usually been justified by those who practice it as a corrective of human vice and folly". See M. H. Abrams, *A Glossary of Literary Terms,* 5th ed. (Fort Worth: Holt Rinehart Winston, 1988), 166.

59. Schuyler, *Black No More,* 95.

60. Schuyler, *Black No More,* 90.

61. Schuyler, *Black No More,* 91.

62. Schuyler, *Black No More,* 90.

63. Schuyler, *Black No More,* 102–3.

64. Schuyler, *Black No More,* 25.

65. Gates, 42.

66. Hill and Rasmussen, 268.

67. Williams, xiii.

68. Hill and Rasmussen, 261. *Black and Conservative* offers a very different picture of Schuyler in the thirties. Schuyler casually dismisses the opinions that "the Garveyites and 'black nationalists'" have of his work on Liberia (186). And as noted before, he criticized the International Labor Defense's involvement with the "Scottsboro Boys" case (187–214).

69. Hill and Rasmussen, 261.

70. Schuyler, *Black and Conservative,* 120.

71. Quoted in Hill and Rasmussen, 260.

72. Quoted in Hill and Rasmussen, 266.

73. Hill and Rasmussen, 260.

74. Donna J. Haraway, "Situated Knowledges," in *Simians, Cyborgs, and Women: The Reinvention of Nature* (New York: Routledge, 1991), 184.

75. Haraway, "Situated Knowledges," 184. See also Paul Feyerabend, *Against Method* (New York: New Left Books, 1975, 1993); Thomas Kuhn, *The Structure of Scientific Revolutions* (Chicago: International Encyclopedia of Unified Science, 1962); Andrew Ross, *Strange Weather: Culture, Science and Technology in the Age of Limits* (London: Verso, 1991).

76. Haraway, "Situated Knowledges," 184.

77. Haraway, "Situated Knowledges," 184; idem, "Cyborgs at Large," in *Technoculture,* ed. Constance Penley and Andrew Ross (Minneapolis: University of Minnesota Press, 1991), 4.

78. To its credit, the *Newsweek* article does present interracial union as a fact of life and of American history instead of an unnatural phenomenon. Schuyler himself married Josephine E. Lewis, the daughter of a white Texas family. Their daughter, Philippa Duke Schuyler, was a child prodigy as a classical pianist and was also known as a journalist. Schuyler documented the history of interracial union in the United States and advocated it as an inevitable solution to racial antagonisms. See "The Caucasian Problem," 290, 295.

79. Tom Morganthau, "What Color Is Black?" *Newsweek,* February 13, 1995, 63.

80. Sharon Begley, "Three Is Not Enough," *Newsweek,* February 13, 1995, 67.

81. In July 1995, the Board of Regents of the University of California system voted to end affirmative action hiring and admissions policies. One of the regents, black businessman Ward Connerly, defended the vote with familiarly black neoconservative claims about what he saw as the need to avoid racial issues: "Race is the raw nerve of the nation. That nerve is always exposed. When you touch it, there is going to be a reaction" (A27). Connerly wants the university to (somehow) "create an inclusive university community without taking race into account" (A28). See Kit Lively, "Preferences Abolished," *Chronicle of Higher Education,* July 28, 1995, A26–28.

82. Kwame Anthony Appiah, "Illusions of Race," in *In My Father's House: Africa and the Philosophy of Culture* (New York: Oxford University Press, 1992), 30.

83. Appiah, 45, 46.

84. Appiah, 45. Du Bois's statements and Appiah's readings of them clearly deserve a more thorough analysis than I am able to provide in this essay.

85. Lucius Outlaw, "Toward a Critical Theory of 'Race,' " in *Anatomy of Racism,* ed. David Theo Goldberg (Minneapolis: University of Minnesota Press, 1990), 74.

86. Outlaw, 74.

87. Michael Omi and Howard Winant, *Racial Formation in the United States* (New York: Routledge, 1986), 69.

88. W. E. B. Du Bois, "The Conservation of Races" (1897), in *Writings,* ed. Nathan Huggins (New York: Library of America, 1986), 825.

9

MARGARET ROSE VENDRYES

HANGING ON THEIR WALLS

AN ART COMMENTARY ON LYNCHING, THE FORGOTTEN 1935 ART EXHIBITION

Countless art exhibitions have been held in New York City in any given year since the second decade of the twentieth century, when the metropolis began to claim its place as art capital of the world. But before 1935, no gallery had hosted an exhibition specific to issues concerning African-American men. With the opening of *An Art Commentary on Lynching* that year, art became, for the first time, an experimental vehicle for countering negative attitudes toward black men. An orchestrated effort of this caliber would not be seen again in New York City until 1994, when the Whitney Museum of American Art hosted *Black Male: Representations of Masculinity in Contemporary Art.* Well over half a century after *An Art Commentary,* several works in the Whitney exhibition reflected the persistence and pertinence of lynching as a theme relevant to black men even though literal lynching had been obliterated. Lynching's manifestations in American visual art began with one man's brainstorm in 1934. What was intended as an overt yet measured method of popularizing the protest of lynching (overt because the purpose was deliberate and political; measured because under the protection of the "fine art" label, the volatile topic became tempered for public consumption) inspired the creation of objects reflecting an unequaled variety of attitudes toward African-American men and the race conflicts in which they figured.

An Art Commentary on Lynching took place at the Arthur U. Newton Galleries on East 57th Street in New York City; it opened on February 15, 1935, and ran for two weeks (see catalog cover, figure 1). The number of visitors far exceeded expectations. This was due, in part, to the last-minute cancellation of the exhibition by its original host, Jacques Seligmann Galleries. The cancellation served to stir up public interest in these art objects that had caused the owner concern about "keep[ing] the galleries free of political or racial manifestations."[1] One hundred eighty-three patrons allowed their names to be listed in the exhibition's catalog as evidence of tangible support. This display of visual art was assembled specifically to draw attention to the need for a nationwide antilynching law under the sponsorship of the National Association for the Advancement of Colored People and the College Art Association.[2]

Although efforts were made to intellectualize the cause and effects of lynching in order to inspire support for *An Art Commentary,* African-American fears of white retribution and the white "tendency to translate [white] barbarisms and deceptions into virtues" came through loud and clear in the art.[3] The 1930s had witnessed an increase in incidents of mob violence against African Americans in the South after a significant decrease since the turn of the century. Increased visibility of blacks in the workplace made possible by New Deal legislation seemed to inspire a resurgence of violence, historically the most virulent form of racial oppression. *Lynchings and What They Mean: General Findings of the Southern Commission on the Study of Lynching,* published in 1931, offered a contemporary look at the state of this issue. In sober and frank language, this thin publication presented data ranging from historical statistics to candid descriptions of lyncher types and techniques.

The commission concluded that "We expect lynchings ultimately to be eradicated by the growth of a healthy public opinion that will no longer tolerate them."[4] Walter White, then director of the NAACP, tirelessly and with steadily increasing militancy investigated methods of promoting the protest of lynching. The operations of the NAACP gained urgency in 1934, when the Costigan-Wagner bill was under consideration by the new Congress.[5] Using various procedures aimed at the typical urban art gallery visitor, White led a city-

AN ART COMMENTARY ON LYNCHING

THE FUGITIVE
by John Steuart Curry

Arthur U. Newton Galleries
Eleven East Fifty-seventh Street
New York City

February 15 — March 2, 1935

Galleries open 10:00 A.M. to
5:00 P.M. daily, except Sunday

Price of Catalogue: Twenty-five Cents

Figure 1. Catalog cover for *An Art Commentary on Lynching*. Hale Woodruff Papers, Amistad Research Center, Tulane University, New Orleans, Louisiana.

centered campaign to uncover the lynch mobs' covert practices.[6] The effectiveness of visual material slowly began to take hold. The earliest method was advertising in national magazines, using texts emphasizing the hypocrisy of the American Constitution as it related to African Americans accompanied by rather explicit photographs of actual lynchings. Another was to hang a black flag from the NAACP New York office window announcing each incident, which read, A MAN WAS LYNCHED YESTERDAY. In 1935 alone, the flag appeared twenty times. Several major magazines published even more gruesome photographs, planting a visual image of the practice in the American mind.

In 1935, those concerned about lynching considered the practice to be primarily a result of ignorance and economic oppression.[7] At the time, lynchings were not critiqued as cultural phenomena in light of the urgency of the need to condemn their continued occurrence. However, Walter White candidly identified lynching as one in a line of American "folk-ways."[8] Today, the distance of sixty years allows for an involved analysis of the exhibit that probes beneath lynching's surface manifestations.

Although the depiction of violence and torture in western art dates back to antiquity, its blatant use as a theme in American art had been almost exclusively propagandistic or pornographic. These two contradictory aims collided in the artistic expression of lynching. The art objects discussed here are telling displays of the important roles perspective and the artist's position play in visualizing a social theme.

Thirty-eight artists submitted their work to *An Art Commentary*.[9] Of this number, one woman, Peggy Bacon, and ten African Americans were represented. Given the premise of the exhibition, those who participated were undoubtedly considered radicals. Although this was a blatant call for artists to apply their talents to realize White's aim to "delicately ... effect a union of art and propaganda," the resulting objects reveal an unanticipated diversity of approach to the subject of lynching.[10] With the exception of Peggy Bacon's caricatures of two notorious hanging judges, *An Art Commentary* was a display of what *men* thought about *men's* deeds. The exhibition, therefore, represents what Robyn Wiegman refers to as a "culturally complex relation between black men and white men and their claims to the patriarchal province of masculine power."[11] The race, class, religion, gender, and sexual orientation of the artist often play a pivotal role in the handling of subject matter in general. But a theme as loaded with social and political significance as lynching tended to exaggerate the artist's expression of self-involvement. Analysis of the art must rightly take into account the background of the artist to enable the most thorough extraction of meaning possible. Hence, an African American's opinion about lynching will understandably contain an autobiographical tone, because as Pearl Buck made clear in her opening address for the exhibition, every black man was a potential victim of the lynch mob.[12] During the years of its use, lynching without a doubt inspired fear in all African Americans, but especially the men. Further, this collection of art serves as an example of lynching's later perpetuation by artists' critiquing broader notions of African-American masculinity and sexuality, issues that were always present in American art.

Several of the works displayed in *An Art Commentary* did not survive. Many have gone the way of cultural ephemera, failing the test of time given to objects of fine art. American art containing sociopolitical commentary during the early twentieth century was closely tied to the graphic media favored by newspapers and magazines.[13] Therefore, many of the *Art Commentary* entries were in black and white media: lithographs, drawings, and cartoons. The paintings and sculptures submitted to the exhibition were, for the most part, larger and more elaborate pieces created prior to the announcement of White's exhibition. These independently conceived objects in particular reveal an interest in the depiction of this macabre practice by celebrated artists as different in temperament as Isamu Noguchi and Thomas Hart Benton.

Noguchi, needing a model, used a photograph published in 1930 for his metal sculpture, *Death (Lynched Figure)* (figure 2). The violence of this subject was considered so uncharacteristic of Noguchi that his biographers have assumed it was created exclusively for *An Art Commentary*.[14] Although the sculptor did approach White for help in finding an appropriate photograph, the idea to depict a lynching was Noguchi's alone. Noguchi, born in Los Angeles and raised in Japan, occasionally faced overt racism from his white American critics. Henry McBride called *Death* "just a little Japanese mistake"; he found Noguchi's adept use of abstraction and figuration to comment on American barbarism irritating at best.[15] Without specific reference to Noguchi, *Art News* pointed out the "strong atmosphere of sensationalism" and "a sort of aesthetic opportunism in capitalization on the dramatic values of the subject" at hand in *An Art Commentary* and finally judged *Death* in that context as "closely approaching the bizarre."[16]

Noguchi's participation in the NAACP exhibition was a feather in the organization's cap. By 1935, he had already enjoyed twelve one-man exhibitions. Noguchi's professed interest in communist issues figured into the criticism of his art. As a humanitarian, he was perhaps expected to be less abstract in his handling of lynching. According to Matthew Baigell, "Noguchi has wanted his materials to express themselves through their textures and physical properties as well as to imply meanings suggested by the configurations of their forms."[17] Slightly smaller than life size, the seamless, faceless metal figure, suspended by actual rope, was frozen in an impossible position that implied struggle when

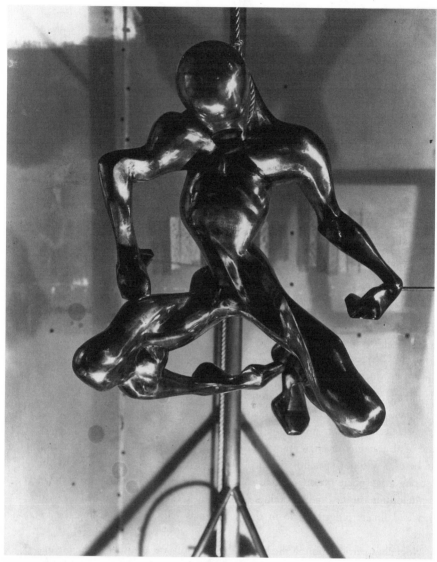

Figure 2. Isamu Noguchi, *Death (Lynched Figure),* 1934, Monel metal, rope, 39 x 29¼ x 21 inches, (base not included). Photograph by Bernice Abbott/Commerce Graphics Ltd., Inc.

struggle would have been futile. The idea of violent death was alive and glistening (as a black body would be over flames or under the lash), attracting even the unwilling viewer, who became a witness to the crime in its presence. Embracing what the eye encountered, this powerful work of art effortlessly

158

dominated the Newton Galleries. Within four days of *An Art Commentary*'s opening, Noguchi, perhaps angry at the omission of his name in the catalog or fed up with the tone of the recent criticism of his work, removed *Death* from Newton Galleries without explanation.[18]

Although Thomas Hart Benton's painting, *A Lynching* (see figure 3), came out of the Midwest Regionalist tradition characterized by a somewhat literal and documentary style; it nevertheless had an uncanny similarity to Noguchi's work. Benton became celebrated as an artist who found optimism in the life of those Americans who continued working the soil. He approached the subject of lynching with similar zeal, picturing able American men at work. Although wielding a log against a jailhouse door, Benton's figures could just as easily have been collaborating to build it. Both artists chose an awkwardly animated pose for the lynched figure, highlighting the morbidity of the victim's final breath— a plastic suspension of life that exaggerated the inevitability of death. Noguchi and Benton also found the appeal of placing the event in an urban-inspired environment more effective than the allusion to the backwoods common to other works. The telephone pole in Benton's picture, from which the hanging body is suspended, brings home the irony of civilization still accommodating savagery. Benton carefully composed his painting with expert use of lights and darks, adding a frenzied rhythm to the scene. Art executed with skill and attention to detail—aspects celebrated in most contexts—had a short public life when it addressed disquieting subjects. The creators of socially oriented painting and sculpture in the 1930s were hard pressed to find private patronage in America. Although both Noguchi's and Benton's lynching works remained unsold in the artists' collections, these men were willing to make humane statements in an arena where few were willing to become publicly involved.[19]

Another picture, painted in 1934 under the auspices of the Public Works of Art Project, was Samuel J. Brown, Jr.'s *The Lynching* (figure 4). Using a style bordering on caricature, Brown, an African American born and raised in North Carolina, left no doubt about his perspective on the subject. Brown had studied to become an art educator at the Pennsylvania Museum of Art. His clever adoption of a folk-like style to present a serious subject became the mark of his artistic work. Separated from the spectators on the ground, the hanged man in *The Lynching* and his viewing audience in the art gallery become one. The bracketing tree trunk and branches are patterned and positioned like a menacing reptile. The black man's incisors, bared as if about to bite down, are pointed, adding an animalistic quality to what we assume was an innocent man. Rather than a reflection of internalized self-hatred, the implied bestiality of the black figure provides commentary on prevailing white judgment of African Americans' subhuman status. Ironic details abound in this picture, but few saw beyond the

DIXIE HOLIDAY
by William Mosby

THIS IS HER FIRST LYNCHING
by Reginald Marsh

A LYNCHING
by Thomas Benton

Figure 3. Illustrated catalog page from *An Art Commentary on Lynching*. Hale Woodruff Papers, Amistad Research Center, Tulane University, New Orleans, Louisiana.

Figure 4. Samuel J. Brown, Jr., *The Lynching,* 1934, watercolor and pencil on paper, 21 x 29 inches. Public Works of Art Project, on deposit at the Philadelphia Museum of Art.

strangled, blue-gray face dominating the center of the frame. The deep pink droplets of blood escaping from the hanging body are suggestive of the smiling, upturned, pink faces of the dense crowd dotting the upper quarter of the picture, as if those droplets created them. A man's blood was shed so that they could live without fear? Countless crucifixion pictures include a ladder leaning against the cross. Although more subtle than others in his use of Christian references, Brown was not able to avoid them altogether. Even the dog tugging playfully at the end of the rope would fare better in life than a black man. Because of Brown's employment by the PWAP, he was free to purposely address a politically loaded, contemporary topic without solely considering its marketability. Subsequently, *The Lynching* can be counted among the large inventory of PWAP artworks that, as one museum official recently expressed it, "nobody wanted."[20] It was clear that, regardless of technical quality, some subjects (lynching probably ranking high on the list) remained unsuitable for expression through fine art. This picture was the boldest commentary to be made by an African American in *An Art Commentary*, but the intricacy of its message was lost in its somewhat heavy use of sarcasm. Winston Burdett described *The Lynching* in the *Brooklyn Daily Eagle:* "It is a decorative grotesque but not very violent, and preciousity [*sic*] is a little out of place in so urgent a subject."[21] Burdett was not alone in his opinion. Yet no critic appeared to be interested in commenting on Allan Freelon's *Barbecue—American Style.* This young black artist chose to depict "that moment when the victim first feels the flames begin to lick at his body."[22] The reverse of Brown's heavenly view, Freelon's victim is buckled up at the feet of his murderers. Not as artistically astute and lacking the calming effects of color, Freelon's drawing, ignored by the critics, was anything but precious.

An Art Commentary received modest news coverage, which tended to highlight the work of the more well-known white contributors: Benton, John Steuart Curry, George Bellows, and Reginald Marsh. Marsh's drawing, *This Is Her First Lynching* (see figure 3), was singled out for its more subtle handling of the subject, where his allusion to the sickness of a mob was enough to disturb most viewers. Remembered for his documentary style and biting clarity, Marsh painted New York in all its urban chaos. He favored the seedier side of life where the overlap of bodies crowded into small spaces made a powerful commentary on modern existence. *This Is Her First Lynching* (there are two fairly similar versions) was no exception. Although the crowd was decidedly made up of country folk, they appear to be dressed for a show and like the "great hives of people," as Marilyn Cohen described Marsh's characters, they continued to be "caught up in a period of national economic disaster, yet still pursuing their leisure or, like the Bowery bums, passing the time, endlessly waiting."[23] A well-educated and financially secure illustrator, Marsh was beholden to none. In 1925, he became one of the original cartoonists for the *New Yorker*.[24] Like a skilled journalist, Marsh offers just enough detail to fuel the imagination. His detachment from the scenes he most enjoyed documenting was obvious. Marsh, living comfortably throughout his life, considered those less fortunate more inventive in their leisure. Lynching was entertainment from the standpoint of the enthusiastic mother holding her child overhead for a better view of the event. Marsh's matter-of-fact handling accentuates the macabre without overt condemnation. Viewer expectations are not met in this picture, and it is for that very reason that it was singled out by the critics as effective. Lacking literal interpretation, such objects invited sustained contemplation.

One standout example of this invitation to contemplate was William Mosby's *Dixie Holiday* (see figure 3). The intuitive style of this folk carver offered an unencumbered meditation on the helplessness of African Americans living in the South. Mosby, the only true black folk artist represented in the exhibition, was a sociology student at Virginia Union University when he carved *Dixie Holiday* out of a solid block of walnut. The sculpture was only about one foot in height, yet it received enthusiastic praise and was eventually purchased by the NAACP for its offices. The popularity of this carving was a reflection of the interest in Negro folk expressions taking hold during the 1930s. The contemporary careers of Horace Pippin and William Edmondson are well-known examples. It was believed that the untainted (read untrained) country artist could best access the true expression of the race. Mosby had never carved before, and it is unknown whether he continued with his art. Without formal training, he skillfully simulated a sense of powerlessness left in the wake of mob violence. In *Dixie Holiday,* the victim's family assemble under the tree like pawns in a chess game, wearing expressionless masks. The religious narrative, equally as subtle as Brown's more sophisticated technique, cannot be overlooked. The Madonna-with-child figure began the chain connecting this narrative to the life of Christ from birth to death. This was the general manner of the African-American artists represented in *An Art Commentary.* The steady quality of Mosby's vertical format and the static, self-contained forms created a quiet complacency—a kind of visual resignation—not conducive to emotional response. Pictures submitted by Hale Woodruff, Malvin Gray Johnson, E. Simms Campbell, and Wilmer Jennings, all African Americans, carried an identical tone. Each included allusions to Christianity coloring their compositions with what would be considered misplaced sentimentality. Stephen Alexander, writing for the *New Masses,* a radical leftist magazine, dismissed *An Art Commentary* as "so permeated by religious spirit as to be little more than prayer in graphic and plastic form."[25] The willingness to make a statement of powerlessness was present but not accompa-

LIVERPOOL JOHN MOORES UNIVERSITY
LEARNING SERVICES

nied by the ability to confront a white-dominated audience with black anger. This of course did not mean anger was altogether absent from the equation.

Alexander's opinion was a reflection of what was expected from art as social commentary. The exhibition was arranged to incite alarm and, with it, action to end lynching through legal channels. Not all visitors to the Newton Galleries went away unmoved. One reporter found a brave female visitor feeling faint while walking through the galleries. Another warned that "You may get a little ill, but it may do you good."[26] Even so, these objects were judged overall as watered down, mere artistic transcriptions of a horrid act, and therefore ineffectual as propaganda. It was apparently not considered possible or necessary for objects of artistic merit to be created under the rubric of lynching. Robert L. Zangrando allotted only a short paragraph to this exhibition in his useful and thorough text, *The NAACP Crusade against Lynching, 1909–1950.*[27] If, then, *An Art Commentary* failed at the levels of fine art and political propaganda, its works nevertheless vividly rendered the violent convergence of race, gender, and sexuality around the phenomenon of lynching.

The life of the mind played an important role in the creation, and in turn the reception, of these works. An artist unable to draw on personal visual experience to create a picture resorts to imagination. Paul Cadmus, an avowed atheist as well as an apolitical homosexual, revealed his opinion by picturing human interaction and intense facial expression. Cadmus created *To the Lynching!* (figure 5) specifically for *An Art Commentary,* using a swirl of fine lines to create a pileup of well-developed male anatomy. The resulting sensation was chaotic. According to Guy Davenport, to understand Cadmus we must recognize that "moral chaos is always shown in crowds" and "once sexuality of any kind becomes a herd activity, Cadmus sees it as vice, chaos, a failure of order and self-control."[28] Many of Cadmus's pictures are overtly sexual. *To the Lynching!* was no exception. Unlike the majority of works in *An Art Commentary,* Cadmus's figures physically interact with the victim's body, clawing his face and arms and touching his abdomen. By making the lynch mob resemble a pack of wolves about to devour their kill, Cadmus covertly implicated the odious nature of the assumption that "Negroes are prone to crimes against women and that unless a Negro is lynched now and then the women in the solitary farmsteads are in danger."[29] In other words, lynching was about correcting supposed sexual deviance, something Cadmus had a talent for picturing. *To the Lynching!* situates the viewer on top of the scene. We are drawn into the confusion, where the figures are disturbingly identical in color. Cadmus's willingness to pull the viewer in so close might be a sign of his awareness that the majority of those who would visit the exhibition would be white. The triangle of white men, in their freedom, are the ones to be feared. This picture frankly accuses its viewers

Figure 5. Paul Cadmus, *To the Lynching!* 1935, graphite and watercolor on paper, 20½ x 15¾ inches. Collection of Whitney Museum of American Art, New York, photograph © 1995, Whitney Museum of American Art.

as participants rather than putting them in sympathy with the victim or, as Benton and others had done, offering a safe distance from which to act as voyeurs.

It was common knowledge that the majority of lynchings of black men were justified by a call to preserve the safety and sanctity of white womanhood. Knowing this, we can recognize the influence of the sexual component behind the actual mutilation of African-American men as well as its depiction in some of the objects created by white artists.[30] Examples range from Jewish sculptor Aaron Goodleman's simple albeit subversive statement that the black man did not have a leg to stand on to the more involved narrative in George Bellows's lithograph, *The Law Is Too Slow* (figure 6).[31]

The Law Is Too Slow was the artistic seed that grew into *An Art Commentary.* Walter White used the lithograph for the jacket cover of his 1929 book *Rope and Faggot: A Biography of Judge Lynch.* However, this picture was originally made in 1923 to illustrate "Nemesis," a short story by Mary Johnston. The title of the piece was inflammatory enough, but the story could have fed the statistics on lynching: "They said that the man, a black man, had done the crime [attacking and murdering a white woman]. Perhaps he had, perhaps he had not. . . . One of the four men lighted the pile, the cane blazed up, and the night turned red and horribly loud—like hell."[32] While the black artist situates the victim on a journey to return to his God, the white artist condemns him to hell on earth. As an artist who embraced nineteenth-century academic tradition, Bellows called to mind works from that century that invoked images of violence and sexual aggression. The subjugated pale woman in art painted by artists from the French School of Romanticists such as Gérôme and Delacroix was replaced with a black man chained here as he was in slavery and glowing from the waist down as if lit from the inside. Rather than assuming the usual masculine position as viewer or active participant, the black man becomes the passive object viewed, the position generally held in art by a female. Bellows's artistic effort, tinged with erotic undertones, attempted to address the gruesome reality of castration of lynching victims but fell amazingly short of that reality. The African-American man in that picture was not presented as a man but a beast whom a national leader such as Woodrow Wilson openly designated as one in a "host of dusky children . . . insolent and aggressive, sick of work, [and] covetous of pleasure," safe in his belief that common consensus was behind him.[33]

The positioning of the black man as not only a victim but a restrained virile beast was not unlike portrayals of the devil in Western art. The seductive quality of "dark evil vanquished" underlying the more sensationalistic handling of the theme by Bellows and others was contrary to the cause of art meant to reflect

Figure 6. George Wesley Bellows, *The Law Is Too Slow,* 1923, lithograph. Gift of George F. Porter, 1925.1567, photograph © 1994, The Art Institute of Chicago. All rights reserved.

the spirit of antilynching propaganda. However distasteful, lynching has interwoven in its meaning issues of sexual morality that most American men could
relate to on some level during that time. These sentiments—bound by fears of
inadequacy—superimposed on lynching produced an antithetical brand of sa-

dism. Hence, we will find the use of black male bodies bound by rope reappearing later as erotica. The idea of manhood/personhood fades away as the black male body claims a space as object of desire.

The manhood of blacks was not an issue during slavery. For all intents and purposes, the slave remained a "boy" throughout his entire life. After the Civil War and emancipation, the African-American man was able to assume a position of masculinity, if only within his own ethnic community. The threat that he might have access to the acts and deeds of "men" was to become the catalyst for the emergence of new and vicious methods of keeping him in his "place." Many of these limitations have been confirmed in American visual arts. The dress and body language of the many anonymous black figures found across the entire historical spectrum of American art prior to the civil rights movement without a doubt reflected the inferior status of the African American.[34]

African-American artists creating works in the 1930s for polite society found it difficult to be as forthright as Cadmus, Bellows, or even Brown. In contrast, most African-American artists, unaccustomed to lashing out at the oppressor, preferred to focus on victimhood and those potential victims left behind. As mentioned earlier, their art possessed the tone of an appeal to the morality of the viewer, often through religious references. Richmond Barthé, a devout Roman Catholic of Louisiana Creole stock, had begun *The Mother* (figure 7) before *An Art Commentary* was conceived.[35] The sculptor emphasized the victim's mother and rendered the black man's body completely nude. Nudity heightened the figure's vulnerability and effected an allusion to familiar images of the crucified Christ while silently highlighting the barrenness of the black man's experience in America. But what is particularly unusual about *The Mother* was that Barthé left the lynched body intact. This was an unlikely state, because when a lynch victim was stripped he was customarily castrated as well. Castration, the literal feminizing of the so-called hypersexual black male, has been pointed out by Wiegman as a "violently homoerotic exchange" bringing out a subconscious white obsession with sexual parity as opposed to gender equality.[36] Further, it has been documented that the penis of the lynch victim became a valuable souvenir. Wiegman convincingly analyzed this practice: "In the image of white men embracing—with hate, fear, and a chilling form of empowered delight—the very penis they were so overdeterminedly driven to destroy, one encounters a sadistic enactment of the homoerotic, indeed its most extreme disavowal."[37] As a black man who openly preferred a homosocial life but never publicly revealed homosexual preferences, Barthé created a sculpture that served as a safe conduit for these closeted sentiments. It is obvious that Barthé meant to cloak a violent crime with the compositional grace and anatomical beauty of the famous Italian Renaissance model, Michelangelo's *Pietà*. But

Figure 7. Richmond Barthé, *The Mother,* 1934, painted plaster, approximately life-sized, destroyed 1940. Photograph from the National Archives, Washington, D.C.

failure to see beneath that cloak renders impotent the social and personal discourse at work in this object.

The religious configuration of art like Barthé's lamentation scene also points to a bold notion taking hold during the period that the son of God was a black man. This idea entered the art arena with works such as the subtle references to lynching in the illustrations by Charles Cullen for Countee Cullen's *Colors* in 1927, and again in 1929 when he published *The Black Christ.* In 1927, a small figure hanging limply from a tree in the background was enough to give an angry edge to an otherwise uplifting picture. By 1929, Cullen boldly created a checkerboard of repeated figures—black-lynched, white-crucified—until the figures begin to merge in the mind's eye. As bold as this work was for its time, *The Black Christ* cover, which introduced a fictional account of a lynching, did not compare to the audacity of Langston Hughes's language in his 1930 poem "Christ in Alabama." Hughes openly called Christ a "nigger" and paralleled his execution with that of a lynch victim. It was apparently easier for some black writers to be forthright in expressing their sentiments on the subject. Most visual artists were using a talent still bound to notions of creating objects of beauty based on Euro-American standards. In 1935, black had not yet become beautiful.

Historically, the impressive strength and beauty of the black male body had not escaped the white artist's brush and chisel. As Michael Hatt has appropriately stated in his essay concerning masculinity and the representation of the black body in American art, "The savage is more animal than human and so clearly cannot be a man, not least because of his excessive sexual nature, lustful and unregulated by socialization."[38] Recognition and appreciation of the black body were given on a level of pure aesthetics excited by the "excessive sexual nature" of the "savage" having nothing to do with endowing blacks with any inherent human qualities.

Harry Sternberg's lithograph, sarcastically titled *Southern Holiday* (figure 8), accentuated the black body while commenting on the ruin of democracy by capitalism. Columns and smokestacks, obvious symbols of civilization and industrialization (offset by the small country church whose steeple the victim touches with his middle finger), also served as phallic symbols emphasizing the missing genitals severed from between the figure's spread legs. The artist recalled being "filled with anger and shame . . . and eventually transmitted these emotions through the finished print."[39] Although we recognize the expression of pain and anguish on the face of the bound figure, his expression does not carry the overall tenor of the picture. Sternberg returned to the lynching theme in 1937, removing the church, enlarging the figure, and obscuring the castration. The sexual language of the writhing, bound body projects a familiar, stereotypical, and hence more powerful message regardless of the symbols surrounding it.[40]

In general, the white artists were more willing to address the spectacle of the lynching act. From their perspective as white men, the artists could conceivably have empathized with the mob. Some of them used a clever compositional tool to avoid such a reading. Whether the use of this tool was a conscious act is unknown. John Steuart Curry's treatment of lynching is a clear example. A Midwesterner known for his sympathetic treatment of the African-American figure, Curry executed several versions of *The Fugitive* (see figure 1) with minor variances between them. Notice how the viewer and by implication the artist are placed outside the manhunt. Safely at a distance, we have a bird's-eye view beyond Curry's black figure gripping the tree branch with his toes like a monkey. Viewers were exempt from the event while being allowed to witness it vicariously. This was also the case with the examples by Benton, Bellows, and Sternberg discussed earlier. In each example, the victim was still alive, as if

Figure 8. Harry Sternberg, *Southern Holiday,* 1935, lithograph, 21¾ x 15¾ inches. Courtesy of Susan Teller Gallery.

rescue might still be possible. In contrast, the black artists more realistically depicted the deed as done.

Advocacy of antilynching legislation was inherent in the invitation to exhibit in *An Art Commentary*. Subtle or hidden symbolism factored into few of the works by white artists, while it was endemic for black artists. White artists fearlessly addressed the absurdities of lynching with the same open-faced audacity that their Southern brothers used to commit the crime. The lynch mob, a gathering usually so large that no single participant was punished, was in most cases addressed as existing out there somewhere beyond the civilized confines of the art gallery. With the exception of Peggy Bacon and Edmund Duffy, white artists willing to point a finger at specific individuals, details were left aside in favor of addressing the larger concern—the act itself. What lynching meant and why it continued to be practiced were thrashed around by a diverse group of artists in *An Art Commentary*. The particulars of lynching included an embarrassing array of perversities. The remnants of *An Art Commentary* are historical documents of a battle of wits between those who saw art as a medium of pleasure and those who wanted it to be an instrument of education.

The persistence of the lynching theme in visual art takes on a new character with the changing attitudes of art makers emerging after *An Art Commentary*. Within less than a decade, writer/photographer Carl Van Vechten, heralded as the enthusiast of the Harlem Renaissance, personal friend and champion of several black artists, and noted patron of *An Art Commentary*, could pose young Allen Meadows in the woods tied to a tree sporting the characteristic arrows of the Roman martyr Saint Sebastian between his legs (figure 9). Admittedly, reported incidents of lynching had all but disappeared by 1940, but did this make such blatant referral to it admissible for purely artistic reasons? [41] Once rendered passive, both in pose and by being a photograph, the black man was no longer an object of fear but one of desire, recalling what Kobena Mercer referred to as "classical racism [which] involved a logic of dehumanization[,] . . . bodies but not minds." [42] Later in the decade, Geoffrey Holder created his untitled photograph of a muscular, dark-skinned torso with heavy-gauge rope cutting into its flesh. [43] Although the model was enveloped in darkness that rendered him anonymous, the mingling tones of sex and violence were unmistakable. The symbolism of lynching, even in the hands of a black artist, had been transformed out of the political realm. Does this mean that time heals all wounds?

Although the literal practice of lynching was eventually stamped out, it continues metaphorically with considerable power. Lynching, a festering sore in American history, has been alluded to by African Americans in reference to all levels of racial injustice. The language used to discuss the recent Thomas/Hill hearings is but one significant example. Lynching's political power as a visual

Figure 9. Carl Van Vechten, Untitled, 1942, black and white photograph. Carl Van Vechten Papers, Beinecke Rare Book and Manuscript Library, Yale University. Courtesy of the Estate of Carl Van Vechten, Joseph Solomon, executor.

tool has disintegrated steadily since *An Art Commentary* was dismantled in December 1935, when its national tour failed to materialize. The vision of a limp figure dangling from a branch had been branded on the American mind. The shock value was wasted on contemporary art audiences. Walter White had no idea how correct he was when he wrote in 1935 that "even a morbid subject can be made popular."[44] Both drawing us in and repulsing us with images evoking disturbing emotional responses, these works (a fraction of the number reflecting American interest in distressing themes) undeniably admit that art maintains a special place for human vice.

NOTES

1. Jacques Seligmann, quoted in "Protests Bar Show of Art on Lynching," *New York Times,* February 12, 1935.
2. For a detailed account of the political underpinnings of this exhibition, see Marlene Park, "Lynching and Antilynching: Art and Politics in the 1930s," in *Prospects* (Center for American Cultural Studies, Cambridge University Press) 18 (1993): 311–65.
3. Southern Commission on the Study of Lynching, *Lynchings and What They Mean* (Atlanta: Commission, 1931), 61.
4. Southern Commission on the Study of Lynching, 63.
5. Robert L. Zangrando, *The NAACP Crusade against Lynching, 1909–1950* (Philadelphia: Temple University Press, 1980), 122–38.
6. Letter to Mrs. George Bellows, December 13, 1934, from Walter White soliciting the use of her late husband's work. White mentions using the example of crusades for anti-prohibition, which swayed the opinion of "snooty society girls and others." NAACP Papers, Library of Congress.
7. A clearheaded approach to investigating the roots of violence against African Americans can be found in Herbert Shapiro, *White Violence and Black Response* (Amherst: University of Massachusetts Press, 1988).
8. Park, 338.
9. Marlene Park numbers the exhibitors at forty-four, following the tally of the newspapers, but neglected to name them. The catalog listed thirty-seven names. It is quite possible that Isamu Noguchi was not the only name missing from the catalog, given the hasty manner in which the exhibition was put together.
10. Letter to Mrs. Harry Payne Whitney, December 13, 1934, NAACP Papers.
11. Robyn Wiegman, "The Anatomy of Lynching," in *American Sexual Politics: Sex, Gender, and Race since the Civil War,* ed. John C. Fout and Maura Shaw Tantillo (Chicago: University of Chicago Press, 1993), 240.
12. Several quotes from the opening address can be found in "Art Goes Educational on Decorous East Fifty-seventh, Near Fifth," *New York Post,* February 18, 1935.
13. Photographs of lynching were taken as early as 1908 and began to be published

in major American magazines by the 1930s. *An Art Commentary* did not include photographs, although initially a ten dollar prize was slated for that medium. Photographs of lynching were seen as gruesomely explicit documents rather than art objects, and more often than not the photographer remained anonymous. The Whitney Museum of American Art's exhibition *Black Male* included *Accused/Blowtorch/Padlock* (1986) by Pat Ward Williams, which questions photographs of torture and why a photographer might not want to own up to being present at a lynching.

14. Bruce Altshuler, *Isamu Noguchi* (New York: Abbeville Press, 1994), 102.
15. Altshuler, 29.
16. Park, 32.
17. Matthew Baigell, *A Concise History of American Painting and Sculpture* (New York: Harper and Row, 1984), 321.
18. NAACP Papers.
19. Apparently, this painting was not favored by Benton. The canvas was left neglected in his leaky summer cottage and subsequently became damaged beyond repair. No color reproductions are known to exist. Letter to R. L. Zangrando from T. H. Benton, March 1963, in Zangrando, 254.
20. Anita Duquette, manager of rights and reproductions of the Whitney Museum of American Art, telephone conversation with author, February 9, 1995.
21. Winston Burdett, "Artists Call Attention to the Gentle Art of Lynching," *Brooklyn Daily Eagle,* February 15, 1935, NAACP Papers.
22. Letter to Walter White from Allan Freelon, undated, NAACP Papers.
23. Marilyn Cohen, *Reginald Marsh's New York* (New York: Whitney Museum of American Art, 1983), 1.
24. Cohen, 3.
25. Quoted in Park, 343.
26. Michel Mok, "Art Show Depicts Horrors of Mob Lynching Hysteria," *New York Post,* February 15, 1935, NAACP Papers.
27. Zangrando, 125–26.
28. Guy Davenport, *The Drawings of Paul Cadmus* (New York: Rizzoli, 1989), 9.
29. Southern Commission on the Study of Lynching, 42.
30. The two African Americans, Mosby and Richmond Barthé, who used complete nudity in their works depicted the male body intact.
31. Goodleman's truncated torso of polished, wood-stained ebony was made more powerful by his adaptation of carved, African representations of the body.
32. Mary Johnston, "Nemesis," *Century Magazine,* May 1923.
33. This statement was made in 1901 and is quoted in Earl Ofari Hutchinson, *The Assassination of the Black Male Image* (Los Angeles: Middle Passage Press, 1994), 11–12.
34. For a visually stimulating excursion of this kind, see Guy C. McElroy, *Facing History: The Black Image in American Art, 1710–1940* (Washington, D.C.: Corcoran Gallery of Art, 1990).

35. Although White courted Barthé heavily to have him exhibit in *An Art Commentary,* Barthé withheld the sculpture, preferring not to implicate himself in the political web of the NAACP program. *The Mother* was a centerpiece in his one-man show held in New York a few weeks after White's show closed.

36. Wiegman, 243.

37. Wiegman, 243.

38. Michael Hatt, " 'Making a Man of Him': Masculinity and the Black Body in Mid-Nineteenth-Century American Sculpture," *Oxford Art Journal* 15, no. 1 (1992): 21–35.

39. Sternberg, quoted in Park, 347.

40. The 1937 version, titled *The Lynching,* was reproduced in Alain Locke, *The Negro in Art: A Pictorial Record of the Negro Artist and of the Negro Theme in Art* (1940; New York: Hacker Art Books, 1968), 197.

41. Jessie D. Ames, *The Changing Character of Lynching: Review of Lynching, 1931–1941* (Atlanta: Commission on Interracial Cooperation, 1942).

42. Kobena Mercer, *Welcome to the Jungle* (New York: Routledge, 1994), 138.

43. This 1942 photograph was published in Geoffrey Holder, *Adam* (New York: Viking, 1986).

44. Letter to Mrs. Harry Payne Whitney.

10

JOHN L. JACKSON, JR.

THE SOLES OF BLACK FOLK

THESE REEBOKS WERE MADE FOR RUNNIN' (FROM THE WHITE MAN)

(for brothers fred hampton & mark clark, murdered 12/4/69 by chicago police at 4:30 a.m. while they slept) . . . were the street lights out? / did they [the police] darken their faces in combat? / did they remove their shoes to creep softer? / could you not see the white of their eyes, / the whi-te of their deathfaces? / or did they just turn into ghost dust and join the night fog?

> —Don L. Lee (Haki Madhabuti), "One Sided Shootout"

There was no deceiving him [the slavemaster]. His work went on in his absence almost as well as in his presence; and he had the faculty of making us feel as if he was ever present with us. This he did by surprising us. He seldom approached the spot where we worked openly, if he could do so secretly. Such was his cunning that we used to call him, amongst ourselves, "the snake." When we were at work in the cornfield, he would sometimes crawl on his hands and knees to avoid detection, and all at once would rise nearly in our midst, and scream out, "Ha, ha! Come, come! Dash on, dash on!" This being his mode of attack, it was never safe to stop a single minute. His comings were like a thief in the night. He appeared to us as being ever at hand. He was under every tree, behind every stump, in every bush and window on the plantation. . . . He seemed to think himself equal to deceiving the Almighty.

> —Frederick Douglass, *Narrative of the Life of Frederick Douglass, An American Slave*

Overseer, overseah, oviseah, ofiseah, offiseah, officer. They both ride horses.

> —KRS-One, "The Sound of the Police"

POLICING THEORY

This essay is an attempt beyond myself, outside myself: a trying out of new techniques ("new" for me, at least), new "voices." It is an excerpt from an ethnography (of sorts) on Crown Heights, where I live, and on the folks who live there with me. But it is not a writing about all of Crown Heights and may not even be, in the final analysis, about any of it. It is more about "the State" in (and of) Crown Heights, about the ways that "State" is thought about and talked about by a few of the people who call this section of Brooklyn home. But this piece is also about theory, about theorization, about the ways we often theorize our lives, our worlds, out of existence, out of this world and into an "other" world many conceptual dimensions removed from our own—the difference between a "model" and the thing "modeled" after.

Theories often serve to displace and subsume the subjects about which they comment and contend. The wonderfully complicated world in which we live is relegated to the calm, cool, and calculated lines of sociological manuscripts that tie up all the loose ends of analysis such that "the theory" ignores the ways in which lived lives exist beyond the hypothesis, outstretch it, outlive it. Indeed, Nietzsche seems right on the mark when the dude says, "All philosophers have handled for millennia has been conceptual mummies. Nothing actual has escaped their hands alive."[1] It is, indeed, not our hands that we have to worry about in this case, but our minds: minds capable of creating a world and destroying it in the very same instant. Surely, to theorize is often a homicidal act, a killing of the heterogeneity of the world, a knife thrust into the very heart of life. With some of this in mind, I will be writing as much about writing as about some of the people in a small section of Crown Heights where I've conducted fieldwork. Ralph Ellison, discussing the ways scholars have theorized about the inner city, once said,

> I don't deny that these sociological formulas are drawn from life, but I do deny that they define the complexity of Harlem. They only abstract it and reduce it to proportions which the sociologists can manage. I simply don't recognize Harlem in them. And I certainly don't recognize the people in Harlem whom I know. Which is by no means to deny the ruggedness of life there, nor the hardship, the poverty, the sordidness, the filth. But there is something else in Harlem, something subjective, willful, and complexly and compellingly human. It is that "something else" that challenges the sociologists who ignore it. . . . It is that something else which makes for our strength, which makes for our endurance and our promise. This is the proper subject for the Negro American writer. Hell, he doesn't have to spend all that tedious time required to write novels [or ethnographies] simply to repeat what the sociologists and certain white intellectuals are broadcasting like a zoo full of parrots.[2]

What was true about the sociological depiction of Harlem then is probably even truer now. And Harlem, in my mind's pineal eye, ain't but a theoretical hop, skip, and jump from its cousin Crown Heights. As different as the two places are, they have an inner sameness that I often recognize (a recognition, let me be quick to add, that shouldn't be misconstrued as a nod to ethnic absolutism). Furthermore, much of Ellison's critique rings true for attempts at talking about both places in the here and now of the late twentieth century.

But how do you talk about and "represent" that "something else" to which Ellison refers, a "something else" that has escaped treatment in traditional academic discourse on the inner city? I use "represent" in the sense of not only "to depict," but "representin' " in the sense evoked in "street" vernacular (bandied about by b-boys and b-girls alike), which means that one is speaking for (and as one of) those commonly left unrepresented in public forums: representin' for the peoples! The complexity and richness of Crown Heights circa 1990, of the "something else" in Crown Heights (a something else that escapes traditional social science discourse as a chameleon does its attacker) are not easy to represent in either sense of the word. I can't begin to grasp ways of doing it accurately. By retheorizing theory, maybe? By tactilizing theory? Praxisorizing it? Exorcising it of its nineteenth-century demons? These are some of the rhetorical feats that this essay (in the true sense of an attempt) is pretending to do: To slip its words in and out of knots, through and around the impossible, so as to arrive at a rendering of Crown Heights as alive, complex, and ungraspable as the wonderfully somethingelsical place itself. Nineteenth-century writing modes, God bless their tired soul, don't cut it. Feigned authority and objectivity just won't do either. Not for the something else. We have to make writing right, or at least more right, before we are left with nothing of importance. I must take Cixous's approach to writing seriously. It resonates with me:

> When I write, I become like a thing, a wild beast. A wild beast doesn't look back when it leaps, doesn't check that people are watching and admiring. Those who do not become wild beasts when they write, who write to please, write nothing that has not already been written, and forge extra bars for our cage.[3]

We need new (dare I say, bestial!) ways of writing to capture our new, ever changing ways of being in the world. That is my belief, and this offering is an attempt, a try (a necessary failure) in just that very endeavor: my representin' of my peoples, an attempt to capture, however inexhaustively, the multilayered lives lived by real people who (it can be argued) often have to make up their worlds and their lives as they go along. And an ethnography/essay/theory that keeps up with people in such a protean world must be just as fluid, as ever shifting, as chameleon-like as they are. Or at least will try to be.

THE LAW-MAINTAINING SILENCE AND THE LAW-FOUNDING SILENCE

It begins with a scene. Of cops and criminals. Of sirens and sounds. The police always seem to be playing hide-and-seek with the public. One moment it is a silent night, dark, almost dank; the police are ever cloaked and camouflaged, waiting to pounce on any wrongdoer. The next minute, presto, like the prover-

JOHN L. JACKSON, JR.

bial rabbit out the hat, there are roaring sirens accompanied by flashing blues to reds to blues to reds.

It was a hot summer night in Crown Heights; in the rest of the city as well, I suspect. Some of the folk living in my mom's housing project complex (my "informants") are outside their buildings: several standing on porches, a few dangling from fire escapes, and even more aligning front walkways, all in an attempt to escape the sweltering apartments inside. (Point of clarification: it is "my mom's housing project complex" because she pays rent there, not because she owns it.) Anyway, I too am out on a walkway, shuffling cards and fellowship-ping with neighbors. My mom's apartment has to be well over 130 degrees, and I'll be damned, I tell myself, if I'll be cooped up in that kind of uncomfortable heat all night.

A car speeds through the 12:00 A.M. street in front of my mom's building and stops on the corner. Eyes crawl up from "spades" and "bullshit" card games (played with red and white checkered cards on foldout tables) to see "whah de fuck is goin' on out dere!?" Stokes is sixty-one and has lived in Crown Heights for some fifteen years. He is the first person to vocalize everyone's preoccupation with that car's sudden screeching. Before Stokes came to Crown Heights, he was in Harlem for another twenty years, but he is originally from Jamaica. Most of the black folks in this area, myself included, are no more than one or two generations removed from the Caribbean. (In fact, I ain't been to Antigua—where my mom was born—but once, and still there are moments when I feel as Caribbean as I do American.) Stokes continues speaking as the now silent automobile rests momentarily motionless across the street.

"What de hell is goin' on in dis muddahfuckah?" he asks.

"You ain't really asking, cause you know we nah know!"

The quick retort is from Kyrle, my spades partner on this night. The two men then begin to theorize about the driver of the car. He is at first said to be a drug dealer, but then it is decided that he could not be, because the car is only a Honda and everyone knows that dealers make enough money for Benzes and BMWs. He is next deemed an undercover cop, but once again they remind themselves that it is a Honda, and police—undercover or not, the men decide—drive American cars.

What happened next was high drama, even for Brooklyn. A man and a woman were in the car, and then spilled out onto the sidewalk screaming and yelling at one another. The man began to hit the woman and wouldn't stop. The police must have been called as soon as the suspiciously screeching car made its entrance on the block, because within a few minutes, they arrived from every direction. The silent block rang out with sirens and flashing blues to reds to blues. But that is not even when the real criminal apprehending began. The cops surrounded the vehicle. Put the man who was driving the Honda (now handcuffed) into the backseat of one squad car and the woman into the backseat of another. They took statements from some passersby and arranged for the car to be towed. The cops were just about done when a sound rang out in the streets. It was a rap song: "Fuck the Police," by the group Niggas With Attitudes. The shocked police began to scurry to and fro attempting to identify the source of the musical disturbance. The officers began to move in our general direction, in the direction of the projects. A dozen or so cops dashed up the steps of the building from which the music was emanating, a blue flood flowing together in an almost poetic unison. Trying to catch the sound bandit, they shot right by us and into the bowels of another building, the one adjacent to ours. "Whah de hurry?" Stokes asked, laughing and shuffling cards. I thought, "Yeah, what is the hurry? It isn't to get there before the music stops, is it? I mean, do they feel that this blasting of anti-cop rhetoric damages them in any way? Maybe this is the police public relations department trying to squash bad press." In any case, we simply continued to play cards that night. Long after the police came down the steps with their handcuffed culprit (Tyrone, one of my homies from junior high school). Long after the blue and white police cars, the hide-and-seek cars, took off their flashing lights and disappeared back into the night. Long after the sun came up. We were still playing card games and trying to beat the heat. It was summertime, and the living was easy.

BLACK OR WHITE

Desmond Robinson is a black cop. But he was shot because he was almost too good a cop, someone able to go so deep undercover that he looked too unlike a cop for his own good. His fellow officers called him "the Phantom." His bald-headed, bearded, earringed face was deemed so unlike the look of the proverbial police officer that he was said to simply blend into the "fluid mass" of commuters that is New York City's subway system, the site where he did much of his undercover police work. For some of the residents in my mom's apartment building, to talk about black cops at all is to talk about the ways Uncle Sam and Uncle Tom are blood brothers.

"They said he didn't look like a cop," Clarence, Stokes's thirty-something-year-old son, says to me as we walk into my mom's building. "Didn't look like a cop?!! He sure didn't, but that was before he took off the uniform. He didn't look like a cop when he was born. He came out his momma's womb and the doctor was like 'damn, you don't look nothin' like a cop.' Got no business in that shit. Like fighting a war for these fuckers. Hell no!!"

"What do cops look like?" I ask him, pressing the buzzer down in the lobby for my mom to let me up.

"Shit, not like us!"

But like what? Maybe those two men who came to the car door weren't impostors, impersonating police, but police impersonating police. They had badges dangling from white strings around their necks. I was all of eleven (or twelve) at the time and was sitting in my mom's car in the parking lot of a Key Food Supermarket not too far from Crown Heights. I used to hate going into those stores because when they were packed (as they usually were when my mom shopped), she made me hold a place for her on one of the lines. So on this evening, I pleaded my case and won: I stayed in the car, reading comic books and listening to the car's tape deck. I hadn't been alone ten minutes when two plainly dressed white men (in jeans, T-shirts, and denim jackets) came up to the car, one on each side, and tried the locks. They were locked; I wasn't no fool. The men then knocked on the car's window, displaying their badges (hung, remember, neatly around their necks), and motioned for me to unlock the doors. I froze. All of a sudden I was scared shitless. It was a preteen terror that I, in retrospect, often dismiss as ridiculous. But was it? I never did unlock the car doors, and when they saw that I would not, they simply left, vanished, went back into the world, into the night, from which they so mysteriously came. To this day I imagine that they were criminals with fake badges trying to take advantage of some unsuspecting soul—my own. But maybe they were worse: cops trying to take advantage of some unsuspecting soul. In the movies (and from that fact alone, I'll assume, in "real life," too) what a cop most dreads to hear are the words "hand in your badge and your gun!" But which is more deadly and/or important? Aren't the badge and the gun connected? Doesn't the one only have its full power with the other to back it up? If a gun had come out of one of the pockets of those badge-necklaced men, then surely their gestures to unlock the door would have carried more weight with my eleven- or twelve-year-old self, no? But instead, I froze—didn't respond. The two men eventually left, and I merely waited nervously for my mother to return—never telling her what had happened, mind you, because that would have been a surefire way of precluding any possibility of my ever escaping those supermarket lines again. And in some strange way, those lines seemed a bit more menacing than anything else I could have possibly been thrown from across the thin blue one.

CASES OF CROOKED COPS

Were those two badge-donning men cops, thieves, or some weird mixture of the two? Some of the cases that make their way from person to person in Crown Heights on cops are incredibly interesting stuff. Scary examples of "cops gone bad," bureaucratic corruption, the "all going to hell in a handbasket" argument. The stories are told during card games, on hot summer nights, in front of buildings and fire escapes. They are passed around at the dinner table, almost a Malinowskian-described kula ring, where I pass mom the tale of the cop who beat up Charles ("Yeah, mom, Charles, that one you are always calling the pretty Indian-looking one!") for no reason at all and she reciprocates with an anecdote about her stepfather being framed by police in Manhattan about twenty years ago for some crime he could never have committed because he had only been in the United States all of six minutes at the time. And the tales that are passed on get bigger and bigger. Grosser and grosser. More and more horrifying. It becomes a kind of storytelling potlatch always resupplied with newer and fresher tales. Like the three cops in Brooklyn's Seventy-third Precinct, about ten minutes from my mom's window (within a siren's earshot), who were charged with (and convicted for) conducting some one hundred illegal shakedowns of drug dealers; one cop even threatened to feed a drug dealer to a pit bull unless the dealer turned over hidden crack and cash (that incredibly dynamic duo). But nefarious police exploits didn't need the Mollen commission to get police corruption unto the lips of Crown Heights residents. The Rodney King fiasco was also icing, though not the cake itself. Police Commissioner Kelly evoking Durkheimian notions of anomie at a press conference to talk about sections of the police force wasn't necessary either. Nor was the media's oversaturated coverage of other shakedown rings in the city, the most notorious being the Seventy-fifth Precinct bunch spearheaded by Police Officer Dowd, by now a legend in his own time.

Indeed, the police are assumed by many people in the area where I live to be corrupt; that is considered the norm. And this was before all the hoopla and media attention. It may not have always been the perception, but it tends to be now. Even the good cop is a crooked officer, because there is no fundamental disconnectedness between the good and the bad one. They are the same animal, one and the same: both bad because the system allows even one bad cop to exist at all.

"A good cop ain't but a little less bad than da bad," Stokes says to me over another card game on another hot night in Crown Heights. "Don't be fooled. A good cop de rock and a bad cop is de fuckin' hard place, as God my witness." He says this and I think (strange as it may sound) of Walter Benjamin: the law-maintaining violence of the police force is so congenitally connected with its law-founding violence that the two become inextricably one. Indeed the police do become like Madhabuti's "ghost dust," periodically merging with fog and then condensing to perform heinous acts (like the killing of a sleeping Fred Hampton and Mark Clark) only to disperse once again into the fog (especially in a fogless summer) from whence they came. Even the shiny, silver-colored badge is hidden in the fog, merges with the white opaqueness of the foggy night, only to lose some of its access to the light of truth, justice, and the American way. Is the badge no longer sacred to the cop or to the non-cop in Crown Heights? The sacredness of the badge is constantly being contested, but that is a qualified contestation—because the badge is still important, still special. Is it the mark of the beast? The badge of corruption? The police badge cannot be allowed to be soiled, which is why it is given in when a cop is discharged or suspended: those dreaded words, "hand in your badge and your gun." Not one or the other, but the two together. Should the badge be sacred? Must it be so for the "good cops" to do their jobs? To profane the badge, to have it thought of as less-than-sacred, to be de-badged, is that reminiscent of Elias Cannetti's unmasking? Is the police officer always already a phony, a fake, a charlatan? "You were put here to protect us," raps KRS One, at a crowded hip-hop club on the mysterious Crown Heights/Flatbush border, "but who protects us from you?"

COINTELPRO FOCUS GROUP

I organize a meeting (one cold Sunday afternoon in November) with several of the young folk in the community. I am really being the anthropologist now, or at least a sociologist, I think to myself—collecting data on people's subjective realities. It will be taped, and I have a few pages of questions I am itching to ask.

Damon, one of my most talkative informants, wasn't there. He was supposed to be, but he didn't show up. Thomas and Carl did show, along with two of their friends, Ray and Tick, guys I had never met before. The focus group was in my mom's apartment, and we talked a little bit about a bunch of topics. Some here and some there. At times the entire affair seemed out of control. The television, tuned to a basketball game, made the entire endeavor damn near impossible. The Knicks were playing, and folks were more interested in the game than in me. "But I am gathering data," I told myself. "So this is gonna be invaluable." *(Cut to the end of the focus group.)*

"Yo, have you ever heard of COINTELPRO?" Thomas asked me as he opened the front door to leave. "You need to check that shit out. You interested in the police and the government and shit, you gotta be checkin' that bad-boy out."

"I do have the book," I replied. "At least I think I do." I went to my junky bookcase. "I ain't read this shit, yet. Give me an overview!"

"It is like, blowing shit up like the World Trade Center on shit like the ways that the Black Panthers and shit were fuckin' totally infiltrated and shit. Like how folks was like bein' framed by the government and the government be knowin' that shit but won't do shit about it. Deep shit!!"

"Make a motherfucker go crazy." Chuck got up to stretch as he spoke. "A niggah read that shit and start tweakin' out. Wanna Colin Ferguson motherfuck-ers and shit."

"What ya'll think about that shit?" I ask, ever the question-hurling Anthro-Man (I should have carved an "A" onto my chest). "I mean 'bout that whole Colin Ferguson shit?"

"Damn, that was a while back, huh," Charles said and stepped a little ways back into the apartment. "Shit, time be flyin. That was like a year ago."

"More than a year, I think, but what do you think about it?" — Anthro-Man again.

"What do you think?" Charles asks, doing the old informant switcheroo.

"I don't know. Blood must've had some serious problems."

"Nah, that niggah was just handlin' his business. Fuck around and lay me off, and I'll be a subway-shootin' motherfucker, too."

Charles laughs. I am ever the graduate student, and my own laughter is muffled by thoughts of Kafka's Joseph K. Of the differences and similarities between him and Colin F.: that Colin may have known something that Joseph did not. Or vice versa?: That to escape the power of the law, if only for a second, is to transgress it. In the end you still lose, but you go out with a bang and not a whimper. I think of Jean Genet, that superthief who chose to be a criminal. To remove his mask. The fellahs leave, and I finish watching the basketball postgame show.

UNMASKING

If de-badging can be said to be akin to unmasking in many ways, what does the Colin Ferguson LIRR massacre and the Desmond Robinson shooting (not to mention the Rodney King extended-play) unmask about the police and those people being policed? How do masks fool their wearers as well as onlookers?

> We wear the mask that grins and lies, / It hides our cheeks and shades our eyes, / This debt we pay to human guile; / With torn and bleeding hearts we smile, / And mouth with myriad subtleties / Why should the world be overwise, / In counting all our tears and sighs? / Nay, let them only see us, while / We wear the mask. / We smile, but, O great Christ, our cries / To thee from tortured souls arise. / We sing, but oh, the clay is vile / Beneath our feet, and long the mile; / But let the world dream otherwise, / We wear the mask.

This famous poem distills and articulates poetically the often mentioned notion of the masking of black identity. Paul Laurence Dunbar is attempting to articulate the ways African Americans can be said to shield their (our) true selves from the rest of America. We smile and shuck and jive and laugh around white people when, he argues, as a function of our blackness in a white world, we are never truly happy human beings. The mask fools the rest of the country, in Dunbar's opinion, but can it also be said to fool those who wear it? But what would happen if we took off that mask? If we no longer let it fool anyone? Attorney William Kunstler uses the term "black rage" to describe Colin Ferguson's horrific act. If it is a black rage, is every black person, as a function of their blackness (a slavery-exploited blackness) prone to such pure rage in the dark recesses of their (our) "tortured souls"? Do we still see the slave overseer/master, Massa Covey, behind every tree? How much of masking ourselves is about fooling ourselves? Is to know the truth to gun down people on the LIRR? Do the rumors unmask? Like the one Damon told me (a fact, he says, not a rumor) about Snapple beverages being owned by the Ku Klux Klan? Or the other one I heard from my cousin about representatives from Procter and Gamble appearing on Donahue to tell the world that proceeds from their products go to Satanic cults—and that it doesn't matter what people think about that fact because their products are everywhere? Or another one about Reebok sneakers being made by a South African company to support the Apartheid effort with black U.S. dollars (a rumor so pervasive that Reebok had to take out a full-page advertisement in a national magazine to dispel it)? Are rumors more powerful than facts? Are they more true than "the truth"?

"I wouldn't fuck with Tropical Fantasy," Richard, who lives across the hall from me, says as I go with him to the corner store and pick out one of the bright, tropically colored bottles from the freezer.

"Why not?"

"I heard that they be putting shit in there to sterilize us. Sterilize black men."

"Where did you hear that shit?"

"Fucking all around. You know it is probably true. They only sell that shit in black neighborhoods. Like malt liquor and shit. If motherfuckers wanted to wipe us the fuck out, which you know they do, they know to hit us with the fried chicken and the fuckin' alcohol."

"White folk drink alcohol and shit," I reply, still holding the bottle of Tropical Fantasy in my hand but keeping the freezer door ajar.

"Yeah, but I bet they ain't drinkin' shit like this." He points to bottles of Olde English Malt Liquor and Red Bull, served in forty-ounce containers. "And you damn well know they ain't got no Tropical Fantasy in they shit, either. Pepsi. Coke. That is the shit that they drink. And I ain't gonna be the niggah caught out there when the eleven o'clock news starts talking about some scandal at Tropical Fantasy and shit. By then it would be too late for you muggs. Shit, and if that stuff ain't fucked with by whitey, Sprite, Coke and the regular shit tastes better than all them cheap shits anyways."

I put the soda back and get Poland Spring bottled water.

"I am glad you ain't pick up that Evian," Richard chuckles and grabs a box of Philly Cigar blunts. "You know what KRS-One said 'bout that shit, 'it is naive spelled backwards.' You betta recognize."

Evian *is* naive spelled backwards, I think to myself. And oddly enough, the Boston tea party iconography on Snapple bottles does look a little like the landing of a slave ship on U.S. shores (and what's to say that the "K" by the picture doesn't, in fact, stand for, as the theory goes, Ku, Klux, Klan?). Rumors speak the unspeakable. They talk about the world in ways that are unsettling. Unmasking? And they have a wonderfully proficient way of co-opting more official truths to their cause. For surely, as many informants have told me, the Tuskegee experiments (where black men with syphilis were allowed, by W.H.O. doctors, to die untreated in the name of science—so that science could have its data) were, in fact, real. And isn't there documented proof, some informants asked me, that the first settlers gave peace offerings to the Native Americans that were blankets laced with smallpox? So why would the rumor of AIDS as manmade, U.S. government-engineered, black-people-killing disease seem strange—especially when AIDS rates in Africa are said to be astronomically high? Rumors use all of that, sift through the facts, and come out clearer, truer, stronger.

"When we steal, we take tangible shit," Damon says to me. "A TV, a stereo and shit. Objects and shit. When white folks steal they steal souls and shit, they steal cultures. We kill people, they kill peoples. That's the difference. Look at all that shit they done did to us and tell me they ain't evil."

SOULTHEFT

"But people don't really believe that stuff, do they?" One of my colleagues at Columbia asks me this question over some Ethiopian food at Massawa's in Manhattan. "They don't believe that that is true, do they?" About as much as they believe the smallpox blankets, I reply. Or the Tuskegee experiments. Or the Atlantic slave trade, for that matter. Are the so-called paranoid feared because they have an ultra-finalized view on the world, one that is not open to discussion or change? There is obviously some Soulstealing going on in this world of sirens and red/blue/red/blue flashing lights, but where do we reasonably draw our line in the sand? All substance can dissolve into nonsubstance, into mere idea. There is power in conspiratorial finality. It is what the scientist is looking for. The chemistrial-conspiracy that makes all chemical reactions and equations clear. It is what anthropologists long for: that metanarrative, meganarrative, which explains all mankind in a few sparse lines. They all want conspiracy. They want the power of paranoia. Aren't conspiracy theories simply Structural Functionalism on acid? Structural Functionalists want their analyses to read like "who shot JFK?" where everything fits snugly in its place and no rock is left unturned, no hand remains unsoiled. When forty-ounce bottles of Olde English Malt Liquor are swallowed, passed, and poured for the folk not present (because snuffed out by the very real unreality of violent inner-city life), conspiracy is more than a belief, more than a mere idea. It becomes incontestable, doxa, habitus. It becomes a given. All else can be added to it or taken away, but it is beyond modification. The particularities and justifications (the evidence) are immaterial, unimportant, unnecessary. That Snapple could be owned by the KKK is as real as the death rates of young black men in Harlem. And a search for answers to horrific questions (like why are black folk where they are in America now?) answers become as horrifying as the questions. And Snapple, Reebok, or some other commodity cum traitor is as reasonable a culprit as any other.

I met Damon and his homeboy, Thomas, on an early Saturday morning in January. Thomas is a black Hebrew Israelite and about twenty-five years old. The young folk in the neighborhood don't have no beef, no static, with his ass cause they know he is, as one person put it, "all about some serious shit, being a black Hebrew Israelite and all." This day he laughed and said that I was trying to look like an Israelite. I had not trimmed my beard for a while, and the Black Israelites believe, based on their biblical teachings, that one shouldn't. Thomas tells me that he wants me to read with them, to go to some meetings with them. He wanted to convert a "niggah" to the truth, he said.

"Black folk gotta realize, they ain't African," he tells me as we part company. "We are from the twelve tribes of Israel. All that Egypt, Africa shit is bullshit. But don't worry, I'm gonna show you the light."

HOLLYWOOD

"Yo, come here," Thomas says, "check this commercial out." The TV is on in the apartment that Thomas shares with a friend of his, another Black Hebrew Israelite, Bigs. It is a McDonald's commercial set in an apartment building full of black folks.

"Yo, you know I been to Hamburger University?" I mutter over the television advertisement. "McDonald's college for Hamburgerology."

"Where the fuck is that?" Bigs asks.

"Near Chicago," I answer, my eyes still glued to the commercial. Bigs nods and continues pouring Fruit Loops into a glass bowl.

The commercial is a trip and a half. The bags of McDonald's food give off a mist/vapor that circulates through the building and forces other tenants to crave the "twoallbeefpattiesspecialsaucelettucecheesepicklesonions on a sesame-seed bun." The tenants don't seem to know why they suddenly crave McDonald's. They can't see the white mist (visible to the TV audience) flowing through the building. They just want McDonald's and don't seem to know why. And why should they? They are not smelling the food, not using their nostrils. They are getting hypnotized by the very power of the food. I think of Marx's notion of commodity fetishism, about how the magic of the McDonald's food is being played up in this commercial. Bigs tells us that he thinks McDonald's food sucks, but Thomas begs to differ. Our collective interest in the television commerical leads to a discussion of TV shows and movies. When the focus of our conversation lands on films, Thomas decides to "school me" on Hollywood.

"It is actually the wood that witches and warlocks used in the olden days to make magic wands and broom sticks. Straight up."

"How you know that?" I ask.

"Man, we got mad info on these folk. They be tellin' on themselves left and right. You can get that shit from they own books. Like I told you before, this shit is about wars. About good and evil. About God and the Devil and which side you choose. The founding fathers and shit was Masons. Every one of them. Washington on down. You heard of the skull and cross bones shit that Bush was a member of at Yale or Harvard or some shit. That shit is all tied to the same thing. It is about Satanism. These motherfuckers are about the Devil, man. They cast spells! You think this shit ain't real you better do your own research. It is like I done told you, it is not about converting and shit to a particular religion or being an African. God has a chosen people, Jacob's seed. Us. And he has peoples he hates: Esau's offspring, the children of Edom, white people. And he describes who is who in the Bible. And God is gonna destroy these Satan worshippers. But for now they trying to fortify they ranks and shit. To cast their spells on the masses. Keep them stupid and ignorant. Hollywood is straight-up about casting spells. Do you notice that every time some shit comes out in movies it is only some time later and it is out in real life. They be using that shit to get us ready for what they gonna do to us. They want to get us prepared for what is to come, for the ways they are gonna come out of the closet with they wicked shit. Man, don't sleep on these motherfuckers. This shit is real. They want us to accept anything as okay. You be watching those talk shows and seein' how they are gettin' us ready for a Sodom and Gomorrah of blasphemy against God. It used to be that just being homosexual was wrong. Now that shit is accepted, and they got ya'll accepting that shit as normal so they doin' more and more crazy shit. Geraldo got shit like lesbian sisters in love, or men who turn into women and shit, 'cause they want you ready for the perverted world of chaos they are gonna institute, their new world of chaos. That is the new world order they lookin' for."

Thomas promises to bring me the documentation for his Hollywood stuff. And he stands by its authenticity. He claims that he can back it up, that he can back it all up. He says that the Black Hebrew Israelites understand what is going on with black folk in America, about this very literal casting of spells on the populace. He talks a little more about talk shows and motion pictures, about the country's top grossing movie at that time, *Stargate*. Jaye Davidson, the male actor who played a man who fooled the audience into thinking he was a woman in *The Crying Game*, is Ra here, a god of ancient Egyptian fame. The movie makes Ra an alien from outer space with a raspy, coarse ("devilish," says Thomas) voice and glowing eyes. Not a god, but a space alien. Thomas finds this alteration particularly meaningful.

"They want us to know they got folk comin' from outer space for our asses. And all day, man, all day, with their movies, their television and their music, they are trying to fatten us up for the slaughter."

NOTES

1. Friedrich Nietzsche, *Twilight of the Idols; and the Anti-Christ* (Baltimore: Penguin, 1968), 45.
2. Ralph Ellison, "A Very Stern Discipline," *Harper's Magazine*, March 1967.
3. Hélène Cixous, "We Who Are Free, Are We Free?" in *Freedom and Interpretation*, ed. Barbara Johnson (New York: Basic Books, 1993).

four

CRACKING THE CODE

EXPOSING THE NATION'S RACIAL NEUROSES

11

FELICIA A. KORNBLUH

WHY GINGRICH?

WELFARE RIGHTS AND RACIAL POLITICS, 1965–1995

Briefly, let me explain how I arrived at the topic of this essay. I am writing a study of the welfare rights movement of the 1960s and 1970s and legal efforts to codify a right to welfare in the United States. The movement for welfare rights was a loosely federated organizing effort among recipients of Aid to Families with Dependent Children (since 1935, AFDC has been the primary welfare program for unmarried, divorced, or separated mothers and their children) and other public assistance programs.[1] Most of the activists were African-American or Puerto Rican; about half lived in New York City.[2] In an effort that peaked between 1968 and 1970, these low-income activists worked closely with a mostly white cohort of poverty lawyers, many of whose salaries were paid by the federal government's Office of Economic Opportunity (OEO). Together, the activists and lawyers sought to change the legal status of poor people in the United States, both by expanding poor people's access to quotidian legal services and by raising constitutional questions in higher courts about poverty as a source of discrimination comparable to race or ethnicity.[3]

In my background reading for this project, I found that there are three main ways that the welfare rights movement has been discussed in the literature: as a movement of black women, by black women's historians;[4] as a radical movement of the poor, by scholars of U.S. social movements;[5] and as a terrible disaster, by people who write about the Democratic Party and the rise of conservatism in recent U.S. politics. I found that I was comfortable with the approach of the black women's historians and that of the social movement scholars, but profoundly uncomfortable with the way writers on the rise of conservatism presented the facts about welfare rights and interpreted them. I was also impressed by the great distance between the first two schools of interpretation and the third, and by the degree to which different communities of scholars seemed to be writing past one another on this issue. I decided to begin locating myself within the literature on welfare rights by explicating some of the assumptions of the third school (which has, of the three, by far the most political cachet and largest readership), and unravelling some of the myths on which it appears to be based.

Distorted memories of the welfare rights movement like those that appear in the literature on the rise of conservatism—which presents welfare rights as an out-of-control excrescence of black politics in the late 1960s—are significant in part because they are often called into service in arguments over welfare retrenchment. In January 1995, the conservative political scientist Lawrence Mead drew on fears of a renascent welfare rights movement to argue in favor of tight controls over the behavior of welfare recipients, but against the Republican congressional leadership's plan to redistribute authority over AFDC to the states. The welfare rights movement, Mead said, "has been in retreat for twenty years. If anything could refire it, it would be the abandonment of national welfare standards.[6] In a major magazine profile that emphasized his national leadership on cutting welfare, Governor Tommy Thompson of Wisconsin remembered that his conversion to the antiwelfare faith occurred on the day in September 1969 when the Milwaukee welfare rights group demonstrated for higher benefits on the floor of the Wisconsin statehouse.[7]

Recent journalistic and scholarly writing on the rise of conservatism is important not only because of the way it distorts the history of welfare rights. Although I have a high estimate of the power of this writing—which largely holds African Americans and their white liberal allies responsible for the enmity that pervades U.S. politics, and sees an excessive emphasis on race as the central problematic of our times—even I was surprised to see how frequently its central argument was invoked in public debate between the time I began thinking about this essay and the time I completed it. To take only one example: in an April 3, 1995, cover story, Richard Kahlenberg of the *New Republic* called for affirmative action based on "class, not race." Like the authors of the books on conservatism discussed below, Kahlenberg implicitly contrasted the supposedly race-blind policies of the New Deal with the racial specificity of the Great Society, and explicitly contrasted the "morally unassailable underpinnings and . . . relatively inexpensive agenda" of the civil rights movement prior to 1964 with the supposed excesses that came later.[8] He twisted Martin Luther King, Jr.'s words from *Why We Can't Wait* to draw King into support for his own policy of obliterating race-based affirmative action. In fact, King wrote, "Whenever this issue of compensatory or preferential treatment for the Negro is raised, some of our friends recoil in horror. The Negro should be granted equality, they agree; but he should ask nothing more. On the surface, this appears reasonable, but it is not realistic."[9] Following Kahlenberg's logic, the Board of Regents of the University of California system voted in July 1995 to obliterate race and ethnicity (and gender) as criteria for admitting students to their colleges, but to preserve economic background as a criterion for admissions.

I do not know where these very powerful interpretations of recent history will lead, but I do know that they are too important for race-conscious scholars to ignore.

In 1969, in a book dedicated to President Richard Nixon and Attorney General John Mitchell, a young political analyst put forth what was then a novel argument. "The principal force which broke up the Democratic (New Deal) coalition," wrote Kevin Phillips on the morning after Nixon's historic presidential victory, "is the Negro socioeconomic revolution and liberal Democratic ideological inability to cope with it." He continued: "*The Negro problem,* having become a national rather than a local one, is the principal cause of the breakup of the New Deal coalition."[10]

This argument, which seemed so original, and so conservative in its implications, when Phillips first committed it to paper, has now become the standard. Commentators from across the left-right political spectrum—from self-described social democrats like *Newsday's* Jim Sleeper, to centrist liberals like the independent journalist/historian Nicholas Lemann and the *Washington Post's* Thomas Edsall, to ardent conservatives like the think tank intellectual Charles Murray—now share essentially the same understanding of why the Democratic Party's national electoral coalition has collapsed and why politicians like Nixon in 1968, and Gingrich in 1994, have come to power.[11]

What I will call the "Negro Problem" thesis or the Phillips thesis blames an alliance of militant African Americans and misunderstanding or pernicious white reformers for making race a central issue in U.S. politics. The "Negro Problem" thesis suggests that black civil and social rights claims went too far in the mid- and late 1960s, and that white liberals and radicals were at fault for indulging those claims. White working- and middle-class voters, especially men, departed from a national Democratic Party supposedly dominated by African Americans and their white supporters.

This argument has been inestimably important. Beyond forming the basis of Republican strategy in presidential elections, the logic of the Phillips thesis has also driven *Democratic* strategizing since at least the Reagan ascendancy in 1981, and certainly including the Clinton presidential race of 1992. Because of its emergence as consensus common sense in Washington, the Phillips thesis has become one of the most powerful historical arguments in the contemporary United States.

But it is not entirely coherent.

Counter to the claims of the "Negro Problem" school, race did *not* meaningfully enter national politics in the United States only in the mid-1960s. Politics in the United States has been racialized since its inception. Certainly, the New Deal state—to which adherents of the "Negro Problem" thesis look back with such nostalgia—was racially specific. It disproportionately favored *white* Americans. Politics in the New Deal period relied on racially exclusive citizenship; the three-quarters of African Americans still living in the South were not represented, and the under one-quarter who were recent migrants to Northern cities could not yet make substantial demands on either national political party.

At the very least, a study of the historical record suggests that Phillips's phrase "Negro problem" is a misnomer for the strains that ultimately undermined the Democratic Party's ability to win presidential elections. So an interesting riddle emerges: How to explain the gap between the credibility of the Phillips thesis, at least to this historian, and its importance in much recent thinking on U.S. politics?

I will proceed in three ways. First, I will describe the contours of the "Negro Problem" thesis, gleaned from a number of important recent texts by historians and political journalists. I will take a short detour to underline treatments of the National Welfare Rights Organization of 1967–73 in this thesis. Second, I will explain why the argument lacks coherence, and I will suggest an alternative. Third, I will suggest some reasons for the strength of this interpretation despite its incoherence. Taking a methodological hint from Nell Irvin Painter's recent work on distortions in especially white feminist remembrances of Sojourner Truth, I will explore the "work" the Phillips thesis does ideologically for an interpretive community of extremely influential writers of the left, center, and right.[12]

THE "NEGRO PROBLEM"

The "Negro Problem" thesis is structured as a narrative of decline. It claims that national politics—at least *liberal* politics—used to be about class, the appropriate source of political identities and coalitions. Beginning during the Depression, Democrats represented the majority of voters, who were those at the bottom of the income ladder and in the middle. Since the mid-1960s, politics has been mostly about race, purportedly an inappropriate source of political identities and coalitions. Republicans represent the majority of voters, who are white, but also are either on the top or in the middle of the income ladder. As Thomas and Mary Edsall summarize the thesis,

> race as a national issue over the past twenty-five years has broken the Democratic New Deal "bottom-up" coalition. . . . The fracturing of the Democrats' "bottom-up" coalition permitted, in turn, those at the top of the "top-down" conservative coalition to encourage and to nurture. . . . the most accelerated upwards redistribution of income in the nation's history.[13]

The Edsalls and others hold race, and those who brought racial issues forward in the 1960s and beyond, responsible not only for popular racial enmity, but also for recent shifts in the class bases of electoral politics. The centrality of race has kept Democrats from the presidency, and harmed ordinary citizens by facilitating the aggrandizement of the rich.

The Democratic Party dominated national politics from Roosevelt's election in 1932 through Johnson's in 1964. The party's electoral victories were built on the joint allegiance to the Democrats of white urban ethnic voters in the Northeast and Midwest, rural and urban whites in the Southeast and Southwest, and, after 1936, African-American voters in the major cities outside the South.[14] Sometime after 1964, Southern and Northern whites, especially Catholics, fled from the party of Roosevelt. The Nixon victories of 1968 and 1972 are said to have proved the power of a new political arithmetic that worked uninterruptedly until at least the 1992 presidential campaign: Southern whites + Northern middle- and working-class whites + the rich = presidential victory for Republicans.[15]

What drove the white Southerners and urban Northerners away?

Left and right analysts of the demise of the New Deal coalition have coalesced in the terms with which they describe this transformation. They concede that Southern whites became Republicans mostly because of their racism. But the analysts insist that Northern whites were not just racist; they were responding to black claims that had gotten out of control, particularly after passage of the Civil Rights Act of 1964. The literature mentions three changes:

1. A change in the *geographic character* of the civil rights movement, from a "Southern" movement to a "national" one. Alternately, race itself is

seen to have shifted from a specifically Southern problematic to a "national" one.

2. A shift in the *content* of black or civil rights movement demands, from, for example, a supposed emphasis in the early 1960s on "equality of opportunity" and political participation to demands for "equality of result" in the later 1960s.

3. A change in the *relationship to the state* of black movements for social change. What seems particularly to damn the Black Panthers and the National Welfare Rights Organization, among other groups that emerged after 1964, is their engagement with the national government. Whereas the civil rights movement of the early 1960s, represented by the Southern Christian Leadership Conference and Martin Luther King, Jr., is seen to have been wholly autonomous of state agencies, the Panthers and NWRO are tarred by their occasional receipt of public funds and supposed "dependence" on assistance from laxly managed federal agencies.

But if black militants were illicitly taking succor and cash from Democratically controlled state agencies, why didn't someone do something about it? How could the Democrats themselves, who controlled both houses of Congress and the presidency from 1961 to 1968, have driven away their loyal white voters? Members of the "Negro Problem" school answer by telling stories of "unintended consequences." For the journalist Nicholas Lemann and the historian Allen Matusow, the Democratic Party suffered from the "unintended consequences" of its War on Poverty, particularly Community Action Programs (CAP) spawned by the Economic Opportunity Act of 1964. Unbeknownst to President Johnson and his wise men in Congress, Community Action was a time bomb lobbed into the War on Poverty by those Matusow terms "closet radicals who would infiltrate the [government] and attempt to use it for promoting social change."[16] In an extraordinary passage, Lemann writes of the anti–juvenile delinquency programs that were models for the Community Action Programs:

> Today it is possible to view [the programs] in the same spirit with which the hero of Delmore Schwartz's story, "In Dreams Begin Responsibilities" looked at an imagined movie of his quarrelsome parents' courtship while shouting, "Don't do it!" Here was a Democratic administration, understandably heedless of the full consequences, embarking on the disastrous course of . . . helping to fund organizations that opened fissures in the urban political coalitions on which the Demo-

cratic party completely depended. At the time none of this must have been apparent.[17]

What Lemann calls "organizations that opened fissures in the urban political coalitions" at the center of Democratic Party politics were, at least in part, organizations of the poor and nonwhite, some of them intent on changing the status quo ante.

Somewhat more obscurely, Charles Murray claims that the Democrats drove away base Democratic voters through the "unintended consequences" of social policy expansions, especially the high percentage growth in cash welfare receipt in the late 1960s. "Getting rid of the stigma of welfare was a deliberate goal" of federal policy in this period, according to Murray, "but the unintended consequence was no one could disqualify himself on moral grounds from eligibility for public assistance—whether or not he was ready to help himself."[18] The Edsalls argue similarly, claiming that opposition to racism among Democrats led to a kind of intellectual deep freeze, which ultimately drove white voters away. "The repudiation of racist expression had an unintended consequence," they claim, generating "an almost censorious set of prohibitions" against talking about the supposed moral failings of the black poor—specifically their "absent fathers, crime, lack of labor-force participation, welfare dependency, [and] illegitimacy."[19]

RACIAL TENSION AND WELFARE RIGHTS

Briefly, let me underline the place of the National Welfare Rights Organization in the literature on the fall of the Democratic majority. To several of the authors who write about the Democrats' decline, the welfare rights movement is taken as perhaps the most extreme of the many social movements that flowered among African Americans in the period after 1965 and that found a hearing among liberal Democrats and some members of the white left.

Welfare rights efforts started with the organizing work of black women in Watts in 1963, and with meetings between white students and black women under the auspices of the urban Economic Research and Action Projects of Students for a Democratic Society in cities such as Cleveland, Newark, Chicago, and Boston.[20] However, to the "Negro Problem" school, which is so intent on blaming the federal government for the defection of whites from the Democratic Party, impoverished black women are relatively invisible and without agency in the history of this social movement; instead, welfare rights efforts appear as the end product of federal policy itself, or of white radical manipulation of credulous African Americans. Typically, the only black participant in the welfare rights movement who earns a mention is George Wiley, a onetime chemistry professor who served as executive director of the National Welfare Rights Organization from 1967 to 1972.

To Charles Murray, the idea for a welfare rights campaign came from bureaucrats from the War on Poverty, who "[a]s early as 1965, [were] sending emissaries to spread the word that it was morally permissible to be on welfare. OEO "Community Action grants," he claims, "provided the wherewithal for booklets, speeches, and one-on-one evangelizing by staff workers. Welfare was to be considered a right, not charity." He adds, almost as a coda, "The government's efforts were reinforced by the National Welfare Rights Organization, founded in 1966 and led by George Wiley."[21] For the journalist Jim Sleeper the National Welfare Rights effort was founded in "1965 by the radical white professors Frances Fox Piven and Richard Cloward"—theoreticians allied with the movement, but not its founders—"and by the veteran black civil rights activist George Wiley."[22]

Sleeper, who studies the end of the Democratic coalition on the relatively small stage of New York City, identifies the welfare rights movement as an outstanding culprit in inserting divisive questions of distributive justice across racial lines into an otherwise halcyon political landscape. He grants pride of place to the welfare rights movement in his chapter titled "The Politics of Polarization," in its first subsection, titled "The Elevation of Race." He blames welfare rights activists for making "race the pivot of their strategy." According to Sleeper, a self-described social democrat and sometimes contributor to *Dissent* magazine, welfare activists erred when they "characterized municipal and other unions as racist and therefore part of the problem of minority unemployment." Acknowledging that the charge of union racism was "[v]alid as a generalization," Sleeper insists that "this assertion overlooked . . . the fact that public unions were certain to change racially, anyway, as urban minorities grew in numbers and electoral strength."[23]

Thomas and Mary Edsall discuss welfare rights prominently in their chapter on "The Fraying Consensus" after 1964. They include the movement in a catalogue of excesses that drove whites away from the Democrats, including "The riots, the welfare rights movement, the black power movement, student disorders, the sexual revolution, radical feminism, recreational use of drugs such as marijuana and LSD, pornographic magazines and movies, and higher taxes."[24]

HOLES IN THE FABRIC

The most problematic assumption of the "Negro Problem" school is that "race" entered U.S. politics powerfully only in the mid-1960s. On the contrary, it is easy to argue that, from the first arrival of slave ships in the seventeenth century through the writing of the Declaration of Independence and the Constitution, and from the reinvention of the national state in the Civil War through its New Deal reformation, race-based power has been constitutive of U.S. politics.

If we look only at the state system born in the New Deal—the supposed high point for class-based politics and low point for race-based politics—a pattern of racial specificity emerges clearly. The hallmark legislation of the New Deal, the Social Security Act of 1935, which offered many workers insurance against poverty in old age and during periods of unemployment, deliberately excluded the jobs most frequently held by African Americans. Agricultural and domestic workers, laundry workers, and those employed sporadically were not eligible for old-age or unemployment insurance. Furthermore, the unemployment insurance and Aid to Dependent Children (A.D.C., later Aid to Families with Dependent Children) components of the Social Security Act were designed to be administered by individual states, *not* the federal government. This feature allowed Southern states to deny benefits to applicants during the agricultural harvest season, or, in the case of A.D.C., at any time when a white woman wanted a black housekeeper.

In his magisterial study, *An American Dilemma* (1944), Gunnar Myrdal noted that Southern states used their local power over welfare programs systematically to deny black families access to Aid to Dependent Children. He found a sizable gap between black poverty levels and the numbers of black A.D.C. clients, and pointed to state regulations demanding "suitable homes" for the recipients of public benefits (regulations the federal law allowed) as particular instruments of discrimination.[25] In an oral history of white textile mill workers, one working-class woman remarked on welfare in the 1930s,

> There was always plenty of help in Greenville because there was lots of colored people and lots of them were on welfare. I went to the welfare office lots of times and asked for somebody to do the housework and keep my child. They'd tell them that they'd have to work or they'd be took off the welfare.[26]

The pattern of race specificity that is evident in the history of A.(F.)D.C. extends across the range of New Deal social programs—to agricultural subsidies, mortgage assistance, housing construction, labor law reform, and public employment.

Democrats in the 1930s occupied a unique historical position. They were able to build a race-specific state system and thereby maintain the fealty of Southern whites, while also gaining support from recent black migrants to the urban North. The balance worked (electorally, not morally) because of the relatively small numbers of black voters in the North in the 1930s.

Four million African Americans left the South between 1940 and 1970. Most of them ultimately voted Democratic. However, they continued to lack political power proportional to their numbers. Their votes did not result in the same kinds of gains for black communities that white communities received for white votes: patronage jobs, infrastructural improvement for their urban neighborhoods, employment with construction firms and others under public contract,[27] and social insurance benefits like those offered to some workers by the Social Security Act.

If we keep in mind the exclusion of blacks from effective participation in Northern urban political machines, it is possible to begin constructing an alternative to the Phillips thesis. The "Negro Problem" writers see 1964 as a watershed year that marks the end of a black politics that Northern whites could abide, and even vote for in some national elections. They claim that black politics changed in their geographic location, their content, and their relationship to the state.

First, geographically, they have a point—although rather than calling the change one from a "Southern" to a "national" location for black political struggle, we might more accurately term it a change from a Southern to a specifically Northern focus. Moreover, when it came North, the movement for black civil rights and social advancement encountered hostilities among urban Northern whites and political elites that were perfectly comparable to the hostilities encountered in Birmingham and Montgomery in the early 1960s.

Second, when we examine the supposed change in the content of black demands after 1964, what appears is more continuity than change. Let me take up just the charge that black claims switched from an emphasis on "equality of opportunity" to one on "equality of result" (of course, this is code for affirmative action). In fact, black activists and politicians in the North had been seeking equal access to jobs, apprenticeships, and other job training for decades before the civil rights movement came North in the mid-1960s. White workers, including those in the municipal unions for which Jim Sleeper has such kind words, refused to admit blacks. They refused African Americans access to apprenticeship programs in the skilled trades and kept them out of construction unions. In the urban North, gaining "equality of opportunity" meant breaking the hold of racist unions on public contracts and apprenticeships; affirmative action was one, albeit politically divisive, method for accomplishing that end.

Third, when we examine the relationship of African-American social movements to the national state, what appears is less a transformation of black demands than an effort to overcome the anomalous lack of power that blacks had in cities where they formed an ever-increasing portion of the potential voting public. To take just the Community Action Programs and the African-American community organizations that received money or other help from them: The CAPs offered some community groups support outside the big-city political machines, drawing them into direct relationships with the federal government. When the process was successful, it could make the machine politicians very angry. But was this an "unintended consequence"? To paraphrase Allen Matusow and Nicholas Lemann, was it a tragic, decisive moment in the history of American liberalism? Probably not, given what we know about the likelihood that the political machines would incorporate their black constituents without some prodding from the federal government.

Prior to 1965, African Americans living in the South lacked political power because of effective disfranchisement; those in the North lacked power because of the exclusionary practices of political machines in the cities to which they had migrated. Northern blacks were not as badly off as their Southern counterparts prior to the mid-1960s, but they too needed something like a voting rights campaign—not to ensure their right to register to vote, but to ensure that their votes, once cast, would result in the same gains that white Democrats had already received for their electoral loyalty. Community Action Programs in at least a few localities can be seen as part of that voting rights effort.

Even if we acknowledge—as the literature on the rise of conservatism would ask its readers to do—that a major transformation occurred in the tenor of U.S. politics after 1964, and in the level of distributional conflict between whites and blacks, we might look elsewhere for explanations than solely to the faults of black activists and their white liberal allies. As suggested above, we must look first at the behavior and attitudes of working- and middle-class whites who were, after all, the ones who left the Democratic Party when it became incrementally more responsive to black demands in the 1960s than it had been previously. Second, we might look at the war in Vietnam, the effects of which are strangely understated in the "Negro Problem" literature. The Gulf of Tonkin Resolution passed Congress in August 1964, and U.S. ground troops officially arrived in Vietnam in 1965. The "hot war" in Southeast Asia generated political conflicts that did their own destructive work on Democratic majorities. The war also drained resources from the War on Poverty and supported zero-sum federal domestic policies (like the "Philadelphia Plan" for affirmative action that President Nixon supported expressly because he wanted to set organized labor and African Americans against one another)[28] that sometimes helped blacks gain access to jobs traditionally held by whites but did not create more high-wage jobs for blacks *and* whites who needed them.

THE IDEOLOGICAL WORK OF PROBLEMATIC NEGROES

There are evident holes in the fabric of the "Negro Problem" thesis. Why has it nevertheless been so powerful in U.S. political thinking? Because this historical interpretation performs valuable ideological work for writers who describe themselves as on the right, in the center, and on the left.

For those on the right, the argument of the "Negro Problem" school undergirds an argument for the abandonment of the Democrats in favor of the Republicans. By focusing on white liberals and activist blacks as the culprits in racializing U.S. politics in the 1960s, the Phillips thesis takes the burden of responsibility away from the white voters who switched parties from the conservative politicians, beginning with Barry Goldwater in 1964 and Nixon in 1968, who exploited racial tensions among Democrats in order to win at the polls.

For those in the center, the "Negro Problem" thesis removes responsibility for Democratic defeats from the shoulders of those Democratic centrists who supported the Vietnam War. It focuses attention on the African-American activists and white reformers who opposed the exclusionary practices of white urban political machines, and *diverts* attention from Democratic regulars who coexisted easily with those political machines. For centrists, the lesson of the supposed debacle of the War on Poverty is that it is a mistake to transcend accepted channels, and that too much democracy (for example, the direct participation of communities of color under the Community Action Programs) is a dangerous thing. The Phillips argument underwrites 1990s claims that the Democrats must become more conservative if they are to be politically effective—especially on issues like affirmative action, crime, welfare, feminism, and gay rights. Finally, the "Negro Problem" thesis, with its fictive construction of a class-based New Deal, contrasted with a race-based Great Society, allows centrist writers to cover their own reluctance to take racial power seriously in U.S. politics by making a purely rhetorical stand in favor of a politics of class.

For some analysts from a left-of-center perspective, the "Negro Problem" thesis removes responsibility for the dissolution of Democratic electoral majorities from the shoulders of white male labor unions and members of the white working class. Writers like Jim Sleeper would rather not know about the easily demonstrable efforts of white-dominated (especially AFL) unions in the 1930s, 1940s, 1950s, and 1960s to keep black workers out. As with the centrists, an argument that values the supposed class focus of the New Deal over the supposed racial focus of the Great Society serves the interests of leftists who still refuse to take racial power seriously. Self-proclaimed intellectuals of the left who can see only one vector of power—that of class—can take comfort from the

"Negro Problem" thesis because it makes race-conscious reformers from the 1960s look bad and, by extension, devalues race-conscious or multicultural political work of the 1990s.

Kevin Phillips, circa 1969, was an excellent Republican strategist. But he was not a good historian. A more honest, historically salient, and politically meaningful analysis of race and recent politics can emerge only if analysts depart from Phillips's precedent, cease pretending that there was a time before race mattered in the United States, and stop dreaming of the moment when problematic "Negroes" might disappear. Many voters, especially white heterosexual men, had reached a pitch of anger and frustration by the late 1980s and early 1990s; they felt left out of the major social movements of the time and saw themselves as on the losing end of social policy solutions to distributional inequality. Rather than taking their frustration as the starting point of analysis, scholars might more appropriately treat it as merely one ingredient in a complicated political mix. Such scholarship would not satisfy mainstream pundits, but it might lay the groundwork for a political arithmetic that counted the rest of us.

NOTES

Thanks to Hendrik Hartog, Daniel Rodgers, and Elizabeth Kiss for their thoughtful comments.

1. When originally included in the Social Security Act of 1935, the program was known as Aid to Dependent Children. In 1962, mothers were added as explicit beneficiaries, and the title of the program was changed to Aid to Families with Dependent Children.
2. In fact, members of the welfare rights movement ran the gamut of ethnic and racial identities, ages, and geographic regions. They included Native Americans on reservations who sought reforms in welfare programs targeted at them; Irish-American senior citizens from Boston who sought improvements in Old-Age Assistance, the federal program for the aged poor; Appalachian whites who sought better benefits under the Aid to the Totally Disabled program; and many others. However, the model welfare rights activist was a black female AFDC recipient from one of a handful of Northeastern cities.
3. For the lawyers' perspective, see Edward Sparer, "The Right to Welfare," in *The Rights of Americans: What They Are, What They Should Be*, ed. Norman Dorsen (New York: Vintage Press, 1970), 65–93; and Rand Rosenblatt, "Legal Entitlement and Welfare Benefits," in *The Politics of Law: A Progressive Critique*, ed. David Kairys (New York: Pantheon, 1982), 262–78. For an overview of the lawyers' engagement with welfare rights, see Martha Davis, *Brutal Need: Lawyers and the Welfare Rights Movement, 1960–1973* (New Haven: Yale University Press, 1993).
4. See Paula Giddings, *When and Where I Enter: The Impact of Black Women on Race and Sex in America* (New York: Bantam Press, 1984), 312–13; and

Jacqueline Jones, *Labor of Love, Labor of Sorrow: Black Women, Work, and the Family, from Slavery to the Present* (New York: Vintage Press, 1985), 306–7. Deborah Gray White's forthcoming work on black women's organizing will begin with a discussion of late nineteenth-century women's clubs and end with welfare rights.

5. See, for example, Frances Fox Piven and Richard Cloward, *Poor People's Movement: How They Succeed, Why They Fail* (New York: Pantheon, 1978); Guida West, *The National Welfare Rights Movement: The Social Protest of Poor Women* (New York: Praeger, 1981); Susan Handley Hertz, *The Welfare Mothers Movement: A Decade of Change for Poor Women?* (Washington, D.C.: University Press of America, 1981); and Lawrence Neil Bailis, *Bread or Justice: Grassroots Organizing in the Welfare Rights Movement* (Lexington, MA: Lexington Books, 1974).

6. Lawrence Mead, "Republican Welfare Reform," testimony before the U.S. Senate, Committee on Governmental Affairs, January 25, 1995, 9.

7. Norman Atkins, "Governor Get-a-Job: Tommy Thompson," *New York Times Magazine,* January 15, 1995, 24.

8. Richard Kahlenberg, "Class, Not Race," *New Republic,* April 3, 1995, 27.

9. Martin Luther King, Jr., *Why We Can't Wait* (New York: Penguin, 1964), 134. King called for a "Bill of Rights for the Disadvantaged" modeled on the GI bill of rights after World War II, which would not have been at all inexpensive. While King wanted to reach some whites as well as blacks with programs that were not explicitly race-based, he also assumed that the vast majority of recipients of the programs funded under such a bill of rights would be African-American.

10. Kevin Phillips, *The Emerging Republican Majority* (New Rochelle, NY: Armonk Publishing, 1969), 37, 39.

11. Although he is not so easy to place on a left-center-right spectrum, I mean to include also the historian Allen Matusow, in *The Unraveling of America: A History of Liberalism in the 1960s* (New York: Harper Torchbooks, 1984).

12. Nell Irvin Painter, "Representing Truth: Sojourner Truth's Knowing and Becoming Known," *Journal of American History* 81, no. 2 (September 1994): 461–92.

13. Thomas Edsall, with Mary Edsall, *Chain Reaction: The Impact of Race, Rights, and Taxes on American Politics* (New York: Norton, 1992), 5–6.

14. On the shift in black political allegiances in the 1930s, see Nancy J. Weiss, *Farewell to the Party of Lincoln: Black Politics in the Age of FDR* (Princeton: Princeton University Press, 1983).

15. Jimmy Carter's election in 1976 is seen as an anomaly, a result of Watergate on the one hand and Carter's Southern evangelical Christian background on the other.

16. Matusow, *The Unraveling,* 243.

17. Nicholas Lemann, *The Promised Land: The Great Black Migration and How It*

Changed America (New York: Knopf, 1991), 129. "In Dreams Begin Responsibilities" was a landmark of the modernist short fiction of the interwar period, and was published in the first issue of the magazine *Partisan Review*. On Delmore Schwartz and his short fiction, see *In Dreams Begin Responsibilities* (Norfolk, CT: New Directions, 1938); James Atlas, *Delmore Schwartz: The Life of an American Poet* (New York: Farrar Straus and Giroux, 1977); and Saul Bellow's novel *Humboldt's Gift* (New York: Viking Press, 1975).

18. Charles Murray, *Losing Ground: American Social Policy, 1950–1980* (New York: Basic Books, 1984), 181–82.

19. Edsall and Edsall, *Chain Reaction,* 15.

20. See Sara Evans, *Personal Politics: The Roots of Women's Liberation in the Civil Rights Movement and the New Left* (New York: Vintage Press, 1980), 142–47; and Jennifer Frost, "Community and Consciousness: Women's Welfare Rights Organizing in Cleveland, 1964–1966" (unpublished paper, Berkshire Conference on the History of Women, Douglass College, New Jersey, June 1990).

21. Murray, *Losing Ground,* 181.

22. Jim Sleeper, *The Closest of Strangers: Liberalism and the Politics of Race in New York* (New York: Norton, 1990), 91.

23. Sleeper, *The Closest of Strangers,* 93–94.

24. Edsall and Edsall, *Chain Reaction,* 72.

25. Gunnar Myrdal, *An American Dilemma* (New York: Harper and Brothers, 1944), 359–60. Winifred Bell found the same thing twenty years later. See *Aid to Dependent Children* (New York: Columbia University Press, 1965). On the legislative debates that produced this version of Social Security, see Linda Gordon, *Pitied but Not Entitled: Single Mothers and the History of Welfare* (New York: Free Press, 1994), 253–85.

26. Jacqueline Hall et al., *Like a Family: The Making of a Southern Cotton Mill World* (Chapel Hill: University of North Carolina Press, 1987), 157.

27. Notwithstanding Sleeper's claim that municipal unions were changing on their own volition, some of the workers who were most resistant to racial integration in the 1960s were those working under public contract. See Jill Quadagno, *The Color of Welfare: How Racism Undermined the War on Poverty* (New York: Oxford University Press, 1994), chap. 3.

28. On this, see H. R. Haldeman, *The Haldeman Diaries: Inside the Nixon White House* (New York: G. P. Putnam's Sons, 1994).

12

KAREN HO
and WENDE ELIZABETH MARSHALL

CRIMINALITY AND CITIZENSHIP

IMPLICATING THE WHITE NATION

One hundred years ago, racial separation, stratification, and white supremacy were the de jure and de facto laws and customs of the land. The struggle to
undo these laws and enact new legislation toward the promise of greater equality
has been one of the major political projects of the twentieth century. The
significance of recent, implicitly pro-white federal and state legislation such as
California's Propositions 184 and 187, the various federal crime bills, soaring
allocations to the Immigration and Naturalization Service's Border Patrol, and
the "War on Drugs" lies in their impact in sustaining and reinscribing limits to
citizenship and status in the United States. For the full threat of recent pro-
white legislation to be understood, we need to analyze the cultural and political
logics that triggered the launching of these torpedoes in the first place. We argue

that the foundational logic is a thinly veiled, hydra-headed, and well-organized resurgence of white nationalism.

METHODOLOGY

Our collaboration is an attempt to critique white nationalism and to open up a space of dialogue between people of color. In working together, we have realized the limitations of theorizing from a single identity politic. Anthropologists Paulla Ebron and Anna Tsing in their groundbreaking essay, "In Dialogue? Writing across Minority Discourses," demonstrate that in many writings from marginalized groups,

> there has been little precedent . . . for doing anything other than restating the forms of marginalization with which one side or the other is the most familiar—as if attempting to buy one's way to the moral high ground of "most oppressed." In this practice, other marginalized groups are collapsed into the dominant center because they do not share the particular form of marginalization about which one is writing. (Ebron and Tsing 1995, 2)

In our collaboration as an Asian-American woman and an African-American woman who belong to groups often pitted against each other, the "model minority" opposing the "immoral minority," we have created a space of dialogue that decenters the primary white referent. This space provides a view of the workings of a white hegemony that is able to deploy Asian Americans "in an eminently programmatic way against other groups" (Palumbo-Liu 1994, 341). With Asians and blacks fighting each other,

> what is missing in the narrative . . . is any inquiry into the structure of an economic system that historically pits Asians against blacks and Latinos, and which exploits this antagonism in order to construct a displaced rehearsal of a simplified white/black, purely "racial" antagonism. (370)

With whites conveniently missing from the picture, the strategy of white supremacy and its concrete ramifications are removed from the scene of the crime.

To closely interrogate the categories and hierarchies that have defined certain people as problematic, as well as the unreflexive use of dominant, white community standards as normative, we argue that research on American culture and public policy must move toward greater analysis of the dominant and powerful;

dominated or less powerful communities should not be the sole subject of our research. Thus, it is critical to analyze how hierarchies of power are embedded in the ways we theorize race/ethnicity/nationality. In other words, we need to ask not only what constitutes criminality, illegitimacy, illegality, and savagery, but also why and how the powerful have categorized these issues as problematic. In radical scholars' attempts to denaturalize and expose the oppressive contexts that transform black men into criminals, black women into welfare mothers, Asians and Chicanos into illegals, they are often in danger of accepting the very categories of criminal, illegal, and so forth that the dominant society has decided are problems. Descriptions of these sociologically "deviant" contexts tacitly accept the logic of dominant whiteness.

As James Baldwin writes in "Many Thousands Gone" (1951), "The American image of the Negro lives also in the Negro's heart; and when he has surrendered to this image, life has no other possible reality" (38). By incorporating these terms of negatively marked reference and by not questioning what problematically lies in our own hearts, we complicitly believe in and protect a dominant white American value system that has defined these othered realities as anti-American and antiwhite. We uphold the notion that for people of color to be truly human and acceptable, they must refute the "welfare queen" label and search instead for a dominant "self."

Rather than incorporating powerful white Western notions of who we are, instead of accepting these negative markings as valid and apologetically explaining why we are not in fact savages contaminating and bleeding the resources of white America, we must explore the roots of savagery in the constitution of whiteness itself. Following Toni Morrison's work *Playing in the Dark: Whiteness and the Literary Imagination,* we should reject a scholarship founded on the objectification of people of color and use our insights to carefully scrutinize the dominant. According to Morrison, who speaks in this quotation of white male authors,

> The fabrication of the Africanist persona is reflexive; an extraordinary meditation on the self; a powerful exploration of the fears and desires that reside in the writerly consciousness. . . . It was this Africanism, deployed as rawness and savagery, that provided the staging ground and arena for the elaboration of the quintessential American identity. (Morrison 1992, 17, 44)

Retaining whiteness as the dominant position of normativity reinscribes whiteness as the subject position in knowledge production of race. As Richard Dyer observes,

> This property of whiteness, to be everything and nothing, is the source of its representational power. . . . [W]hite domination is reproduced by the way that white people "colonize the definition of normal." Paul Gilroy similarly spells out the political consequences, in the British context, of the way that whiteness both disappears behind and is subsumed into other identities. He discusses the way that the language of "the nation" aims to be unifying . . . but goes on to observe that: "there is a problem in these plural forms: why do they include, or, more precisely for our purposes, do they help reproduce blackness and Englishness as mutually exclusive categories? . . . why are contemporary appeals to 'the people' in danger of transmitting themselves as appeals to the white people?" (Dyer 1988, 45–46)

Making whiteness an unbounded and ill-defined cultural space limits our understanding of how its performance and production are implicated in the (re)production of white supremacy. When white is invisible, a critical interrogation of cultural and institutional white power becomes nearly impossible.

It is important to note, however, that our strategy is not entirely similar to that of Ruth Frankenberg in *White Women, Race Matters: The Social Construction of Whiteness* (1993), a work that challenges a framework of Western scholarship that has ignored the white racial being. Though her critical "inventory of whiteness as a subjective terrain" through an examination of the lives of white women challenges the "colonial construction of whiteness as an 'empty' cultural space, in part by refiguring it as constructed and dominant rather than as norm," she makes the mistake of preserving the centrality of a white point of view. For example, in illustrating that dominant white discourse is characterized by color-blind and power-evasive language, Frankenberg writes that "at this time in U.S. history" only the "far right" "explicitly articulates" "whiteness as a marked identity . . . mainly in terms of 'white pride'" (232). On the contrary, we argue that colored Americans, growing up in households where whiteness was constantly named, critiqued, and challenged, clearly articulate whiteness as a marked identity. Frankenberg's failure to acknowledge that people of color are engaged in knowledge production about whiteness refuses to legitimize people of color as authors, not objects, of knowledge and implicitly normalizes the white point of view. Another point of our collaboration here is also to reinstate agency in Other points of view.

Using the space opened up by our collaboration, we want to identify the intersections of seemingly disparate discourses surrounding crime, poverty, drugs, and immigration. Rather than isolating these issues according to their effects on specific identity groups or geographic areas, we are viewing them as a unified attack on "Others" in the production of what we call the White Nation. In using the conception of White Nation as a cornerstone of our project, we attempt to dislodge whiteness from panoptical centrality/domination. We recognize, however, that in using the crude and monolithic term "White Nation" we evade a nuanced rendering of the agonistic field on which a heterogeneous assortment of constituencies jockey for position. We also recognize that in focusing on this "unified attack on 'Others,' " we are in danger of deleting the varying power differentials and privileges of these "Others." However, *there is* a series of strategies whose aim is to reclaim white power/privilege and the symbolic and institutional structures that sustain it, although overt white supremacist rhetoric is often veiled.

Our naming of the White Nation is an alternative, a strategy to subvert the view that whiteness is invisible, normative, and blameless. It challenges the scholarship on race relations in the United States that defines "differently" racialized bodies as judicial and policy problems, who, having created their mess through individual lack, are deviants, incapable of "self-determination" and shameless enough to continually whine to and shit on the white hand that kindly feeds them. The deliberately provocative term "White Nation" is meant to point clearly to the thinly veiled attempts by policy makers and legislators to reclaim white privilege and maintain white power. When the media discourse on crime and citizenship focuses strictly on the criminal and the "alien," it elides the multiple structures of global capital, militarization, and terror used to bolster the White Nation. In using the conception "White Nation" we hope to evoke and analyze the images of Newt Gingrich on the Capitol steps, Charles Murray in the academy, white male Los Angeles police officers beating Rodney King, Pete Wilson's rallying cry of "Save Our State," Tom Ridge's signature on the death warrant of Mumia Abu-Jamal, the six white male Greenwich, Connecticut, high school students coding "kill all niggers" in their high school yearbook, and the media's shameless assumption that Middle Eastern rather than Midwestern terrorists were responsible for the April 1995 bombing of the federal building in Oklahoma City. We hope that "White Nation" will carry a tropic load as potent as the standard incantations "black underclass" and "illegal alien."

It is also important to situate our theorizing about the White Nation in a transnational and comparative context, for the strategies of the White Nation carry global ramifications, and we can learn much about white nationalism by studying the logic of other nationalisms. In this regard, the recent anthropological literature on national culture making, although rarely applied to the West, offers a clear and useful model for analysis of the White Nation's culture- and power-making process. This literature analyzes the processes of cultural production and the technologies of exclusion on which such concepts as "nation" and "state" are grounded. It explores the plasticity of bounded entities such as race and ethnicity and the contestory field of national imaginings. The anthropologist Richard Fox's essay "Hindu Nationalism in the Making; or, the Rise of the Hindian" (Fox 1990) explores the Hindu national culture-making process in India. Significantly, for our purposes, Fox analyzes the "ideological hijacking" of Gandhism, a competing national ideology that emphasizes tolerance and plurality. Hindu nationalism redefines and appropriates what Gandhi spoke of as God and Truth and makes it a Hindu truth alone. Hidden by the veils of centrality, Hindu nationalism is invisible; Hindu is conflated with Indian. These kinds of analyses of nationalism in the "developing" world provide us with a useful approach to the United States precisely because the process here has become so transparent. If we selectively apply the methodologies of the anthropology of national culture making to the United States, we can begin to discern the production of the White Nation. Like the "hijacking of Gandhism," the reproducing White Nation cloaks its white racist ideology in the rhetoric of patriotism and safe streets, lawfulness and self-determination. And, like Hindu nationalists, many white nationalists are working to achieve consensus and promote a single version of culture, citizen, and truth.

From an anthropological perspective, we recognize that our implication of the active actors bolstering the White Nation and our corresponding attention to the perspective of Others challenges not only U.S. scholarship on race relations but also our discipline. Since our very theoretical tools are founded on humans and places who supposedly fundamentally lack agency compared to "us," we have found it difficult to portray the weavers of culture, to theorize about human agency, even the agency of the relatively powerful. In focusing on the strategies of white nationalists, we are rejecting the white hegemonic viewpoint that denies its own agency in destructively reproducing itself—especially in light of recent social theorists' tendencies to give grand agency to "big" institutions and phenomena. For example, many postcolonial critics, in attempting to talk about the scope of "global capitalism" and "world colonization," have used models in which power and dominations emanate from the West and *onto* "the rest." In this model, global capitalism and Western states are grand institutions set on autopilot without real actors. Also, our implicating the White Nation is an attempt to avoid the vicious trap of concluding that nonhegemonic groups and people are simply dominated, trapped, inferior Others acted on by great white power structures.

The White Nation, however, is neither simply a conspiracy nor an institution. Rather, it is a series of strategies and actors deployed from multiple sites with manifold objectives, always tested by numerous counterstrategies. The White

Nation is not a right-wing militia group or the far-right wing of the Republican Party; its composition is a dynamic network of decentralized webs that deploy multiple processes—judicial, economic, linguistic, military/paramilitary—from varied sites to achieve an always contested hegemony. Michel Foucault's notion of power provides valuable insight into the architectonics of the White Nation. According to Foucault,

> neither the caste that governs, nor the groups which control the state apparatus, nor those who make the most important economic decisions direct the entire network of power that functions in society (and makes *it* function); the rationality of power is characterized by tactics that are often quite explicit at the restricted level where they are inscribed, tactics which, becoming connected to one another, but finding their base of support and their conditions elsewhere, end by forming comprehensive systems. (Foucault 1978, 95)

This Foucauldian notion of power leaves room for the complicated reality of multiracial, multiethnic support of strategies that buttress the White Nation.

THE WHITE NATION IN ACTION

Having set the theoretical framing of our analysis, we want to focus directly on the very tangible technologies of the White Nation. Since part of the strategy of (re)producing the White Nation is precisely to render invisible its own workings of maintaining supremacy and to focus its lens on problematic Others who are balkanizing and depleting the nation, our counterstrategy is twofold. First, we hope to render visible and precisely demonstrate how the very actions and ideas of White Nation actors maintain their own privilege by spreading pain onto others. We hope to illustrate that only by upholding the very systems of white entitlements, protection of white property, and white segregation (to name just a few) are problematic categories such as criminal and illegal constructed and made sensible. We hope to explore how notions of criminality, stealing, and looting would not be possible without the accompanying ideologies of individual property ownership and self-made prosperity. Only from the perspective of the White Nation's protection of its ownership of property and belongingness as citizens would such oppressive systems as ghettoized segregation and Propositions 187 and 184 be necessary. Ironically, white nationalists are so bent on keeping the very systems/categories that make them whole that they are unable to diverge from them, even if they entrap them as well.

Second, we hope to demonstrate that maintenance of the White Nation is achieved most profitably through the criminalizing, medicalizing, or reterritorializing of those who undermine it. We hope to show what is actually happening to these "problematic Others": criminals and aliens are those who, practically or existentially,[1] pose a threat to white hegemony and must therefore be contained, restrained, or eliminated by death or deportation.

Robert Fitch, in an article called "Spread the Pain? Tax the Gain!" (1995), demonstrates how white nationalists such as New York City mayor Rudolph Giuliani and New York governor George Pataki are "energetically engaged in redistributing income upward" (630). Legitimated by conservative white think tanks and using the strategy of "spreading the pain" and "there's no more money," Giuliani and Pataki are hoping to cut city spending for Medicaid and child welfare programs, close down city public hospitals, lay off thousands of workers, shrink benefits to the blind and homeless, "eliminate school loans for most poor students and all graduate students, double tuition at City University of New York and lay off 1,000 tenured faculty, eliminating 15,000 courses" (629, 620). At the same time, they hope to use this money to offer multiyear tax cuts to the rich, subsidize downtown property owners, developers, and multinational corporations, and give big investment tax credits. Obviously, then, elite white actors—even at the expense of the city and state's "economic and fiscal mudslide"—are hoarding much-needed funds in order to support a narrow version of the White Nation: the rich and their growing "economic monoculture—excessive reliance on the finance, insurance, and real estate industries" (628).[2]

This frenetic protection of elite white property comes to the forefront in the 1992 Los Angeles Rebellion. David Palumbo-Liu (1994) demonstrates that in media and dominant portrayals of the Los Angeles debacle, Korean-Americans, who were seen as "white surrogates" because of their model ownership of property, were depicted in *Newsweek* as gun-carrying defenders of the American dream against black and Latino "looters." Just as their gun carrying was legitimized in a sense, for they were protecting sacred property, those who did not have property were constructed as self-stabbing, selfish criminals. At the same time, however, when Korean-Americans in South Central and Koreatown called the Los Angeles Police Department for protection against the fire and looting of their property and homes, no police responded to their 911 calls for help. They were all busy protecting Beverly Hills and Westwood (Cho 1993, 196). In this light, Korean-Americans' machine gun stance was both an upholding of elite white property standards and evidence that the White Nation would not protect them. As Elaine Kim writes, the three days of the rebellion were a "baptism into what it means for a Korean to 'become American' in the 1990s" (1993, 219). Not only are they sacrificed in favor of Westwood, for their "stolen" property does not carry the signature of white entitlement, but they are conveniently scapegoated by the White Nation in order to fragment and polarize the anger of other people of color.

This redirecting of the roots of the White Nation's racism and classism to marginalized peoples and communities and not toward corporate, government, and military strongholds is nowhere more recently evident than in the media's short-lived coverage of the Oklahoma City tragedy compared to its racist love of the O. J. Simpson trial. As a writer in the *Militant* observes, because the Oklahoma City debacle so obviously made the connection for the public between recent right-wing government actions, the military, and the reinvigoration of white supremacy, White Nation actors in the media quickly shifted the heat away from themselves and onto the O. J. Simpson trial. The return focus to the trial is a master's stroke to reinstill racist fears in the country, for the entire drama revolves not around white skinheads but the fear of what happens to white folks when they get too close to black folks. With the national eye focused on the O. J. Simpson trial, viewers get their daily dose of "fear of a black planet."

The system of white segregation is an excellent example of how the White Nation actively fears a black planet and maintains its privilege by delineating racial hierarchies. For example, James Loewen's 1971 study of the Mississippi Chinese who were recruited by Southern planters to exploit as sharecroppers in the Delta explains how the white system of segregation first, allowed the Chinese to open up grocery businesses and thus move in status from Negro to nearly-white-but-not-white status, and second, kept blacks and whites in their hierarchized positions. Because white segregation associated blackness with subhuman-ness, all whites and many blacks, for reasons of status, would not shop in black-owned stores,[3] not to mention that lenders would not lend money to blacks. Similarly, most whites, except lower-class ones, would not open up stores in black or poor neighborhoods, for that meant selling to, associating with, and being courteous to blacks. They were not about to be dubbed "nigger lovers" (Loewen 1971, 50). Thus, with this critical opening caused by white oppression of blacks where no one wanted to buy from or sell to blacks, Chinese immigrants, as foreigners coming from "outside," were able to sell to blacks. "Whites probably would not have tolerated Chinese competition in other fields" (50). Thus, it was a white system of segregation that defines blacks as incapable of buying, selling, or owning property to others and to themselves. It is this system of segregation that puts blacks at the bottom and whites on top, and sandwiches the Chinese somewhere in between, depending on how and where they (the Chinese) can be the most useful for white nationalist needs. Loewen also observes that this system of segregation that bolsters the White Nation is not *always* for the complete best interests of whites:

Whites are clearly on top, yet they cannot take full advantage of their situation, because the system of rationalizations with which they bolster their position and by which they defend their actions interferes. If a different ideology had developed (and alternatives can be imagined), not dependent upon dehumanizing the Negro, then whites might not have been shackled with the corollary denigration of work itself or of avoidance of Negro-oriented trade. (54)

The White Nation, then, is not shatterproof. The system of white segregation, for example, also entraps whites, for they cannot transgress the very tight "system of rationalizations" that makes their positioning possible. In this sense, all transgressions against white property, white citizenship, even from white people, must be contained. At this point, after having explored some of the logics behind the construction of such categories as criminal and illegitimate, we will now turn to our exploration of how people of "lower" color and class are defined and convicted as "criminals" and "illegals" for the survival of the White Nation.

In 1980, the election of Ronald Reagan was a victory that allowed a vicious politics of white resentment, white discontent, and white insecurity to openly flourish. Ideologies that were perfectly legitimate in the 1950s but were marginalized in the 1970s (exemplified by George Wallace) came to the surface again. Now, disciplined, well-organized, and well-financed, the vanguard of the White Nation has pushed a policy agenda whose major focus is the restriction or excision of nonwhite roles and power. In the symbolics of the White Nation, "black welfare mothers," "crack addicts," and roaming "wolf-packs" of jaded black teenagers figure as prominent symbols of a fallen America, while job-stealing sweatshop and migrant laborers, tax-cheating "aliens," and speakers of "foreign" tongues represent the threat to its redemption. As the political scientist Noel Kent has noted, since the restoration of untrammeled white supremacy is unfeasible, the White Nation exerted its energies toward blocking the legitimacy of group (versus individual) rights and redefining the meaning of social and racial equality. Its prominence in the Republican and Democratic parties and in a phalanx of think tanks, lobbying organizations, and churches guarantees enormous influence (Kent 1993, 65).

We must abandon the idea of power as something possessed by one group and leveled against a powerless Other; the networks of actors, practices, institutions, and technologies that make up the White Nation must be read together. The passage of an assortment of federal crime bills, California's Three Strikes Proposition 184 and Anti-Immigrant Proposition 187 needs to be read as a comprehensive strategy for delimiting rank and citizenship in the United States.

In California, the Three Strikes and You're Out Initiative was packaged as punishing violent criminals (read black and Latino), and Proposition 187 was packaged as saving our state from undeserving needy illegals (read Mexican and Asian). Since they were framed as separate propositions and viewed as tackling two separate problems, the fact that they implicate a unified attack on the White Nation's Others was obscured.

In the campaign for the passage of California's Proposition 187, people of color were pitted, and pitted themselves, against each other. Twenty-three percent of Latinas and 47 percent of Asian-American and African-American voters supported the passage of Proposition 187, (Adams 1995, 21), which attempts to deny health care, education, and other social services to undocumented immigrants.[4] Both the "sanctioned" immigrants who have just obtained their "legal" status, perhaps by proving that they are highly assimilable to white mainstream American culture, and many people of color supported the passage of Proposition 187. Believing in the ideology of economic scarcity, they were not about to let new immigrants compete for their hard-earned space at the bottom.

One of the many arguments used by progressives fighting against Proposition 187 was that immigrants are not "burdens" on the United States since they contribute positively to the economy and do not abuse scarce resources. The seemingly innocent logic that immigrants are useful, meager people who do not detract from white space attempts to differentiate immigrants from African-Americans, who have traditionally been seen as "welfare cheats" and "unemployables."[5] This image of the hardworking immigrant is constructed against the image of African Americans seen as immoral, lazy, criminal bodies heavily dependent on state largesse. Many of those fighting against Proposition 187 focus on the ousting of Latinos and Asians but do not connect this with the throwing of blacks, Latinos, and Native Americans into prison through the passage of Proposition 184.

The passage of Proposition 184 occurred in California, a state with the third largest penal system in the world, following China and the rest of the United States. In 1995 the official California prisoner count was 125,842, 66 percent of whom are Latino or black (Davis 1995, 229, 230).[6] The November 1994 passage of this proposition requires the sentences for second felonies to be doubled, while third-time offenders receive minimum sentences of twenty years to life. A felony conviction covers crimes ranging from murder to burglary and shoplifting. Although a spate of studies refutes the notion that high incarceration rates reduce crime,[7] the passage of Proposition 184 follows the enactment of more than a thousand bills designed to toughen misdemeanor and felony sentencing standards between 1984 and 1992. Proposition 184 has already had a disproportionate impact on African Americans. According to urban studies scholar Mike Davis, the new law

> promises a dramatic escalation in racial disparities. In the first six months of prosecution under the . . . law, African Americans (10 percent of the population) made up 57 percent of the "three strikes" filings in L.A. County. This is seventeen times the rate for whites, say public defenders here, *although other studies have shown that white men commit at least 60 percent of all the rape, robberies and assault in the state.* (Davis 1994, 234, emphasis added)

According to professor Sylvia Wynter (1992), the Los Angeles Police Department code word for crimes involving black men was "no humans involved." During Daryl Gates's tenure as commissioner of the Los Angeles Police Department, police officers routinely referred to black drug dealers as Vietcong (Rayner 1995, 50). This double-edged reference to the U.S. occupation of Vietnam during the war there points to the escalating militarization of neighborhoods like South Central and the oppressive conflation of African Americans as foreign enemies. New federal crime laws and the "War on Drugs" have virtually placed the nation's ghettos under paramilitary occupation. The manufacture of crime hysteria, despite data showing significant decreases in violent and property crimes over the last two decades, has provided a convenient cover for a dramatic expansion of coercive government power, limiting the rights of citizens in areas under occupation and monopolizing technologies of violence in the hands of the state (Davis 1990, 267–322). Recent legislation has allocated funds to increase the numbers of police officers, construct new state and local prisons, raise time requirements for sentencing and incarceration, and increase the number of crimes punishable by death.[8]

Other measures allow the prosecution of children as adults and allocate funds to schools for metal detectors and video surveillance. Latino children are the special focus of police in California's Orange County, the birthplace of the Proposition 187 campaign. Despite the rise in violent hate crimes perpetrated by middle-class white youths, Latino youths are systematically targeted by the police, who photograph and classify them as gang members "without probable cause, arrest, or permission." In response, a coalition of Latino, African-American, Asian-American, and Native American organizations have begun documenting the county's "low-intensity race war" and its failure to fully investigate and prosecute white hate crimes. Despite the repeated attacks on African Americans, migrant workers, and Southeast Asians by young white skinheads, Orange

County has failed to mount an attack on the white youth perpetrating hate crimes (Davis 1994, 488–90).

Parallel to the escalation of paramilitary operations in urban ghettos is the intense militarization of the U.S.-Mexico border and the surrounding South-western states. Progressives fighting against Proposition 187—Taxpayers United against Proposition 187, led by Latino state-elected officials—have also used the U.S.-Mexico border as a scapegoat. They blamed the immigrant "problem" on the lack of adequate policing of the U.S.-Mexico border. They played up voter fears that the passage of 187 would lead to "rampaging gangs of (brown) children pushed out of schools; [and] the spread of tuberculosis by untreated 'illegals'" and hence shifted the locus of California's social problems onto the border. The Border Patrol, the military wing of the Immigration and Naturaliza-tion Service, received $345.5 million in federal funds in 1995, a sixfold increase in the past fifteen years. Nearly five thousand Border Patrol agents are stationed along U.S. borders (including the Canadian border, Puerto Rico, Mississippi, New Orleans, and the Gulf Coast of Florida), armed with semiautomatic weapons, radar, night scopes, and helicopters. The Immigration Law Enforce-ment Monitoring Project (ILEMP), a watchdog group, has charged that the Border Patrol lacks "official mechanisms for accountability and oversight." The ILEMP regularly documents incidents of illegal search, document destruction, and vehicle seizure, along with the detention of children, the rape of women, and shooting to kill. ILEMP staff have also documented the Border Patrol's use of hollow-point bullets, "a kind of ammunition that explodes inside the body . . . which [is] outlawed by international law" (Lee 1995, 16).

The destructive path of the Border Patrol reaches deep into the lives of U.S. citizens living in the border states. Author Leslie Marmon Silko, who grew up on the Laguna Pueblo reservation, remembers freely traveling the highways of Arizona and New Mexico. But the rise in anti-immigrant hysteria, coupled with the increased budget for Border Patrol and the greatly expanding number of checkpoints, some as far as ninety-five miles from the border, has hindered the right of U.S. citizens, no doubt usually Latinos and Asians who look and speak "foreign," to freely travel. Silko writes,

> I was detained at Truth or Consequences [checkpoints], despite my and my companion's Arizona driver's license. Two men, both Chicanos were detained at the same time, despite the fact that they too presented ID and spoke English without the thick Texas accents of the Border Patrol agents. While we were stopped, we watched as other vehicles— whose occupants were white—were waved through the checkpoint. White people traveling with brown people, however, can expect to be

stopped on suspicion they work with the sanctuary movement, which shelters refugees. . . . Alleged increases in illegal immigration by people of Asian ancestry means that the Border Patrol now routinely detains anyone who appears to be Asian or part Asian. (1994, 412–16)

In Silko's view, since the 1980s, the southwestern United States has become a "police state."

Although the principal targets of federal crime bills are U.S. citizens (primarily young men of color), the text of a bill recently passed by Congress includes two significant provisions: the first, contingent on longer sentences and less parole, allocates more federal dollars for the building of state prisons. In addition, these guidelines propose the elimination of prisoner sports facilities and the abridgment of the rights of prisoners to institute litigation to challenge prison conditions. The second provision obviously demonstrates the double criminality of the undocumented illegal. The new bill would provide for the immediate deportation of "the undocumented" only after they have served a sentence (Seelye 1995, A1).

The "War on Drugs" is a particular nexus of policies and laws that support the White Nation. Much of the Border Patrol's technological equipment was funded in the late 1980s during the escalation of the "War on Drugs." Also, the logic of the war drives much of the frenzy for new prison construction, as well as the military occupation of the nation's urban communities of color. Clarence Lusane, an analyst of the drug war, described the policies first implemented by the Bush administration as a

> declaration of war on users and dealers [which] threatens their civil liberties and has had virtually no impact on the roots of the drug problem, either internationally or domestically. Mass waves of police actions against street sales into inner city communities have moved drug markets indoors. Drug sales and use in the suites and boardrooms of America's large and small corporations have remained largely untouched. . . . In numerous Black communities, police departments have launched what are essentially full-scale military assaults. With the logistics of the kind usually reserved for invasions of other nations, police raid Black neighborhoods weekly. . . . Not a single White community has been the target of these assaults. . . . By mainly going after street-level dealers, drug enforcement officers perpetuate the myth that the majority of traffickers and users are people of color. In 1988, however, the FBI and the National Institute on Drug Abuse concluded that Blacks constitute only 12 percent of the nation's drug users. Whites

comprise 80 percent of all illegal drug users. . . . Whites are not only the majority of drug users; they are also the most common drug sellers. . . . Whites dominate the drug trafficking industry. Whites also get the lion's share of the profits, as they deal narcotics wholesale and behind the security of closed corporate doors. (Lusane 1991, 5, 46, 45)

One of the drug war's most egregious tactics is the 1986 Controlled Substances Act, one of the most plainly racist pieces of law enforcement legislation in U.S. history. Although crack cocaine and powder cocaine are chemically identical, crack cocaine use is more prevalent in urban areas (although the National Institute on Drug Abuse's 1990 figures estimated that whites comprised 77 percent of America's crack users [Lusane 1991, 45]). Under the federal crack law, however, convictions for possession of small amounts of crack carry mandatory minimum sentencing requirements, while possession of much larger amounts of cocaine carries probation (Washington 1995, 1, 22). Seventy percent of federal inmates are doing time on drug charges, at a cost of $6.1 billion (Lusane 1995, 39). Ninety-three percent of those convicted for use and/or sale of crack in federal courts are African American. In 1992, 78 percent of African Americans convicted under the federal drug kingpin statute were sentenced to death. And in Nebraska, where the African-American population is 3.6 percent of the total, blacks were 92.3 percent of those convicted of crack offenses during a six-month period in 1992 (Washington 1995, 1). David Dudley, a California attorney who represents clients convicted of crack offenses, was quoted in a recent newspaper article analyzing the racism of the federal crack law:

> Today, you don't find people using racist language unless they are Skinheads. . . . No one says they want to "lock the niggers up." They use code words like "criminal." These prosecutors, judges, and Congressmen will deny racism to their graves. (Cited in Washington 1995, 23)

As a blueprint for delimiting rights, these laws and policies are concentrated at significant points: the massive construction of penal facilities for internal exiles, coupled with an intensified mechanism for deportation; and the militarization of urban ghettos and the border areas of the southwestern United States, including the abridgment of the rights of residents of these areas. This method of attacking communities of color through anticrime and anti-immigrant legislation is a central albeit contested strategy. Bringing the discourses on crime and citizenship into the analytic frame of white nationalism provides a view marking the heterogeneous degrees of status that are accorded "Americans" along the racial, ethnic, and class divides. What emerges is a view of the interconnected technologies that strictly limit citizenship and enforce rank. While the discourses are neatly segmented and "marketed" as separate arenas of policy making affecting separate geographic and demographic groups, together they define the White Nation's internal enemy Other.

In our project, we hope we have demonstrated that the White Nation is not a "fixed, natural unit" with "monoracial representation" by showing how white nationalists constantly work to create its ideal community, demand "exclusive political allegiance from its citizens," and suppress the multiple Others that stray from its hegemony (Yanagisako 1995, 292). Our strategy is obviously very different from that of white supremacists themselves, who believe that the White Nation is indeed an ideal, fixed, and natural unit. We end by imagining the launching of counterstrategies and the formation of counterhegemonic concatenations, though we do not see evidence of such a cluster of counterforces at this historical juncture. Both Asian Americans and African Americans in California favored the passage of 184 and 187, opposition to the crime bills is noticeably lacking, and since the victory of Proposition 187 and despite court challenges blocking its implementation, pro-187 activists have been assisting similar campaigns in Florida, Arizona, and Washington. In California, pro-187 activists have launched a campaign for a ballot initiative abolishing affirmative action, and some pro-187 organizations have proposed a constitutional amendment that would restrict citizenship to those "born of an American" and strip foreign nationals of most civil rights (McDonnell 1995, B3). But things can change, as dreams so egregiously deferred have been known to explode.

NOTES

1. People of color are nearly a quarter of the U.S. population and will number 30 percent by the turn of the century. The majority of schoolchildren will be nonwhite (Young 1993, 5).

2. Of course there is rampant resistance to these elite white nationalists. For example, responding to Giuliani and his administration's assumption that CUNY students do not need to go to college but can "do clever things with their hands and their bodies," and that they should get a job when many already work more than twenty-five hours a week, fourteen thousand students left class on March 24, 1995, to protest these cuts in front of City Hall (Fitch 1995, 630).

3. Blacks who could or wanted to "do better" did not want to shop in black-owned stores.

4. According to an analysis of the vote on Proposition 187, although California is on the brink of a nonwhite majority, the registered electorate remains 76

percent white. Proposition 187 "appealed to the racial anxieties of Californians . . . [and] served as the perfect vehicle for [this] overwhelming white electorate to express its unease." Exit polls on the day of the election documented 63 percent of whites voting in support of 187 (Adams 1995, 1–3).

5. In general, the discourse on the United States as a "nation of immigrants" lacks any historical context or analysis of power. It becomes a weightless signifier that any politician can appropriate for her own use. If immigrants are understood as those who "voluntarily" came to the United States in search of a better life, then Native Americans, who were already here, and African Americans, who were enslaved, as well as all other "immigrants" forced here by the trajectory of Euro-American colonialism and economic exploitation, are omitted.

6. Nationally, over one million U.S. citizens are in prison. The incarceration rate in the United States, at 426 per 100,000, is the highest in the world (LaFranière 1991, A3).

7. Although there is much hysterical rhetoric creating the perception that crime rates have risen dramatically, the U.S. Department of Justice Uniform Crime Reports reported a 3 percent decrease in crime index offenses for the first six months of 1994. This decline was preceded by annual declines of 2 percent in 1993 and 3 percent in 1992. The Justice Department's research indicated that the largest drop in crime rates occurred in U.S. cities with populations exceeding 500,000, including Los Angeles, where the 1994 annual crime index declined 14 percent, before the passage of Proposition 184. Crime index offenses include murder, forcible rape, aggravated assault, burglary, larceny-theft, motor-vehicle theft, and arson. (United States Department of Justice, Federal Bureau of Investigation, 1994.)

8. One response to our paper asked whether our discussion could be construed as denying the fears of crime and the calls for more police articulated by African Americans and others. Certainly, communities have expressed both the "longing for crime-free neighborhoods and an equally strong dream of an accountable police force" (Anner 1995, 19). Rod Hampton, the executive director of the National Black Police Association, has argued that people always say, "We need more police," when asked what should be done about crime. However, when they are pushed further,

> you find out that their experiences with the police are usually terrible. They say, "When we call the cops, they never come. And when they do come, they treat us disrespectfully, call us names, and sometime beat us up." . . . Hampton points to a convenient blind spot among those currently defining the terms of the debate over crime and safety: Solutions proposed to combat the problems inevitably call for putting more police on the streets, without looking at what these police officers do once they get there. But as the Rodney King riots demonstrated in the clearest possible terms, anger over police brutality and disrespectful behavior runs at least as deep in many parts of

the country as the fear of being a victim of violent crime. (Anner 1995, 1)

With such a racist police system, recruiting people of color as police can be read as a hegemonic strategy of the White Nation to pacify opposition to police brutality. Neighborhood activists in cities such as Providence, Oakland, Denver, and Orangeburg, South Carolina, have begun to develop organizing strategies to lower both crime rates and police misconduct, which clearly distinguish between socially responsible solutions and the race-based attacks currently pursued by national law enforcement agencies.

REFERENCES

Adams, Jan. 1995. "Proposition 187: What's To Be Learned?" Unpublished manuscript, January 25.

Anner, John. 1995. "Making the Connection between Crime and Police Brutality." Third Force: Issues and Actions in Communities of Color 22 (6).

Baldwin, James. 1951. "Many Thousands Gone." In *Notes of a Native Son.* Boston: Beacon Press, 1984.

Cho, Sumi. 1993. "Korean Americans vs. African Americans: Conflict and Construction." In *Reading Rodney King, Reading Urban Uprising,* edited by Robert Gooding-Williams. New York: Routledge.

Davis, Mike. 1990. "The Hammer and the Rock." In *City of Quartz.* London: Verso.

———. 1994. "Behind the Orange Curtain: Legal Lynching in San Clemente." *Nation* 256 (14), October 31.

———. 1995. "A Prison-Industrial Complex: Hell Factories in the Field." *Nation* 260 (7), February 20.

Dyer, Richard. 1988. "White." *Screen* 29 (4), Autumn.

Ebron, Paulla, and Anna Tsing. 1995. "In Dialogue? Reading across Minority Discourses." In *Women Writing Culture,* edited by Ruth Behar and Deborah A. Gordon. Berkeley and Los Angeles: University of California Press.

Fitch, Robert. 1995. "Spread the Pain? Tax the Gain!" *Nation* 260 (18), May 8.

Foucault, Michel. 1978. *The History of Sexuality: An Introduction.* Vol. 1. New York: Vintage Books.

Fox, Richard, ed. 1990. *Nationalist Ideologies and the Production of National Cultures.* American Ethnological Society Monograph Series, no. 2. Washington, D.C.: American Anthropological Association.

Frankenburg, Ruth. 1993. *White Women, Race Matters: The Social Construction of Whiteness.* Minneapolis: University of Minnesota Press.

Kent, Noel Jacob. 1993. "To Polarize a Nation: Racism, Labor Markets, and the State in U.S. Political Economy." In *The Rising Tide of Cultural Pluralism,* edited by Crawford Young. Madison: University of Wisconsin Press.

Kim, Elaine. 1993. "Home Is Where the *Han* Is: A Korean American Perspective on the Los Angeles Upheavals." In *Reading Rodney King, Reading Urban Uprising,* edited by Robert Gooding-Williams. New York: Routledge.

LaFranière, Sharon. 1991. "U.S. Has Most Prisoners Per Capita in the World." *Washington Post,* January 5.

Lee, Elisa. 1995. "Watching the Border Watchers." *Third Force: Issues and Actions in Communities of Color* 2 (6), January–February.

Loewen, James W. 1971. *The Mississippi Chinese: Between Black and White.* Cambridge: Harvard University Press.

Lusane, Clarence. 1991. *Pipe Dream Blues: Racism and the War on Drugs.* Boston: South End Press.

———. 1995. "A Radical Approach to the Continuing Drug Crisis." *Third Force: Issues and Actions in Communities of Color* 2 (6), January–February.

McDonnell, Patrick J. 1995. "Proposition 187 Backers Take Aim at Other Targets." *Los Angeles Times,* January 31, Washington edition.

Morrison, Toni. 1992. *Playing in the Dark: Whiteness and the Literary Imagination.* Cambridge: Harvard University Press.

Palumbo-Liu, David. 1994. "Los Angeles, Asians, and Perverse Ventriloquisms: On the Functions of Asian Americans in the Recent American Imaginary." *Public Culture* 6.

Rayner, Richard. 1995. "Wanted: A Kinder, Gentler Cop." *New York Times Magazine,* January 22.

Seelye, Katharine Q. 1995. "Two Anti-Crime Bills Cleared by House by Large Margins." *New York Times,* February 11.

Silko, Leslie Marmon. 1994. "The Border Patrol State: America's Iron Curtain." *Nation* 259 (12), October 17.

United States Department of Justice, Federal Bureau of Investigation. 1994. "Uniform Crime Reports, January–June, 1994," December 4.

Washington, Linn. 1995. "American Race War: Blacks Bashed by Biased Crack Law." *Philadelphia New Observer* 29 (24), June 14.

Wynter, Sylvia. 1992. "No Humans Involved: An Open Letter to My Colleagues." In *Voices of the African Diaspora: Aesthetics, Vision, and Urban America* 8 (2), Fall. Center for Afroamerican and American Studies Research and Review.

Yanagisako, Sylvia. 1995. "Transforming Orientalism: Gender, Nationality, and Class in Asian American Studies." In *Naturalizing Power: Essays in Feminist Cultural Analysis,* edited by Sylvia Yanagisako and Carol Delaney. New York: Routledge.

Young, Crawford. 1993. "The Dialectics of Cultural Pluralism: Concept and Reality." In *The Rising Tide of Cultural Pluralism,* edited by Crawford Young. Madison: University of Wisconsin Press.

13

PAUL KRAMER

JIM CROW SCIENCE AND THE "NEGRO PROBLEM" IN THE OCCUPIED PHILIPPINES, 1898–1914

We are betraying a tendency to swagger under the "white man's burden," sometimes in the garb of commercialism, sometimes in the raiment of science.

—James LeRoy, "Race Prejudice in the Philippines"

In 1901, William Freer landed at the port of Manila on the army transport *Meade,* ready to begin service as a school instructor in the newest outpost of the United States. "The sounds of the river and street life, the peculiar odors, the strange sights, were bewildering," he wrote in 1906. "The clouted Chinese coolies laboring on the water-front, the Filipino boys swimming . . . the odd vehicles and emaciated ponies drawing them, Sikhs, Cingalese,—all these made up the most interesting medley I had ever seen. That day and the few immediately following I looked and lingered, and looked again, held by a fascination I could not resist."[1] Freer was not alone in grappling with the diversity of the Philippines. Throughout the U.S. occupation of the Philippines, American colonialists faced the task of making racial sense of the population of the newly acquired territory, as both a symbol and practical instrument of colonial control. Seeking tools in this effort, they often drew deeply on the racial ideas and structures of late nineteenth-century society, specifically, the debate on the "Negro Problem." But while racial thinking saturated debates over colonialism and its institutions, the politics of empire was too contentious for racial thought to settle neatly into any one channel. Rather, "race" in the Philippines came to have meaning only in the context of arguments over America's imperial role, a concept built and rebuilt within specific political climates and institutions of authority. It is the goal of this paper to sketch the competing renditions of the imperial "Negro Problem" that took shape during the early years of the U.S. occupation.[2] As it will show, during the Philippine-American War, political alignments fostered an association between Filipinos and black Americans, including those made by black soldiers questioning their participation in a racialized war of conquest. In the postwar period, the analogy between the "Negro Problem" and the U.S. role in the Philippines continued to impact colonial policy and the behavior of American elites. Efforts were made to temper its most violent aspects, to find more scientific categories, and where useful, to turn it toward the consolidation of a paternalistic civilian government and the establishment of networks of collaboration. For all their elasticity, however, paternalist associations between Filipinos and blacks provoked the resentment of influential Filipinos and were occasionally stretched into more radical interpretations by American officials. After 1907, the political advances of nationalists, institutional changes in colonial science, and the response of American imperialists came together in shaping the work of Robert Bennett Bean, whose scientific research formally joined together the "Negro problem" and the imperial project.

During the Philippine-American War, the idea of a resemblance between blacks and Filipinos emerged on a number of fronts, fitting the "race question" and the debates over colonialism into one another. But while it was often invoked, the political meaning of the metaphor, the proper articulation of the two debates, remained the subject of intense argument. Within anti-imperialist forces, the metaphor came from two competing directions. The largely Northeastern Anti-Imperialist League had drawn some of its support and leadership from faltering abolitionist circles in the late nineteenth century; these members, often the children of midcentury abolitionists, brought with them a powerful denunciation of imperialism as slavery, linking Filipinos and blacks as victims of oppression.[3] At the same time, anti-imperialists based in the Southern Democratic Party played on racial fears to argue that foreign conquest in the Pacific would bring waves of Filipinos to American shores and ballot boxes, contributing to yet another unsolvable "Negro Problem." But the role of white-black racial division in debates on imperialism can perhaps best be seen in the experiences of black soldiers fighting in the Pacific as both agents and critics of the "white man's burden," and in subsequent discussions of the proposed colonization of the Philippines by blacks.

The contours of an imperial "Negro Problem" changed with the recruitment of black regiments for the war with Spain in 1898.[4] While some blacks reasoned that Cuba's liberation should not be undertaken before the United States had fully freed its own neglected citizens, others saw the war as a chance to demonstrate the patriotism and manhood of the race at the darkest hours of Jim Crow and the lynch mob. Optimists like Theophilus Steward, chaplain of the Twenty-fifth U.S. Colored Infantry, held that the war would "greatly help the American colored man of the South, and result in a further clearing of the national atmosphere."[5] Others were far more skeptical. T. Thomas Fortune, editor of the *New York Age,* had held that no possible advancement for blacks could be carried out through the military, as the U.S. Military Academy was "the rankest charity cesspool of snobbery and colorphobia, outside the University of Virginia, in the Republic."[6] Black units that were recruited, as Fortune had warned, faced prejudice from both inside and outside the army. Denied officers of their race despite repeated demands, black troops stationed in tense encampments in Florida faced hostility from surrounding whites, which erupted several times in armed conflict. In spite of the harsh conditions of the camps and their relegation to cooking, hauling, and digging duties, most black soldiers retained their tentative optimism for the war in Cuba. When war broke out against the Philippine Republic in 1899, however, black troops stationed there often wrote home comparing the drawn-out campaign to the savagery of white violence against blacks at home. Facing racism within their own ranks and a "colored" enemy, some blacks reported warm social contacts with the Filipino people and made high assessments of Philippine society. Filipino strategists took advantage of racial divisions within the army, calling on black troops to join them as an army of color against white imperialists. While few chose to switch sides, many black troops returned to the United States deeply troubled about both the imperial project and narrowing avenues for black advancement.[7] Steward, upholder of the U.S. military as the archetypal avenue of black uplift, was nonetheless appalled by the racism he witnessed by white troops in the Philippines, particularly the use of antiblack racial stereotype and insult against Filipinos. Against McKinley's hopes for a peaceful process of "benevolent assimilation" that would accompany American capture of the Philippines, Steward warned that "a deep revulsion will set in as soon as the Filipinos come to understand what the word 'nigger' means."[8]

With Aguinaldo's forces in retreat and eventual control of the islands by American forces almost assured, politicians began to debate the proper racial outlines of the new possessions. Senator John Tyler Morgan of Alabama, senior member of the Senate Foreign Relations Committee and an ardent expansionist, stood against much of his own Democratic Party in rejecting fears that a Pacific colony would send torrents of "Negroes" to the United States. Rather, he argued, white supremacy might be aided by empire, and proposed to secretary of war Elihu Root that black veterans be encouraged to stay in the islands as the core of what he hoped would become a government-sponsored mass colonization by black Americans.[9] Claiming, according to a critic, that "[the 'Negroes'] are the aboriginal inhabitants of the Philippines,"[10] Morgan promised prospective black migrants the protection of the U.S. army, "as many business advantages as possible," and "twenty acres of land to each person." Reaction to Morgan's solution to the "Negro Problem" in the black community was mixed. In 1901, the War Department appointed T. Thomas Fortune a special commissioner to Hawaii and the Philippines to investigate the feasibility of the Morgan proposal. Fortune approved of the plan: blacks were less abusive and harderworking than white Americans, he concluded, and by migrating could escape the oppression of the South, and in the islands be virtuous models for whites and bringers of a "rejuvenation of blood" to the Filipinos.[11] On the other hand, R. B. Lemus, a veteran of the Philippine War, blasted the proposal in the *Colored American Magazine* on a number of levels. Questioning the reliability of Morgan's promises and affirming the Philippine revolutionary struggle, he also questioned the applicability of Morgan's racial scheme, claiming that in early Philippine history, "the archipelago had been peopled by tribes known as Negritos, similar to the African tribes, in the hue of his skin only, and having no more affinity with the twenty African slaves landed at Jamestown, Va., in the seventeenth century, than with Senator Morgan."[12] Lemus concluded on a note of irony: "I am positive that whites . . . would rather have the Negro taxpayer living among them as at present, than to pay taxes for him to live somewhere else."[13] Faced with both domestic and colonial opposition to the plan, Morgan was persuaded to abandon it. The acquisition of the Philippines would not be the answer to the "Negro Problem," and the islands would not become the Jim Crow car of the national territory. But the instance demonstrates how whiteblack racial conflict organized the quarrels and experiences of empire among imperialism's black supporters and dissenters, as well as white abolitionist and white supremacist anti-imperialists.

The end of the war inaugurated the formal transfer of power from military to civilian forces in the Philippines. Under the direction of the Philippine Commission, the architecture of colonial government was established over the next several years, with the formation of municipal governments, courts and constabulary forces, road-building efforts, and school systems.[14] During the early period of the civilian regime, the necessity of consolidating and extending control to new areas and building collaborative links to Manila and regional elites worked against some of the racial analogies that had been forged during the war. Where earlier uses of blackness had emphasized stark divisions in order to create a racial foe for wartime, newer models attempted to attenuate racial hostility into a warmer and more elastic paternalism suitable to the machinery of formal colonial rule. In spite of open antagonism by Americans, a pattern of racial paternalism, built on American traditions and closely tied to the workings of collaboration, took root in the projects of the civilian government, most visibly in its anthropological researches and public school system.

Fueled by the growth of the American population in the Philippines and postwar recriminations, racial prejudice among civilian personnel persisted. While forms of legal segregation appear to have been absent, as James LeRoy, secretary to the Taft Commission, related in the *Atlantic Monthly* in 1902, in everyday practice, Americans in the islands attempted to build a segregated social order similar to that of many Southern cities at the turn of the century.[15] "That the color line would be drawn by some Americans who had to do with the islands could readily have been predicted," he wrote.[16] "Race feeling" against Filipinos by Americans in Manila had begun early on. At a ball held by the Philippine Commission in 1899, for instance, "officers whose wives had joined them did not think of meeting any residents but some of the wealthy Spanish 'left-overs' on anything like terms of social equality."[17] While the "policy of attraction" muted some conflicts, the social atmosphere of the capitals was tense with tolerance. Filipinos were kept off the calling lists of American matrons; in the provinces white teachers were warned before issuing forth "against mingling with the people of their towns."[18] Elements of Jim Crow had found their way into the new public infrastructure of Manila. LeRoy reported that attempts had been made to exclude both Filipino patients and financial patrons from the new Woman's Hospital. At the completion of the American Library, built in part with funds from the Philippine treasury, its builders "made very strenuous protests against having it also thrown open to the Filipinos for a share in its management and use," claiming it as a monument to the American soldiers who had died fighting against Filipinos in the recent war.[19]

While LeRoy's piece chronicled the force of American racial prejudice, it also demonstrated the desire within some administrative circles to lessen its impact. With a degree of outrage, LeRoy attacked the conceptual link between blacks and Filipinos that had been forged by American imperialists during the war. "It is the usual thing among Americans who have been in the Philippines and imbibed a contempt or dislike for the people," he wrote, "to betray in their conversation the fact [that] their theories of the situation are based upon popular understandings at home as to Negro shortcomings and incapacity."[20] LeRoy's frustration was primarily aimed at the fixity of American categories and the incapacity of colonialists to distinguish wealthy Filipinos from the rabble. In exchange for what he believed a ridiculous racial metaphor, he called for a new and more subtle set of categories that would enable Americans to greet respectable, cosmopolitan Filipinos with the dignity and patronage they deserved. "Without in the least justifying the prejudice against negroes in the United States, what possible excuse does that afford for proceeding on the 'nigger' theory among a people largely Malayan?"[21]

As the civilian government built links to the Filipino political class, those categories were supplied by some of the new scientific and administrative organs established by the Philippine Commission. These new categories would give a more precise and authoritative understanding of the Filipino population that would allow easier alliances to be struck in regions still independent of American control, but one that would also supply a rationale for continued American rule. Within the government, these tasks were taken up by the Bureau of Non-Christian Tribes, whose work represented the fusion of research, administrative, and reformist goals within the umbrella of the new collaborationist politics.[22] Established in 1901 by the Philippine Commission, the Bureau of Non-Christian Tribes joined a Spanish colonial category to the institutional models of the Bureau of American Ethnology and the Bureau of Indian Affairs in an effort "[f]irst, to investigate the actual condition of these pagan and Mohammedan tribes, and to recommend legislation for their civil government; and second, to conduct scientific investigation in the ethnology of the Philippines."[23] Consistent with the extension of governmental control into highland regions and the emerging politics of collaboration, the work of the Bureau of Non-Christian Tribes replaced earlier racial generalization that joined Filipinos to black Americans, seeking through fieldwork and publication a more scientific and authoritative racial enumeration of different non-Christian groups and their relative levels of cooperation and "advancement." Gathered by American and Filipino provincial officials and a few amateur researchers at the outposts of American control, knowledge of non-Christians produced by the bureau was aimed toward the dual projects of highland diplomacy and military conquest, dealing with the specifics of individual tribes and their racial, cultural, and political connections with others.

As well as aiding diplomacy, the bureau brought more intense cultural attention to the Philippines' "non-Christian" peoples. The highland populations of the islands had been relatively obscure to earlier American travelers in the

Philippines, who seldom strayed beyond coastal areas. With the fieldwork of the bureau, Secretary Worcester's annual visitations and photographic zeal, and the Louisiana Purchase Exposition (St. Louis World's Fair of 1904), however, the non-Christian tribes in this period became a key element in the structure of American colonial justification.[24] But their symbolic use embodied the tensions between the racial thought of imperialists and anti-imperialists in the postwar period. In official renditions, the balances of paternalism required that the Filipinos be savage enough to require American tutelage and control, but not so backward as to make American efforts pointless. The tensions within paternalist representation emerged during the 1904 St. Louis Expo, where after much debate, tableaux of warlike tribesmen accompanied displays of marching Filipino constabularymen and dutiful children in schools.[25]

But within the proliferation of tribes studied by Bureau researchers and officials, the Negrito population, whose link to black Americans survived earlier debates, took on a special importance, receiving the first monograph published by the Bureau in 1904 (see figure 1).[26] Within the larger racial array that colonialists felt lay before them, Negritos presented special opportunities and conundrums. "The number of problems presented to the ethnologist by these little blacks is almost bewildering," wrote David Barrows, first director of the Bureau of Non-Christian Tribes, in his 1902 report.[27] The draw of the Negritos was in part narrowly disciplinary: historical-minded anthropologists were compelled by the opportunity to study what they believed the primitive ancestor (or forebear) of mankind. But interest may have also derived from broader racial concerns. In 1906, George Dorsey of the Field Museum in Chicago explained to an expedition sponsor that the goal of the Philippine project, the first of its kind mounted by a private museum in the United States, was "the determination of the relationship of these scattered Blacks through this area . . . above all to what extent they have influenced and have been influenced by the lighter skin tribes with whom they have come in contact."[28] Dorsey's sketch, while consistent with academic questions of migration and cultural diffusion, overlapped with preoccupations over racial hybridity and miscegenation. Perhaps in a world so diverse, in which the dreams of white purity and control were undermined by the realities of armed resistance, collaborative tension, and mutual acculturation, the border-ground between races itself was to become the object of study and reordering. But for all the questions of human ancestry and racial purity scholars believed the Negritos would answer, research on them appears to have flagged after the initial study. To the frustration of officials and researchers, Negrito populations moved upland when confronted by parties of scholars and constabularymen, and anthropologists found little in their material culture suitable to the American museum economy.[29]

Figure 1. This bust of a Negrito "type" was produced for the Louisiana Purchase Exposition (St. Louis World's Fair) of 1904. Courtesy Department of Library Services, American Museum of Natural History.

In policy making as well as research, American colonialists continued to draw some direction from paternalist approaches to the "Negro Problem" at home. In search of a model for the Philippine educational system, Frederick Atkinson, the regime's first superintendent of education, seized on the idea of industrial education, which had come to dominate the education of blacks in the United States. In April 1900 he wrote Booker T. Washington, industrial education's leading advocate, that "[e]ducation in the Philippines must be along industrial lines and any and all suggestions from you and your work will be invaluable."[30] The letter was followed by a May tour of Tuskegee and the Hampton Institute, the two core institutions of black industrial education; in his report to the Philippine Commission, Atkinson concluded that "the Filipinos may be taught those things for which they have a capacity, that is, industrial and mechanical pursuits. . . . These instructors should follow the plan of work of Hampton and Tuskegee."[31] In warning against a program of higher education in the colony, he presented his cautions by historical and racial analogy: "We should heed the lesson taught us in our reconstruction period when we started to educate the negro."[32] In a letter to Governor-General Taft that same year, his brother Horace agreed. "Won't you go in for industrial education for the Philippines?" he asked. "Certainly there is no other education for a race like the Negroes that compares with that in its effect upon character and race deficiency."[33]

The political use of non-Christians and the application of American models of paternalism, while they balanced arguments for both control and benevolence and suggested models from the American "Negro Problem," occasionally opened holes in networks of collaboration. In 1904, for example, the emphasis given to non-Christian peoples in American advertisements for empire sparked conflicts between the American government and its Filipino clients. Eager to promote their civilization and "fitness" for self-rule, Filipino politicians criticized connections made by American officials and anthropologists between Filipino elites, non-Christians, and America's racial minorities at the 1904 St. Louis Expo. Filipino collaborators attending the Expo to cement political relations and survey the non-Christian tribes put on display there expressed frustration at the Expo's larger message. As Vicente Nepomuceno, a Filipino official, claimed, the Republican administration had featured the "lowest types" of Filipinos "in an attempt to justify their paternal grip on the islands." As a result, he reported, "the impression has gone abroad that we are barbarians; that we eat dog and all that sort of thing, and no matter how long we [the Honorary Board] stay here we cannot convince the public to the contrary."[34]

Even within the colonial regime, the tensions expressed in the rhetoric of paternalism, its volatile blend of rigid hierarchy and potential uplift, could lead in unexpected directions. In certain contexts, the uplift elements of colonial paternalism drawn from contemporary discussions of the "Negro Problem" could fuse with anti-imperialist antislavery rhetoric in condemnations of the hierarchical Philippine social structure on which American rule was built. In December 1901, Dallas Henderson, an official in San Fernando, Pampanga, reported to Barrows that his commissioned investigation of local Negritos had stirred him to do further work that might "liberate them."[35] Against racial expectation, he had found the Negritos in his province bright and educable, and was shocked to find them oppressed by wealthy planters, often captured and sold as a mobile and tractable labor force. "They are scattered all over the northern part of this Island," he wrote, "and are slaves as much as our Negroes were in the South."[36] The abolitionist impulse present in some colonial paternalism was also found in Denzil Taylor, a young civil engineer in the early years of the occupation. Arriving in the islands in September 1900, he had set to work energetically as a provincial supervisor of public works projects in Ilocos Norte.[37] Within weeks, however, he began to encounter the seamier sides of colonial life: decadent landowners, corrupt American officials, and poverty-stricken peasants. Taylor was particularly angered by the oppressive tributary system in place in the provinces and the forced labor drafts customary under both Spanish and American regimes. Traveling widely with an "unrestrained intercourse with all classes," Taylor learned Spanish and Ilocano and earned the enmity of local elites for his interruption of tribute collection and insistence on paid labor.[38] "This is slavery," he wrote of price-fixing, "the thing must go."[39] On his travels through the region he demanded that Americans stop pressuring local leaders to intimidate villagers into forming unpaid labor gangs. In a diary entry for October 31, 1901, he wrote, "Have been over to San Nicolas, where an American school-teacher had persuaded the Presidente to take some natives from their work in the rice paddies to build some school houses for him. I stopped it—picked into the school-teacher heavy—told him to wait til there was money to pay for building school houses—I was mad."[40] Struggling to complete underfunded public works projects and educate Filipinos in irrigation and agricultural improvement before the rainy season of 1902, Taylor contracted cholera in the epidemic that swept the islands and died August 14, just under a year after his arrival. Taylor had named his target "slavery," and Reverend W. H. Branigan, in delivering the memorial sermon, made explicit the connections between Taylor's activism and earlier abolitionism: "Here was an iniquitous system of slavery which enabled rich and official classes to oppress the poorer and less fortunate. And to the work of righting that wrong—with all the zeal and determination which in the days of the anti-slavery crusade characterized a youthful Garrison or Parker or Wendell Phillips, he gave himself with heart and mind and strength."[41]

Imperial abolitionism of this sort faced hard limits in the colonial context. While they inherited earlier connections between enslaved blacks and colonized Filipinos made by the abolitionist ranks of the anti-imperialist movement, would-be abolitionists within the American empire could also denounce Filipino elites as a corollary to justifications of American intervention. Oppression of the native poor, although fundamentally responsible for the "backwardness" of rural Filipinos, was also made into evidence that neither class was capable of governing itself.[42] In this way, colonial paternalism and its analogies to white-black relations proved resilient. Mirrored to some extent in the hierarchical social evolutionism of bureau anthropologists, such paternalism laid conceptual ground rules for the building of the colonial state, making room for Filipino "advancement" only through careful "tutelage" and collaboration from below. In their insistence that paved roads and open markets, modern schools and remunerated labor would "elevate" the Filipino masses from their conditions of degradation, critics such as Taylor accepted many of imperialism's tenets, underestimated the economic power of Filipino landowners, and overestimated the benevolence of American-owned export agriculture, commercial ventures, and the political institutions that came with them. But critical assessments of Filipino society under American rule—emerging from both the Philippine revolutionary struggle and the battered memories of radical Republicanism—revealed the tensions within paternalism that left space for Filipino nationalists and internal colonial dissenters.

In 1906, the year of the first election of the Philippine Assembly, a young racial anatomist in Michigan laid out his professional vision of the field. "The race question in America has been treated recently," wrote Robert Bennett Bean in the *Century,* "from the standpoint of a former slave-owner, in the light of the Reconstruction period, in a mathematician's statistical way, and as an economic problem."[43] From several of these perspectives, Bean was well suited to approach the question and its implications in the latter years of the Philippines' Taft era. Confronting a rising opposition within the Philippines, the American government slowly opened municipal offices and elections to Filipinos and inaugurated the Philippine Assembly as the legislature's lower house in 1907. These political changes altered the face of colonial scholarly institutions. Faced with a budgetary crisis, the Philippine Commission eliminated the appropriation for the Bureau of Non-Christian Tribes in 1905, first transferring it as a division to the Bureau of Education, then to the Bureau of Science, before turning ethnological researches to private enterprise entirely in 1914. Nationalism and institutional change made for new articulations of the "Negro Problem" in the Philippines, represented by Bean's imperial career.

Born in 1874, Bean was the son of two old and venerable Virginia families; his father had courted his mother when he was a lieutenant in the Baltimore Light Artillery of the Army of Northern Virginia.[44] During his early years,

Bean's family apparently faced "trying circumstances of economic distress in the backwash of the Reconstruction period," and he was educated at home by a devout aunt. When he was thirteen his home schooling ceased, and for the next nine years he took up a series of odd jobs, including work as a guard of convict labor gangs. After graduating from Virginia Polytechnic Institute in 1900, he entered the Johns Hopkins Medical School and took an interest in anatomy, graduating in 1904 and receiving an appointment there. From 1905 to 1907 Bean continued his research as assistant professor of anatomy at the University of Michigan.

During this period, Bean's work centered on the comparative analysis of white and black brain tissue and an attempt to explain intellectual and moral development. Reflecting the racial pessimism of the New South, filtered through contemporary neurological theory, Bean's work shored up arguments for the permanent incapacity of blacks. In a 1906 article in the *Century*, "The Negro Brain," he laid out a popular account of his research, citing "observations made on thousands of negroes throughout the Middle Atlantic and Middle Western States."[45] After breaking the black population into a thicket of subcategories— from the lowest "Hottentots" of the South to the relatively "advanced" mulattos of the North—Bean presented his data that black brains both weighed less than white brains and had less developed front ends, signaling permanent differences in ability, including "sexual instability" and "bumptiousness." Having revealed through advanced science what was by then white Southern common sense, Bean concluded that "the white and Black races are anti-podal, then, in cardinal points . . . the one very advanced, the other a very backward one. The Caucasian and the negro are fundamentally opposed extremes in evolution."[46] Later that same year, Bean followed with a second article, "The Training of the Negro," in which he extended the list of black mental shortcomings but concluded, perhaps referring to his own work as a convict labor guard and recent debates over black officers in the Spanish-American War, that under the proper controls black capacities might be directed toward positive ends: "The negro is a good laborer under compulsion, or a good soldier with white officers, where his one idea is to work and obey."[47] In spite of his limited hopes for racial reform through industrial education, Bean chose to end on an ominous and impatient note of warning: "The negro must work out his own salvation with fear and trembling; for he is at the bar of public opinion, and if tried and found wanting, is in imminent danger of losing all."[48]

In 1907, Bean received an appointment through Michigan patronage networks to the colonial civil service in the Philippines; he traveled to Manila that year to take up the post of assistant professor and director of the anatomy lab of the Philippine Medical School. Probably his growing notoriety as a scholar of racial difference contributed to his selection; having convinced Michigan counterparts of his skill at anatomical interpretation at the very core of the "Negro Problem," he could surely deal with the vexing difficulties of the maturing civilian regime in the colony. With scientific resources available through the medical school and the research subjects he required—from Manila normal schools, villagers encountered on travels, hospital patients, or studies at the Malecon morgue—he eventually published seventeen articles based on his Philippine researches.[49]

But Bean's position in Manila brought to the foreground the problems inherent in Jim Crow's encounter with the racial complexity of the Philippines. Whereas his subjects in the United States had been divided into two easily discernible groups—blacks visiting the Johns Hopkins dispensary and white University of Michigan students—in the Philippines the proper racial categories for his subjects had to be made the ground of research itself. The traditional markers of race that had undergirded his prior research no longer held up in the colony, and new ones would have to be developed. "Color markings have been of no value in the differentiation of Filipino types," he wrote. "Hair form has been of little avail in the study of the Filipinos, because they all have straight black hair, with an occasional wave. The cephalic index has been found unreliable because of possible distortions of the head."[50] As a result, Bean's work, which culminated in *The Racial Anatomy of the Philippine Islanders* in 1910, was self-consciously innovative. Whereas his earlier work had been the comparative study of dead tissues between definite race groupings, this new work was primarily a "racial anatomy of the living" between groups whose boundaries were yet unclear.[51] In describing the book's objective, "to find the exact composition of a mixed population,"[52] he emphasized the thorny problem of type recognition: "The object of this book is to establish definite types of man that may be recognized by ear form, cephalic index, nasal index, and other factors, that such types may be studied in families through several generations to establish their hereditary characteristics."[53]

To do this, Bean joined German racial science and Mendelian genetics to enumerate seven racial types whose average qualities were already established.[54] By measuring individual Filipino subjects and correlating the data with figures from his ideal types, Bean was able to break down each subject into his or her constitutive racial types, tracing the Philippine racial constitution as a whole back to its pure sources by separating out genetic influences; putting a new term in Mendelian genetics to double use, Bean called this process "segregation."[55] To conclude, Bean presented his vision of Philippine racial history, in which successive waves of immigration intermixed the "three fundamental units of mankind,"[56] the old Iberian, Australoid, and Primitive races, into both "Blends" and an entirely distinct racial type, which he called "Homo Philippinensis."[57] Behind the protection of statistics and scientific jargon, Bean had taken his

239

readers into the heart of an American primal scene at the turn of the century, where races crossed and recrossed. The work's last line, however, sounded a contradictory note of segregationist confidence. Even miscegenation over the course of centuries could not obscure the underlying racial divisions of mankind: "Continual intermingling has failed to eradicate, or fuse, or blend the three fundamental types, Iberian, Primitive and Australoid, which continue in comparative purity throughout the Philippine Islands," he concluded.[58]

As the first scientist in the Philippines whose research had focused primarily on black Americans, Bean's own professional path demonstrated the continuities between earlier and later conceptions of the Philippine empire as a "Negro Problem." But his scholarship, as colonial science and racial thought, represented a degree of departure from earlier work in several areas. Whereas the Bureau's primary method was fieldwork, tangled in the politics of highland collaboration, Bean's research represented the rise of metropolitan scientific institutions. The change in site had important intellectual consequences: where Bureau researchers had had to deal with Filipinos as political and diplomatic units, and to their frustration, as interpreters, guides, and assistants who made travel possible, the medical case study model, and Bean's ready access to urban patients and remains, allowed him to measure individual Filipinos along categories of his own devising, ones he had sharpened in research on blacks in the United States.[59] This methodological shift was aided by the transfer of ethnological research from its original reformist and social evolutionist homes to the Bureau of Science, where the quantitative methods of biological, agricultural, and commercial research held greater sway.

Even as Bean's research was shaped by institutional change in science, his application of racial categories may have been a response to nationalist politics. With the passing of the provincial governments that had studied and overseen non-Christians into Filipino hands, the increasing volume of Philippine nationalists, and the rise of the Assembly, powerful claims had been set forth for the reality of a Philippine nation united by historic struggle. Bean's volume, in contrast, was a powerful testament both to Filipino racial division and the exclusive authority of American science to "segregate" its subjects into comprehensible parts. Where to some extent a "Homo Philippinensis" was discovered by both Bean and the nationalists in the late 1900s, Bean's was the backward subject drawn from his earlier racial imaginings of Baltimore blacks in the world of Jim Crow, in sharp contrast to the heroic patriot of nationalist oratory.

"If the Constitution does not follow the flag," wrote R. B. Lemus in 1903, "sentiment does, and as the sentiment of the Stars and Stripes now [seems] to be 'White Supremacy,' it would be the same in the far-off islands."[60] As Americans labored to make sense of Philippine society under American control, the extended patterns of the "Negro Problem," while commonly employed, were never completely agreed upon. The politics of empire were turbulent enough to call on conflicting accounts of race, making the "Negro Problem" malleable to many political ends. During the conduct of the war, the metaphor fired the hatreds of American soldiers, rallied anti-imperialists, and raised troubling questions for the army's black soldiers. In the early occupation, new variants emerged, borrowing on the paternalistic models of evolutionary science and industrial education. Consistent with forms of Jim Crow in the colony, Bean's eugenics hitched together researches on blacks and Filipinos, fracturing Filipino society into an anti-nation of distinct racial types. These colonial revisions of the "Negro Problem" in the Philippines then returned to domestic soil in a variety of forms. Black soldiers, disillusioned with the American struggle for empire and the pressures it had placed on them, wrote of their experiences as correspondents for hometown newspapers. Denzil Taylor, like many American colonialists, died in the islands, leaving only a memorial echo. Robert Bennett Bean, returning to the United States in 1910, took a position as professor at Tulane and in 1916 was appointed head of anatomy at the University of Virginia.[61]

NOTES

The author would like to thank Daniel Rodgers, Cynthia Petrites, Kevin Gaines, and Stephen Kantrowitz for their critical comments on early drafts of this paper, and Eileen Scully, Arcadio Díaz-Quiñones, Paul Taylor, Patricia Afable, Judith Kramer, and Oscar Kramer, for their continual support and encouragement.

1. William B. Freer, *The Philippine Experiences of an American Teacher* (New York: Charles Scribner's Sons, 1906), p. 5.
2. The themes of race and American empire, which I take up here, have been explored repeatedly by historians, with a variety of conclusions. The Wisconsin School's work, with its emphasis on the search for Asian markets as the driving force of imperialism, saw "social Darwinist" and "Anglo-Saxonist" rhetoric as an instrument of cynical political manipulation, either a distraction from the true economic bases of imperialism or an intellectual reflection of material imperatives. See Walter LaFeber, *The New Empire: An Interpretation of American Expansionism, 1860–1898* (Ithaca: Cornell University Press, 1963). More recent accountings see racial ideas as a causative element in imperialism, and focus on the congruence of racism and imperialism. See Nell Painter, "The White Man's Burden," in *Standing at Armageddon: The United States, 1877–1919* (New York: Norton, 1987). This piece sets out with the assumption of the latter work—that race figured prominently in the workings of imperialism—but unlike this work, I wish to undermine the idea that racism and

imperialism marched always together. At no point in American history has "race" ever had one stable or homogeneous meaning; rather, it has been a site of tremendous conflict. We should expect no less of this conflict for its imperial setting. American imperialism, far from a consensual arrangement, took place through a contest over which racial ideas were to matter and how, over what "race" itself was to mean. In the colonial setting, inheritance, experimentation, and transformation were present in equal parts: established racial ideas and institutions, many of them drawn from the "Negro Problem," were applied, fought over, reworked, and sometimes abandoned in new contexts.

3. James McPherson, "Women's Rights and Anti-imperialism," in *The Abolitionist Legacy: From Reconstruction to the NAACP* (Princeton: Princeton University Press, 1975). For an account of anti-imperialism, see Richard Welch, *Response to Imperialism: The United States and the Philippine-American War, 1899–1902* (Chapel Hill: University of North Carolina Press, 1979). For profiles of members of the anti-imperialist movement, see Robert Beisner, *Twelve against Empire: The Anti-Imperialists, 1898–1900* (Chicago: University of Chicago Press, 1985). For examples of anti-imperialist argument, see Philip S. Foner and Richard C. Winchester, *The Anti-imperialist Reader: A Documentary History of Anti-imperialism in the United States* (New York: Holmes and Meier, 1984).

4. The best treatment of black soldiers' conflicted experience in the Spanish-American and Philippine-American Wars remains Willard Gatewood, *Black Americans and the White Man's Burden* (Urbana: University of Illinois Press, 1975). For written testimonies by black soldiers, see Willard Gatewood, *"Smoked Yankees" and the Struggle for Empire: Letters from Negro Soldiers, 1898–1902* (Urbana: University of Illinois Press, 1971). See also Amy Kaplan, "Black and Blue on San Juan Hill," in *Cultures of United States Imperialism*, ed. Amy Kaplan and Donald Pease (Durham, N.C.: Duke University Press, 1993).

5. Theophilus Steward, *Cleveland Gazette,* May 18, 1898, as quoted in Gatewood, *"Smoked Yankees,"* p. 26. For a broader description of black uplift ideology, see Kevin Gaines, *Uplifting the Race: Black Leadership, Politics, and Culture in the Twentieth Century* (Chapel Hill: University of North Carolina Press, 1996).

6. T. Thomas Fortune, "Unjust Treatment of Afro-American Soldier," *New York Age,* editorial, February 13, 1892, p. 2., cited in William Seraile, "Theophilus Steward, Intellectual Chaplain, 25th U.S. Colored Infantry," *Nebraska History* 66, no. 3 (1985), p. 278.

7. While the solidarity of black soldiers with Filipinos was often limited by their own tenuous position and wartime suspicion, in a few notable cases, black soldiers rejected imperial conquest and sided with Filipino forces resisting the American army. For one such case, see Michael C. Robinson and Frank N. Schubert, "David Fagen: An Afro-American Rebel in the Philippines, 1899–1901," *Pacific Historical Review* 44, no. 1 (February 1975), pp. 68–83.

8. Theophilus Steward, *Cleveland Gazette,* April 21, 1900, cited in Gatewood, *"Smoked Yankees,"* p. 262–63.

9. Joseph O. Baylen and John Hammond Moore, "Senator John Tyler Morgan and Negro Colonization in the Philippines, 1901 to 1902," *Phylon* 29 (spring 1968), pp. 65–69.

10. R. B. Lemus, "The Negro and the Philippines," *Colored American Magazine* 6 (February 1903), p. 314.

11. T. Thomas Fortune, "The Filipinos: Some Incidents of a Trip through the Island of Luzon," *Voice of the Negro* 1 (June 1901), pp. 240–45.

12. Lemus, p. 314.

13. Lemus, p. 317.

14. For a detailed account of the American colonial project and relations between the U.S. government and the Federalista and Nacionalista parties, see Glenn A. May, *Social Engineering in the Philippines: The Aims, Execution and Impact of American Colonial Policy, 1900–1913* (Westport, CT: Greenwood, 1980); Peter Stanley, *A Nation in the Making: The Philippines and the United States, 1899–1921* (Cambridge: Harvard University Press, 1974); Peter Stanley, ed., *Reappraising an Empire: New Perspectives on Philippine-American History* (Cambridge: Harvard University Press, 1984); Ruby Paredes, ed., *Philippine Colonial Democracy* (New Haven: Yale University Southeast Asia Studies, 1988).

15. While there appear to have been no legal barriers, segregation as a means of institutionally defining colonial rulers and subjects seems to have been common. It may not be too far-fetched to use the term "Jim Crow" to describe this process. In using the term "Jim Crow," I refer to the racial segregation of public facilities, by both law and custom, which transformed relations between blacks and whites in Southern states at the turn of the century. The classic text on Jim Crow remains C. Vann Woodward, *The Strange Career of Jim Crow* (New York: Oxford University Press, 1965).

16. James LeRoy, "Race Prejudice in the Philippines," *Atlantic Monthly,* July 1902, p. 101.

17. LeRoy, p. 101.

18. LeRoy, p. 102.

19. LeRoy, p. 102.

20. LeRoy, p. 101.

21. LeRoy, p. 101.

22. The practice of American anthropological science and its relationship to administration in the highland Philippines is the larger subject of my work. For existing research, see Karl Hutterer, "Dean Worcester and Philippine Anthropology," *Philippine Quarterly of Culture and Society* 6 (1978), pp. 125–56; Frank Jenista, *The White Apos: American Governors on the Cordillera Central* (Quezon City: New Day Publishers, 1987).

23. David P. Barrows, "Report of the Chief of the Bureau of Non-Christian Tribes for the Year Ending August 31, 1902," in *Reports of the Philippine Commission* (Washington, D.C.: Government Printing Office, 1902), p. 679. As I hope to demonstrate in my larger work, interwoven with extensions of the "Negro

Problem" to the Philippines were the institutions of Indian policy and ethnological research. For an interesting discussion of legal categories brought to the Pacific from the experience of Western expansion and Indian policy, see Walter Williams, "United States Indian Policy and the Debate over Philippine Annexation: Implications for the Origins of American Imperialism," *Journal of American History* 66, no. 4 (March 1980), pp. 810–31.

24. The role played by Philippine non-Christians in colonial rationale has been explored in Robert Rydell, "The Louisiana Purchase Exposition, Saint Louis, 1904: 'The Coronation of Civilization,'" in *All the World's a Fair: Visions of Empire at American International Expositions, 1876–1916* (Chicago: University of Chicago Press, 1984); Vicente Rafael, "White Love: Surveillance and Nationalist Resistance in the U.S. Colonization of the Philippines," in *Cultures of United States Imperialism,* ed. Amy Kaplan and Donald Pease (Durham, N.C.: Duke University Press, 1993); Renato Rosaldo, "Utter Savages of Scientific Value," in *Politics and History in Band Societies,* ed. Eleanor Leacock and Richard Lee (Cambridge: Cambridge University Press, 1982). Worcester's role as showman of primitivism is central: see Rodney Sullivan, *Exemplar of Americanism: The Philippine Career of Dean C. Worcester* (Ann Arbor: University of Michigan Press, 1991). For a discussion of the role of "slavery" in discussions of non-Christians and Filipino "fitness" for self-rule, see Michael Salman, "The United States and the End of Slavery in the Philippines, 1898–1914: A Study of Imperialism, Ideology and Nationalism," 2 vols. (Ph.D. diss., Stanford University, 1993), chaps. 10–18.

25. Rydell, pp. 171–77.

26. William Allan Reed, *Negritos of Zambales,* Department of the Interior, Ethnological Survey Publications, vol. 2, pt. 1 (Manila: Bureau of Public Printing, 1904). For a discussion of early research interest in the Negritos from a disciplinary perspective, see Rudolf Rahmann, "The Philippine Negritos in the Context of Research on Food-Gatherers during This Century," *Philippine Quarterly of Culture and Society* 3 (1975), pp. 204–36.

27. Barrows, p. 680. Barrows's own complex political thought requires greater discussion than is possible here. As the Philippines' second superintendent of education, he began a campaign of literary and practical education that he hoped would liberate the enslaved Philippine peasantry from the grip of the cacique system. His thought joined critiques of New South political economy to an attack on Indian policy as he had encountered it as a California anthropologist, all within the rubric of a defense of American prerogative in the Philippines. For a discussion of Barrows, see Kenton Clymer, "Humanitarian Imperialism: David Prescott Barrows and the White Man's Burden in the Philippines," *Pacific Historical Review* 45, no. 4 (November 1976), pp. 495–517; and May, chap. 6.

28. Letter from George Dorsey to R. F. Cummings, June 2, 1906, Records of the Cummings Expedition, Field Museum of Natural History Archives, Chicago.

29. Often ignored in studies of anthropology and colonial ideology, as much from the difficulties of source materials as from theoretical orientation, is the reluctance or open resistance by colonized peoples to becoming assembled pieces of colonial expression. To understand better the politics of colonial science, researchers must try to read around the edges of imperialist narratives more carefully to see the limits placed on their projects, including anthropology, by the responses of studied peoples.

30. May, p. 92.

31. May, p. 92.

32. May, p. 93.

33. May, p. 92.

34. *St. Louis Post-Dispatch,* July 18, 1904, cited in Sharra Vostral, "Imperialism on Display: The Philippine Exposition at the 1904 World's Fair," *Gateway Heritage* (Spring 1993), pp. 29–30.

35. Dallas Henderson, Report to David P. Barrows, December 7, 1901, Beyer Collection of Original Sources in Philippine Ethnography, Tozzer Library, Harvard University.

36. Henderson.

37. "Biography," in *In Memory of Denzil Hollis Taylor, 1877–1902* (Boston: n.p., [1902?]), pp. 7–8.

38. "Biography," p. 11.

39. Quoted in Reverend W. H. Branigan, "A Memorial Sermon," in *In Memory of Denzil Hollis Taylor, 1877–1902,* p. 32.

40. "Extracts from Denzil's Letters," in *In Memory of Denzil Hollis Taylor, 1877–1902,* p. 143.

41. Branigan, pp. 31–32.

42. Salman traces in great detail the evolution of antislavery discourse from the language of anti-imperialism to a "hegemonic ideology" and one of the central justifications for American retention.

43. Robert Bennett Bean, "The Negro Brain," *Century,* September 1906, p. 778.

44. William Bennett Bean, "Obituary, Robert Bennett Bean, 1874–1944," *Science* 101, no. 2623 (April 6, 1945), p. 346.

45. Bean, "Negro Brain," p. 779.

46. Bean, "Negro Brain," p. 784. For a criticism of Bean's scientific procedures, see Stephen Jay Gould, *The Mismeasure of Man* (New York: Norton, 1981).

47. Robert Bennett Bean, "The Training of the Negro," *Century,* December 1906, p. 949.

48. Bean, "Training of the Negro," p. 953.

49. Most of Bean's work was published first in the *Philippine Journal of Science,* the organ of the colonial government's Bureau of Science, although several of his pieces appeared in more popular journals like *American Anthropologist* and *Science.*

50. Robert Bennett Bean, *The Racial Anatomy of the Philippine Islanders* (Philadelphia: J. B. Lippincott, 1910), p. 219.

51. Bean, *Racial Anatomy*, p. 7.

52. Bean, *Racial Anatomy*, p. 207.

53. Bean, *Racial Anatomy*, pp. 8–9.

54. Bean's use of these methods and theories can be located in the institutions of his training. Founded in the late 1870s, Johns Hopkins was the first American university established along the lines of the German research university, and intellectual connections and travel between Hopkins and German universities were common. For a detailed account of the intellectual current of "polygeneticism" that Bean inherited and in turn based his innovations on, see George Stocking, "The Persistence of Polygenetic Thought in Post-Darwinian Anthropology," in *Race, Culture and Evolution: Essays in the History of Anthropology* (Chicago: University of Chicago Press, 1968). On the retreat of Lamarckian thought and the rise of genetics, see Carl Degler, *The Search for Human Nature: The Decline and Revival of Darwinism in American Social Thought* (New York: Oxford University Press, 1991).

55. The *Oxford English Dictionary* records the first use of the term "segregation" to refer to the differentiation of organic cell materials in 1902. Bean's use of the term to mean the division of individual organisms—rather than cells—into their hereditary components may have been a new application of the term.

56. Bean, *Racial Anatomy*, p. 221.

57. Bean, *Racial Anatomy*, pp. 227–29.

58. Bean, *Racial Anatomy*, p. 224.

59. Warwick Anderson has stressed the emergence of the laboratory and its impact on colonial medicine in the Philippines in " 'Where Every Prospect Pleases and Only Man Is Vile': Laboratory Medicine as Colonial Discourse," *Critical Inquiry* 18 (Spring 1992), pp. 502–29; idem, "Colonial Pathologies: American Medicine in the Philippines, 1898–1921" (Ph.D. diss., University of Pennsylvania, 1992).

60. Lemus, p. 317.

61. Bean, "Obituary," p. 347.

14

RUSTY L. MONHOLLON

BLACK POWER, WHITE FEAR

THE "NEGRO PROBLEM" IN LAWRENCE, KANSAS, 1960–1970

Throughout the 1960s, Lawrence, a small community of forty-five thousand in northeast Kansas and home to the University of Kansas (KU), was racked by protests and demonstrations by students and civil rights activists. For more than a decade, Lawrencians agitating for civil rights, for more control over their personal lives, and against the war in Vietnam clashed with the rigid and at times hostile response of those opposed to their desires, creating tension in the town. Through their frequent sit-ins, marches, and vigils, many young Kansans, like their peers across the country, expressed their disenchantment with American society. Responding to these demonstrations, other residents of Lawrence expressed their own concerns about the new activism—they saw a breakdown of law and order, a flippant disregard for moral values and standards; they felt a creeping fear of a communist takeover of society. These conflicting views divided Lawrence, limiting cooperation, sharpening differences, hardening conflict, and hindering efforts at reconciliation. By 1970 the threat of violence, which had loomed since the beginning of the decade, had become a reality. Bombings throughout the community, racial fights at Lawrence High School, a devastating, multimillion-dollar arson at the University Memorial Union, and a three-day curfew thrust Lawrence into the national spotlight and created confusion for its residents. This chaos culminated in the shooting deaths of two young men— one black, one white—by Lawrence police during one week in July 1970.

Rick "Tiger" Dowdell, a nineteen-year-old native of Lawrence and a member of Lawrence's militant black community, died on July 16, 1970, from a bullet wound to the head, fired by Officer William Garrett of the Lawrence Police Department (LPD), after a car chase involving Dowdell. In 1968 Dowdell had participated in a protest at Lawrence High School, and later became a member of the Black Student Union (BSU) while a student at the University of Kansas. After the shooting Garrett claimed Dowdell had fired shots at him, and a gun was found near the body. The slain teen had had many altercations with Lawrence police, and previously had complained of police harassment.[1] Dowdell's brother claimed that Garrett had threatened to "get one of you Dowdells yet" when he stopped Rick for a broken taillight the night before the shooting.[2]

At Dowdell's funeral service at St. Luke's African Methodist Episcopal Church, the Reverend A. N. Larkin implored the congregation to employ nonviolence in their struggle for civil rights. "Violence after violence solved nothing," the lean preacher extolled, evoking the nonviolent spirit of Martin Luther King, "Freedom was never gained with a gun in the hand or violence in the heart." Conversely, the Reverend Oquisa Benefee of the McKissick Liberation School in Milwaukee, in attendance at the funeral, spoke of centuries of black struggle "as related in the Bible . . . and of the lifestyle of a young revolutionary" like Dowdell. "Such a person's life," he said, "does not belong to the individual but to the struggle, and in this context Rick Dowdell died."[3] Despite this rhetoric, Helen Kimball, a 1966 Lawrence High graduate, believed that Dowdell died not as a martyr nor as a revolutionary, but "in self-defense." At "that particular instant" and "with the particular officer that was involved," Kimball claimed, any black in Lawrence might have died in Dowdell's place.[4]

An all-white panel at a coroner's inquest exonerated Garrett in the shooting. The black community largely rejected the verdict; its militant faction threatened retaliation. The Black Student Union at the University of Kansas vowed that Garrett "shall reap what he has sown."[5] A letter to city officials purportedly written by Leonard Harrison, the director of the Ballard recreation center in

North Lawrence, promised that the black community would "no longer allow Black people to be brutalized" by whites and that it would "avenge the death of our beautiful brother by any means necessary. We are saying if it is necessary, we will kill . . . any other muthafucka that gets in the way of the total liberation of our people. . . . Lawrence will become a police state if justice is denied us."[6] White radicals, who, like blacks in Lawrence, believed they were denigrated by the mainstream white community and harassed by the police, also condemned Dowdell's death. The underground newspaper *Vortex* published Garrett's photograph above the caption "Wanted for Murder," which outraged many local residents.[7] The night of the shooting and the following night, snipers shot out car windows and street lights, and fired at police officers and firefighters responding to calls. An LPD officer was wounded in a gun battle with blacks "employing guerilla tactics" near the Afro-House, a black cultural center established by the BSU.[8]

The violence set the stage for yet another death. The following two days remained quiet, with only minor incidents, mostly in a section of town called Oread, an area adjacent to the university and home to many of the so-called street people. There, on July 20, fire hydrants were opened and cars were overturned and set afire. Police attempted to disperse the people gathered there by firing above the crowd. In the confusion, Nick Rice, a teenaged white male who had just finished his first year at KU, lay dying in the street. By all accounts Rice was an innocent victim; he was not a radical, nor had he had previous encounters with the police, nor had he been involved in the infractions that led to the police's being called to the area. Following Rice's death, Kansas Governor Robert B. Docking placed the city under an emergency curfew and sent Kansas Highway Patrol troopers to relieve weary Lawrence police officers from routine traffic duty.[9]

Outrage came exclusively from the black community or the radical fringe when Dowdell was killed. Some whites even justified the shooting. A business owner circulated a petition that expressed "our gratitude and sympathy" to police wounded by sniper fire, and praised the "courageous action of the police officer who fired the shot that killed Dowdell."[10] The state senator from Lawrence remarked that Lawrence "hadn't lost a thing" when Dowdell died, which the black community decried as symptomatic of whites' general indifference to blacks.[11]

Some white residents of Lawrence had also become radicalized. A group calling itself the Loyal American Whites (LAW) demanded $500 billion from the "Negro race," to pay for the "expense of educating them from slavery into the American mainstream."[12] Raymond Vandeventer claimed he headed a secret vigilante organization that included "300 members in Lawrence and 1600 backup people." Vandeventer promised to use "guerilla warfare" to halt the "nigger and hippie militants."[13]

How had Lawrence become so polarized, and why did such tragic events happen there? The sources of the violence were many, but they all stemmed from the nation's encounters with contemporary social issues: racism, the Vietnam War, campus unrest, women's liberation, the counterculture. Although Lawrence witnessed conflicts over all these social issues, its problems were most deeply entrenched in the extant racial tensions. The bloodshed in Lawrence was primarily the consequence of the reactions, from both blacks and whites, to the emergence of black militancy, and specifically the Black Power movement in Lawrence, as an alternative to mainstream civil rights activism.

"The problem of the twentieth century is the problem of the color line . . . the relation of the darker to the lighter races of men," W. E. B. Du Bois wrote in 1903.[14] White Americans, Du Bois argued, defined the existence of African Americans and their failure to assimilate into white American society as the "Negro Problem." African Americans have had to fight against not only virulent racism and structural barriers, but also white indifference to that struggle. But since white Americans have dictated the terms of the debate, as Du Bois noted, and with little compelling reason for whites to reform all of American society, responsibility for finding a solution has historically fallen to black Americans. This has created a paradox for blacks: how far could they go in demanding their legitimate rights as American citizens before whites claimed they were moving too far and too fast? If blacks did not push at all for racial and social equality, they remained confined to second-class citizenship. If they pushed too hard and threatened the status quo, white society resisted even their most legitimate of claims.

This was as true in Lawrence as anywhere. In 1965, Lawrence Paper Company president Justin D. Hill complained about a recent civil rights demonstration at the University of Kansas. "Before Negroes will be accepted by whites as equals," he wrote, "they will have to raise their standard of living to the accepted level of the community." This conviction, shared by many whites in Lawrence, held that African Americans already had an equality of opportunity—protected by law—with whites. Social inequality was due to blacks' failure to exploit their opportunities; therefore it was the responsibility of black Americans—not whites—to resolve the problem. It was, Hill claimed, "up to the Negro and Negro leaders to raise the standards of their race."[15] Therefore, many white Lawrencians were either vehemently hostile to the black freedom struggle or, more commonly, completely indifferent to the cause, arguing that the movement's moderate goals of legal, political, and social equality already existed. This constructed view of American society ignored the very real indignities blacks suffered and the institutional and economic obstacles they encountered. Hill, like most other whites in Lawrence, refused to acknowledge that his antipathy was an impediment to blacks' exercising their equality of opportunity. Despite the ongoing efforts of civil rights activists, blacks in Lawrence confronted segregated facilities, clustered substandard housing, limited educational and employment opportunities, and the indignities of racial slurs and social exclusion.

With the passage of the Civil Rights Act of 1964 and the Voting Rights Act of 1965, it seemed that the civil rights movement was redeeming its promise of racial equality. But as the historian Harvard Sitkoff notes, "the movement created aspirations it could not fulfill," which pushed many young activists toward the nascent vision of Black Power.[16] In 1966, Stokely Carmichael's cry for "Black Power" quickly became an exhilarating ideological alternative to the traditional civil rights movement. A year later, Carmichael and Charles Hamilton defined the inchoate concept as a call for blacks to "unite, recognize their heritage, and build a sense of community," and "to define their own goals" and "lead their own organizations."[17] The historian Clayborne Carson writes that Black Power "formulate[d] a political vocabulary that expressed the previously unarticulated anger of many blacks, particularly the young and urban poor."[18] Many African Americans in Lawrence, lured by Black Power's emphasis on cultural and racial self-identification, and armed with a vocabulary that allowed them to release their own anger, quickly embraced its ideology and reshaped the terms of the debate on the "Negro Problem" in Lawrence.

A young African-American protestor remarked in April 1970 that whites in Lawrence were unconcerned with social issues until they personally affected them. "When it comes through your front door, you worry about it," he explained.[19] What young blacks in Lawrence wanted was to be treated with respect and to be allowed to express their pride in being black. The impressive record of victories in the courts and civil rights legislation neither raised the economic or social status of African Americans in Lawrence nor significantly contributed to a sense of racial pride or self-identity. Threatening to overthrow the white power structure—however futile that exercise may have seemed to whites—was psychologically liberating and produced a sense of cultural pride and identity for African Americans.[20]

Whites literally had to be shaken out of their complacency. The white community's perceived threat of violence by blacks initially was a powerful spur to progress toward racial equality in Lawrence. The historian Steven F. Lawson has noted that "burgeoning racial pride among African Americans was instrumental for black political mobilization."[21] Traditional civil rights efforts in Lawrence, similar to the nonviolent, direct action employed by Martin Luther

King, were by themselves insufficient to eliminate segregation, combat inadequate housing, and enhance employment opportunities in the city. As the
sociologist Herbert H. Haines has suggested, Black Power "generated a crisis in
American institutions which made the legislative agenda of 'polite, realistic,
and businesslike' mainstream organizations more attractive to societal decision
makers." Rather than "hindering the cause of civil rights," these "strident
voices" instead "enhanced the moderates' bargaining power," a proposition that
Lawrence's example substantiates.[22]

Despite having been a haven for runaway slaves in the nineteenth century,
Lawrence in the twentieth century was a segregated town. Grassroots civil rights
organizations struggled for racial justice there at least as far back as World War
II. In the 1940s, the liberal, predominantly white Lawrence League for the
Practice of Democracy (LLPD) and the Lawrence-Douglas County chapter of
the National Association for the Advancement of Colored People (LDC-
NAACP) fought to pass local antidiscrimination laws. Between 1951 and 1960,
University of Kansas chancellor Franklin D. Murphy, by threatening to show
first-run movies and open barber shops and cafés on campus that would compete
with Lawrence's segregated businesses, convinced many businesspeople to open
their doors to blacks.[23] Murphy's quest was aided by the towering presence of
Wilt Chamberlain, the seven-foot KU basketball star, who claimed he "single-
handedly integrated . . . every damn place within 40 miles of Lawrence."[24]

But even this apparent progress was illusory. In 1960—after Murphy and
Chamberlain had left Lawrence—white Lawrence business owners and city
officials ignored antidiscrimination laws, and African Americans again were
denied service in restaurants, skating rinks, bowling alleys, and swimming pools.
Although blacks had voted freely in Lawrence since the end of the Civil War,
they could buy or rent only substandard housing in clustered neighborhoods
scattered around the town. They typically earned a third less than did whites—
mainly from jobs confined to domestic service—but still suffered higher rates of
unemployment and underemployment, and limited educational and employment opportunities.[25] Like other African Americans in the North, those in
Lawrence had all the trappings of equality but were not afforded the opportunity
and respect of first-class citizenship.

The 1954 *Brown v. Board of Education* decision and the Greensboro sit-ins in
1960 inspired Lawrence freedom fighters, both black and white, to continue to
press for equality in their town. Continuing a fifteen-year struggle to integrate
Lawrence's swimming pools, in 1960 the LLPD unsuccessfully challenged the
racially exclusive policies of the Jayhawk Plunge, a privately owned swim club.

The KU student-based Civil Rights Council in 1961 tried—again, unsuccessfully—to compel local businesses to comply with the Kansas Public Accommodations Law. Throughout the decade, the LDC-NAACP, along with local churches and the LLPD, lobbied for fair housing legislation and to improve employment opportunities for blacks in Lawrence, with only moderate success.[26]

Hindering these efforts was a prevailing attitude of apathy and hostility. Ed Abels, the conservative editor of the weekly *Lawrence Outlook,* disapproved of all civil rights protests. He claimed that racial tension would persist "as long as the principal appeal" of civil rights activists continued "to be the emotion of the Negroes as they are induced to form mobs in which there is singing, praying, cheering and resistance to law and order." According to Abels, communist agitators were exploiting "the economic situation," which was "the ideal situation for the trouble makers to fan the flames of hatred and to play on the emotions of the Negro, and many whites."[27] Justin Hill agreed, incredulous that blacks were "demanding housing in suburbs developed by whites, jobs in companies developed by whites, the right to eat in restaurants and go to stores owned and developed by whites. . . . white people must earn the right to these things, it is not given to them. The coloreds should earn the right to these things."[28]

Because of white antipathy, even successful civil rights demonstrations—typically measured by favorable court decisions or legislation—were limited in what they could accomplish. For example, after a student-led sit-in in Chancellor Clarke Wescoe's office in March 1965, the University of Kansas removed racially discriminatory advertising from campus publications, removed racist landlords from university-approved housing, agreed not to work with school districts that would not hire black teachers, forced all campus organizations to affirm that race was not a consideration for membership, established a human relations committee to redress racially motivated grievances, and restated the university's commitment to equal opportunity for all.[29] Unfortunately, these gains were only a hollow victory. Because of legislation and court victories, for decades civil rights had been perceived—by whites and blacks alike—as improving. Racism in Lawrence persisted, however, and although the sit-in in Wescoe's office could be called a legislative and administrative success, it still did not, or could not, break down racist attitudes. One year after the sit-in, a protestor, Norma Norman, was called "nigger" by a group of white fraternity men dressed in blackface and wearing bones in their wigged hair. Indeed, Norman believed a "backlash" against blacks resulted from the protest.[30] Believing that blacks had been given equality rather than earning it, whites in Lawrence hardened their opposition to what they perceived as a disruption of society and a threat to their own security and status.

It was this kind of "success" that contributed to the disillusionment of many blacks, which pushed them to other means of protest. Norman stated that "by the time it had filtered down" to the next generation of African Americans, "all this other stuff had been tried. They saw our generation struggling with it, [and] made no gains." Militancy was "the next logical alternative."[31] Black Power advocate Charles V. Hamilton wrote in 1968 that "there comes a point beyond which people cannot be expected to endure prejudice, oppression, and deprivation, and they *will* explode."[32] By 1967 it appeared that many young African Americans in Lawrence had reached that point and were ready to consider other ways of achieving equality.

Frustrations among and tension between blacks and whites were apparent across the United States in 1967, when almost two dozen American cities experienced racial violence. Enraged over the continued lack of summer recreational and employment opportunities and the apathetic attitude of Lawrence's city officials and whites in rectifying the situation, early in August 1967, a large group of teenage blacks gathered downtown and, according to the Lawrence teacher and civil rights leader Jesse Milan, threatened to burn the town.[33] Lawrence escaped violence that summer, but the Lawrence Human Relations Commission and other whites perceived a threat, whether or not it was as serious as Milan remembers. Lawrence Police Chief Bill Troelstrup scoffed at suggestions that the city had been on the threshold of a race riot, claiming that his department did not "act on rumors."[34] This comment diminishes Milan's claim that a riot was imminent, but it reinforces the notion that many people in Lawrence feared such an event. Milan, the first black teacher hired in the integrated, post-*Brown* Lawrence schools, knew most of the young blacks, having taught them in school, and sincerely believed that the youths "were ready to riot."[35] Moreover, Milan's concerns were shared by many whites in Lawrence, their fears intensified by accounts of urban rioting in Newark, Detroit, and Wichita, Kansas. That summer, the *Lawrence Daily Journal-World* ran disturbing headlines: "Negro Outburst Follows Order Setting Curfew," "Wichita Feels More Violence during Curfew," and "Gangs of Negroes Shake U.S. Capital." This gathering of young blacks so concerned a part of the community that a special meeting was arranged between the Lawrence Human Relations Commission and young African Americans on August 8, 1967.

An important aspect of this LHRC meeting was the forum it provided for African-American youths to express their views. John Spearman, Jr., a senior at Lawrence High School, was not present among the throngs of black students gathered on Massachusetts Street. Like most of his peers, however, he was angry at the lack of progress in race relations in Lawrence. Moreover, Spearman was now willing to express that anger, which he did at the LHRC meeting. He had reached a point in his life where he was weighing alternatives to the mainstream civil rights movement, which he believed "had failed to get it done."[36] Within a year, Spearman was a committed and radical proponent of Black Power, using his rage to try to unite the black community and gain political power for blacks. The meeting also produced some immediate results. Civil rights activists had been trying since the 1940s to integrate Lawrence's swimming clubs and to build a municipal pool open to all residents. The Lawrence City Commission agreed to lease temporarily an unused swimming pool open to all Lawrence citizens, regardless of race. Later that fall, Lawrence voters agreed to finance the construction of an integrated municipal swimming pool, which was completed in 1970.[37]

Black anger became a crucial factor in the decision to lease the temporary pool and the passage of the pool bond issue. The threat of violence—actual or perceived—by angry young African Americans helped bring about change. The LHRC's willingness to hold a special meeting to hear the black youths' grievances attests to this. Even if all that actually happened was that a group of young African Americans congregated in the downtown area, the need for a public meeting to discuss that nonevent is a powerful testament to the depth of white fears, exacerbated by the growing unrest and militancy among urban African Americans elsewhere. The threat of violence compelled local officials to provide temporary swimming facilities accessible to the entire community, and the residual effects of that threat contributed to the passage of bonds to finance a permanent municipal swimming pool in November. Additionally, the LHRC began holding weekly rather than monthly meetings. Without the threat of violence, it is doubtful that this sudden activity would have occurred when it did. Black youths in Lawrence had tapped into the dynamic force of Black Power, which was reshaping civil rights activism.

This was apparent the following year at Lawrence High School (LHS). In May 1968, about fifty black students and their parents met with Lawrence High principal William Medley and six counselors and teachers. The students raised several issues: discrimination by the faculty and staff, the racially biased selection process for athletic teams and cheerleaders, the lack of communication between black students and officials, and the possibility of adding black history and cultural studies courses to the curriculum. Additionally, black students objected to the insensitivity of white students and teachers. One black student reported that a teacher had cursed her, after she was unable to finish an assignment properly by saying, "You niggers can't do anything right." Medley excused the teacher's behavior as "a slip of the tongue that doesn't necessarily indicate prejudice." John Spearman told school officials that only another black would understand the feeling of being oppressed.[38] Medley rejected the students' claims of oppression, remarking that "all people were oppressed"; he personally had experienced it because he was "redheaded."[39] Nothing came of this meeting except a promise from Medley to work with black students in improving race relations at the school.

Medley believed conditions at LHS were improving; many African Americans, however, disagreed. On September 25, 1968, thirty-seven black students demanded of school officials assured black representation on the cheerleading squad, a black homecoming queen, additional black teachers and administrators, black history and culture courses, and a black student union—the same items discussed at the May meeting. They then walked out of school in protest. Medley suspended them, saying that they would not be reinstated until each student and his or her parents had met with him.

The students were inspired by the Black Power movement. The national movement had an intangible quality that appealed to many young blacks, and it exuded a certain excitement. While this did not stimulate all black students to action—the protesting students constituted only about one-third of all blacks at LHS—the cultural aspects of the movement, evident in their demands, were persuasive to those who did walk out. The influence of the Black Power movement was apparent in the militancy of the students' protest. They refused the help of white KU students, stating that whites "should worry about their own problems as white members of the community."[40] The students insisted that they would "not return to" school until officials agreed to their terms, and that they were "not just asking for these things" but were "demanding them." If their conditions were not met, they would resort to "other means."[41] This implied threat concerned many whites, fifteen of whom wrote to superintendent Carl Knox, urging him to give them a chance to be heard, fearing that "killing their spirit . . . may incite violence."[42] This effort at reconciliation clearly was not the dominant view. Moreover, it is not clear whether these writers were motivated by altruism or merely wished to avoid violence.

The response of school administrators more accurately reflected the mood of the white community. Selecting cheerleaders "according to race is not consistent with the principles of our American way of life," Medley said. "We don't discriminate neither do we go out of our way to hand pick for special consideration because of race, color or creed."[43] Other comments were less tactful. A typical complaint read, "the demands of Negro students at Lawrence High School, as well as the demands of national Negro leaders, have reached a state of unbelievable irrationality . . . they are demanding that there be racial quotas established. They want Negroes assigned to these positions for reasons of their race."[44] Knox received petitions signed by over six hundred "tired tax payers" approving of the suspensions and condemning the walkout. According to LHS student president Mike Roark, "most white students disapproved" of the protest. If their demands were granted, Roark said, the black students would want more and would never be "satisf[ied]."[45] Ed Abels claimed the protestors were merely imitating "radical and ignorant college students," and that the walkout "placed renewed emphasis on the need for more industrial and practical courses in the high schools for those who do not want to go to college," which presumably referred to African Americans.[46]

Even as it enraged whites, the walkout helped unify the black community. Fifty black students, their parents, and other African Americans formed a "symbolic black school," which included black "volunteer teachers, some parents, and some [accredited] teachers."[47] The KU Black Student Union (BSU) sent advisors.[48] This unity was most evident at the October 7, 1968, school board meeting, devoted entirely to a discussion of the walkout. The students' parents said they were "proud" that their children had "the awareness, the pride and the determination to make the effort through traditional democratic processes to fight against racism and discrimination." The students, "after having exhausted all orderly and conventional means of protest," had no other choice but to walk out.[49]

The walkout abruptly ended on September 29, when the black students, without explanation, returned to classes according to the administration's conditions. Administrators made no guarantee of black representation on the cheerleading squad, although they did agree to amend the selection process so that ability, and not solely popularity, would be a factor. Officials also agreed to increase efforts to hire more black teachers, coaches, and administrators and to consider creating a black history course.[50] While most whites believed that the "concessions" given to the black students were more than adequate, they clearly fell short of their demands.

The protest had made clear the change in attitude among many young African Americans in Lawrence, first apparent in August 1967, and even more so in September 1968. The black students had taken direct action in pursuit of their demands through a militant attitude. The students demanded change, were less polite and respectful toward authority, and were contemptuous of the label "Negro." Their demands reflected an identification with Black Power, a display of pride in being black, and an effort to work together to take control of their own lives. The protest also illustrated the antipathy of whites to black militancy. Although the 1968 protest produced no immediate results, it established a foundation for future action and empowered both students and parents in the black community by infusing them with a sense of self-identity and racial pride. This was the real strength of Black Power. As an ideology, it was as much a cultural and psychological movement as it was political, and in this sense the walkout was successful. The students had forced school officials and whites in Lawrence to take notice of their demands, and their actions had unified a large portion of the black community.

This essay paints a pessimistic picture of race relations and progress in Lawrence during the 1960s. While progress toward racial equality could be claimed in the post–World War II era, that progress was not that of Martin Luther King's dream of complete racial integration and the acceptance of African Americans by whites as social equals. Between 1960 and 1967, there was a clear transition in Lawrence from the traditional, liberal, integrationalist/assimilationist approach to civil rights to an increasingly separatist, confrontational, and sometimes violent movement led primarily by young African Americans. Many blacks in Lawrence, although not all, moved away from a desire for integration into white society and embraced the Black Power movement. Traditional civil rights activity in Lawrence continued, but the emergence of activists committed to Black Power, and the accompanying fearful reactions from the white community, escalated long-standing racial tensions and contributed to the bloodshed.

This is not to say that Black Power, or blacks, bore all, or even principal, responsibility for the violence. There was a tension and ambivalence to Black Power; it meant different things to different groups and individuals. Most white Lawrencians were utterly hostile to Black Power. Because the prevailing attitudes and institutional structure of white, middle-class society were indifferent even to modest black demands, this should not be surprising. The apathy and antipathy of white society were perhaps the most onerous barrier confronting African Americans in their quest for equality. The combination of indifference and hostility was a powerful force to overcome. Moreover, Black Power's sometimes inflammatory rhetoric would have been impotent if the heat of racial oppression were absent; the crucible of white racism in Lawrence made militant words very relevant to young blacks.

Moreover, as Lawrence's African Americans embraced Black Power, they redefined the "Negro Problem" on their own terms. The results, like American race relations in general, were paradoxical. While it was empowering for blacks, it also contributed to a polarization of the entire community along racial lines. Most whites could not understand the rhetoric and actions of Black Power, nor could they understand why some African Americans were dissatisfied with the civil rights "progress" that had been made. More important, however, most whites refused to acknowledge that any problem had ever existed, or if they did, they charged blacks for creating their own problems. A white service station attendant in Lawrence unwittingly expressed the essence of the "Negro Problem" in 1970 when he proclaimed, "What I don't understand is they call me a racist.

Hell I don't even know what a racist is. I do a lot of business with niggers.[51]

William Van Deberg suggests that the Black Power movement was necessary because "there were too many barriers of too many kinds and they were toppling too slowly. Black people . . . wanted to know the time and the place of their own triumph over both institutional racism and the burden of everyday insults."[52] Was there a need for a Black Power movement in Lawrence? The answer is a resounding yes. African Americans in Lawrence also wanted to know the time and the place of their triumph, and using Black Power as their guide, they struggled for that goal on their own terms. Black Power, even before it was articulated nationally, was in Lawrence a seminal element in the black freedom struggle, and contributed to significant political and civil rights victories. Those gains, however, were not without costs. In Lawrence, Kansas, Black Power and white fear proved a deadly combination.

Although Black Power was psychologically empowering for African Americans, for most whites it generated fear and distrust. This ambivalence suggests that the study of race relations, rather than a narrow focus on Black Studies, might be a more useful approach in examining the past, especially the civil rights movement. Black Power was not only what blacks claimed it to be, but also what whites believed it to be, a construction of the social boundaries and limits prescribed by both blacks and whites. Considering race relations in this way allows us to better understand the issue of race in America, the nature of the struggle for social equality, and what it means and has meant to be black, and white, in America. Additionally, blacks and whites in America confront each other in a society they have constructed together and in which they share a common history, as well as similar religions, values, ideals, and cultures. Understanding the reactions to the civil rights movement from all sides allows for black and white Americans to better understand the limits of both peaceful and militant protest, and the consequences of apathy to the legitimate claims of citizenship of minority populations.[53]

NOTES

1. Cited in Bill Moyers, *Listening to America: A Traveller Rediscovers His Country* (New York: Harper's Magazine Press, 1971), 96.
2. Kansas Attorney General Kent Frizzell, "Lawrence Investigative Report," August 21, 1970 (hereafter, "AG Report, 1970"), in Robert B. Docking Papers (hereafter, RBD Papers), box 41, folder 10, Kansas Collection (hereafter, KC), Spencer Research Library, University of Kansas. Many blacks claimed that a revolver was planted on Dowdell's body, although paraffin tests conducted by the Kansas Bureau of Investigation confirmed that Dowdell had recently fired a weapon.

3. "Respectful Silence for Slain Youth," *Kansas City Star,* July 24, 1970.

4. Helen Kimball, interview transcript, Douglas County Historical Society (hereafter, DCHS), Lawrence, Kansas.

5. *Harambee,* July 19, 1970. Both the Kansas Collection and the University of Kansas Archives have copies of *Harambee.*

6. Typed statement, attached to Governor's Office Memo to Robert B. Docking, July 22, 1970, RBD Papers, box 41, folder 10, KC.

7. *Vortex,* n.d., n.p. (probably July 1970), KC; "Courthouse Scene of Trouble," *Lawrence Daily Journal-World,* July 22, 1970.

8. "AG Report, 1970."

9. "AG Report, 1970."

10. "Massive Ideological Chasm Apparent in Lawrence," *Topeka Daily Capital,* July 22, 1970; "Petition Backs Officer Garrett," *Lawrence Daily Journal-World,* July 22, 1970.

11. "Schultz Statement Repudiated," *University Daily Kansan,* September 23, 1970.

12. "Kansas Highway Patrol Report," September 18, 1970 (hereafter, "KHP Report 1970"), RBD Papers, box 41, folder 10, KC.

13. "Fear Forms in Kansas Community," *San Francisco Chronicle,* December 26, 1970.

14. W. E. B. Du Bois, *The Souls of Black Folk,* with an introduction by Henry Louis Gates (1903; New York: Bantam Books, 1989), 10.

15. "City Moves to Desegregation," *University Daily Kansan,* January 20, 1961.

16. Harvard Sitkoff, *The Black Struggle for Equality, 1954–1980* (New York: Hill and Wang, 1981), 167.

17. Stokely Carmichael and Charles V. Hamilton, *Black Power: The Politics of Liberation in America* (New York: Vintage Books, 1974), 44.

18. Clayborne Carson, *In Struggle: SNCC and the Black Awakening of the 1960s* (Cambridge: Harvard University Press, 1981), 244.

19. Dennis Embry and John Miller, "Racial and Student Disturbances: Documentary, Lawrence, Kansas, 1970" (audio tapes), tape 5, side A, KC.

20. William L. Van Deberg, *New Day in Babylon: The Black Power Movement and American Culture* (Chicago: University of Chicago Press, 1992), 26.

21. Steven F. Lawson, *Running for Freedom: Civil Rights and Black Politics Since 1941* (Philadelphia: Temple University Press, 1991), 121.

22. Herbert H. Haines, *Black Radicals and the Civil Rights Mainstream, 1954–1970* (Knoxville: University of Tennessee Press, 1988), quoted in Van Deberg, *New Day in Babylon,* 306.

23. For more on civil rights during this period, see Kristine M. McCusker, " 'The Forgotten Years' of America's Civil Rights Movement: The University of Kansas, 1939–1961" (Master's thesis, University of Kansas, 1993), chap. 5 and epilogue.

24. Wilt Chamberlain and David Shaw, *Wilt: Just Like Any Other Seven-Foot Black Millionaire Who Lives Next Door* (New York: Macmillan, 1973), 51.

25. For more on the socioeconomic status of blacks in Lawrence, see Rusty L. Monhollon, " 'Away from the Dream': The Roots of Black Power in Lawrence, Kansas, 1960–1970" (Master's thesis, University of Kansas, 1994), 22–41.

26. On the Jayhawk Plunge picket, see Monhollon, " 'Away from the Dream,' " 42–65; for the CRC's activities, see 66–92; on fair housing legislation, see 94–105.

27. "Comments on Local Affairs," *Lawrence Outlook,* June 20, 1963.

28. Justin D. Hill to W. Clarke Wescoe, March 10, 1965. Chancellor's Office, Executive Secretary, Case Files, 1959–65, "Easton Dismissal, Bookstore Petition, Civil Rights Demonstrations," series 2/01/1/, box 9, "Hate" folder, University Archives, University of Kansas (hereafter, UA).

29. For details of the sit-in, see Monhollon, " 'Away from the Dream,' " 111–45.

30. Norma Norman, interview with author, Topeka, Kansas, May 25, 1994.

31. Norman, interview.

32. Charles V. Hamilton, "An Advocate of Black Power Defines It," in *Black Protest in the Sixties: Articles from the New York Times,* ed. August Meier, Elliot Rudwick, and John Bracey, Jr. (New York: Markus Wiener, 1991), 155.

33. Jesse Milan, interview with author, Kansas City, Kansas, May 27, 1994.

34. "Police Policies Topic of Meet of Rights Body," *Lawrence Daily Journal-World,* August 24, 1967.

35. Milan, interview.

36. John Spearman, Jr., telephone interview with author, October 9, 1994.

37. See Monhollon, " 'Away from the Dream,' " 146–62.

38. "Negroes at LHS Air Concerns," *Lawrence Daily Journal-World,* May 22, 1968.

39. Spearman, interview.

40. "KU Group Meets to Discuss LHS," *University Daily Kansan,* September 27, 1968.

41. "Black Students Walk Out to Protest LHS Policies," *Lawrence Daily Journal-World,* September 25, 1968.

42. "White Group Voices Plea to Schoolmen," *Lawrence Daily Journal-World,* September 26, 1968.

43. "Negroes Will Meet with LHS Officials," *University Daily Kansan,* September 27, 1968; "Black Students Walk Out to Protest LHS Policies."

44. Letter to editor, *Lawrence Daily Journal-World,* September 28, 1968.

45. "White Student Reaction: LHS Black Walkout Hurt Cause," *University Daily Kansan,* October 2, 1968.

46. "On the Street," *Lawrence Outlook,* September 26, 1968; "Ed Abels' Column," *Lawrence Outlook,* September 30, 1968.

47. "Negroes Set Up School: Blacks Leave LHS," *University Daily Kansan,* September 26, 1968.

48. Spearman, interview.

49. Statement read by June Walker, Unified School District 497 board meeting, October 7, 1968, in "Black Walkout 1968" folder, DCHS.

50. Lawrence Human Relations Council, "Study of the Lawrence High School Confrontation in April, 1970," December 1970, Lawrence Public Library, Lawrence, Kansas; Ephemeral material, "Black Walkout 1968" folder, DCHS.

51. Quoted in Moyers, *Listening to America,* 92.

52. Van Deberg, *New Day in Babylon,* 31.

53. Social constructionism emphasizes the "ways in which ethnic or racial boundaries, identities, and cultures are negotiated, defined, and produced through social interaction" among groups and individuals inside and outside ethnic communities. See Joane Nagel, "Constructing Ethnicity: Creating and Recreating Ethnic Identity and Culture," *Social Problems* 41, no. 1 (February 1994): 152–76; the quote is from Nagel, "Constructing Ethnicity," 152. For recent assessments of social constructionism, see James A. Holstein and Gale Miller, *Reconsidering Social Constructionism: Debates in Social Problems Theory* (New York: Aldine de Gruyter, 1993); or Gale Miller and James A. Holstein, *Constructionist Controversies: Issues in Social Problems Theory* (New York: Aldine de Gruyter, 1993).